Person-Centred Counselling Psychology

An Introduction

D0074657

Ewan Gillon

SAGE Publications

Los Angeles • London • New Delhi • Singapore

Ewan Gillon © 2007

First published 2007

Apart from any fair dealing for the purposes of research
or private study, or criticism or review, as permitted
under the Copyright, Designs and Patents Act, 1988, this
publication may be reproduced, stored or transmitted in
any form, or by any means, only with the prior permission
in writing of the publishers, or in the case of reprographic
reproduction, in accordance with the terms of licences
issued by the Copyright Licensing Agency. Enquiries
concerning reproduction outside those terms should be
sent to the publishers.

 SAGE Publications Ltd
1 Oliver's Yard
55 City Road
London EC1Y 1SP

SAGE Publications Inc.
2455 Teller Road
Thousand Oaks, California 91320

SAGE Publications India Pvt Ltd
B 1/I 1 Mohan Cooperative Industrial Area
Mathura Road, New Delhi 110 044
India

SAGE Publications Asia-Pacific Pte Ltd
33 Pekin Street #02-01
Far East Square
Singapore 048763

British Library Cataloguing in Publication data

A catalogue record for this book is available from the
British Library

ISBN 978-0-7619-4334-1
ISBN 978-0-7619-4335-8 (pbk)

Library of Congress Control Number: 2006939131

Typeset by C&M Digitals (P) Ltd., Chennai, India
Printed and bound in Great Britain by Athenaeum Press, Gateshead
Printed on paper from sustainable resources

Contents

Acknowledgements

Lots of different people contributed to this book, and I am indebted to each of them for their support, assistance (and tolerance!) during the time it took for me to research and write it. In particular I would like to thank Mick Cooper and Alan Frankland for their insightful and thoughtful feedback on various chapters, as well as their immense support and encouragement from beginning to end. I would also like to thank colleagues and friends at Glasgow Caledonian University for giving me the time and opportunity to focus on something like this. The following also deserve a particular mention for their assistance and encouragement, in so many different ways. Without them, I would undoubtedly still be planning Chapter 4 or 5. They are: Jeremy Hoad, Lindsey Fidler, David Melhuish, Keith Sutton, Kirsten Jardine, Richard Payne, Paul Flowers, Brian Johnston, David Craigie, Jean Stewart, Lisa Marshall, Heather Macintryre, members of the Division of Counselling Psychology (Scotland), Nicola Stuckey, Angie Fee, all at the Southside Centre in Edinburgh, Sylvia Russell, Mike Marsland, all at the University of East Anglia Counselling Service, Dave Mearns, Conor McKenna, Helen, Angus and Kirsty Gillon, and Ann Hodson. I would also like to express a huge thanks to colleagues at Sage for their never-ending encouragement and assistance, particularly in the face of my constantly changing deadlines. Most of all I would like to thank Julia for her unstinting love and support, as well as her gentle reminders of a life outwith work. The book is for her, and for our wonderful little boy, Ferdie.

Introduction

Introduction

In the opinion of Dorothea Brandt, author of the famous *Becoming a Writer* (1981), all writing is autobiographical in one way or another. Hence this book may be seen to represent not only something about its topic, person-centred counselling psychology, but also something about me, as its author. Certainly, the focus of the book evolved from the disparate strands of my own career, firstly as an academic psychologist, then, as a person-centred counsellor, and now as a counselling psychologist.

During the time I spent in these different professional domains, I grappled with many questions asking how each related to the other, and in particular, how the person-centred approach fitted within the field of contemporary psychology, a field which so often prioritises empirical methods and scientific expertise in trying to understand and attend to the human condition. Although, as a counselling psychologist I was well acquainted with difficulties in reconciling different world views, what I missed, even from within this setting, was a clear understanding of how the person-centred approach could be understood from a *psychological* point of view.

The purpose of this book is to address this shortfall by providing a clear, thorough and up-to-date appraisal of the person-centred approach as a form of *psychology*. It offers an exploration of the history, theory, practice/s and context/s of person-centred therapy from a psychological perspective, and is written for readers who have an interest in the area of contemporary counselling psychology but who are perhaps less familiar with the complexity of person-centred concepts and methods, as well as the challenges these present and the opportunities they afford.

Person-centred therapy is often misunderstood and simplified within contemporary psychology, a process that has had some very significant consequences over the years. Hence an added intention of the book is to touch upon the areas of the approach that are often ignored, misinterpreted, forgotten or neglected (e.g. its research tradition), and bring these back into focus. However, the book is not a historical narrative. Far too many developments have occurred within the person-centred framework in recent years to allow for this. Consequently, as well as its development, the book highlights the dynamic and evolving status of the person-centred approach as a contemporary form of psychological therapy, focusing upon its unique contribution to psychological theory and practice, as well as the areas of overlap the approach shares with other psychological traditions and domains.

Undoubtedly, my account of person-centred therapy will stir a range of reactions. It is very much a personal reading of the approach which, for some, will be neglectful and for others, insightful (I prefer to think that the majority will tend toward the latter!). However, irrespective of such responses, I hope the book conveys at least some of the excitement that person-centred therapy often generates among practitioners, as well as clients, in offering a stance valuing personal experiences above all else. In the context of contemporary (Western) psychology, the person-centred approach offers a radical, even revolutionary, standpoint that, among other things, challenges the individual practitioner to offer himself to his clients, first and foremost as a *person*, rather than as a scientist or 'expert' on psychological well being. This is unlike what is often encouraged within many areas of the therapeutic domain, a domain where professional rivalries as well as the cultural pressure to demonstrate scientific status and power can also get in the way.

The person-centred approach offers an alternative point of view which, in many ways, accords with many of the values underpinning the growing discipline of counselling psychology. It is the intention of this book to demonstrate this by providing, for counselling psychologists, students, trainees and others within the area, a clear marker of how the person-centred theory and practice is situated within the contemporary psychological domain.

What is counselling psychology?

Counselling psychology is a form of applied psychology. It was formally welcomed into being in the UK by the British Psychological Society (BPS) in 1982 via the formation of its Counselling Psychology Section. Although counselling psychology is now a Division within the BPS, with equivalent status to areas such as clinical and occupational psychology, what distinguishes it from these and all other forms of applied psychology are its philosophical standpoint and emphasis on the client's subjective experiencing. This translates, in practice, to the following areas of interest (Strawbridge and Woolfe, 2003: p.9):

- The value basis of practice.
- Subjective experience, feelings and meanings.
- The empathic engagement of the psychologist with the world of the client.
- The acceptance of the subjective world of the client as meaningful and valid in its own terms.

- The need to negotiate between perceptions and world-views without assuming an objectively discoverable 'truth'.
- The qualitative description of experience.
- The development of insight and the increased capacity for choice.
- The primacy in practice in generating knowledge.

On the basis of attributes such as this, it is clear that counselling psychology assumes a stance which is highly sensitive to the experiences and values of its clients in their own terms, rather than in the form of empirically derived, 'objective' knowledge so commonplace within psychology more generally. Any reader with some prior exposure to psychology will recognise this as a somewhat humanistic standpoint (e.g. Maslow, 1954), and as such may conclude that counselling psychologists are primarily humanistic practitioners. However, this is an overly simplified view, for counselling psychology promotes a multiplicity of therapeutic 'truths' (Frankland and Walsh, 2005) and values a wide range of therapeutic approaches located within each of the main traditions or 'paradigms' in psychology: cognitive-behavioural, psychodynamic, existential-phenomenological, as well as humanistic.

Indeed it goes further than this, in actively encouraging practitioners to work in a way that recognises the impossibility of one therapeutic 'right' answer that may be applied to each client in every circumstance. Hence counselling psychologists attend to different client needs by drawing on a range of therapeutic approaches and methods in a theoretically and clinically coherent manner. While such a practice may raise a multitude of dilemmas for any therapeutic practitioner with a strong commitment to a single therapeutic approach, these are counteracted by the intention of counselling psychology as a discipline to locate itself within a social constructionist framework emphasising the contestability of psychological knowledge and the multiplicity therapeutic 'truths' (i.e. no one approach being 'right'). As a result counselling psychologists are constantly invited to reflect on their practice as inevitable series of contesting possibilities, rather than a series of rights and wrongs. This invitation is one of the features that often differentiates practitioners from counsellors and psychotherapists, who often train in, and align themselves to, a single model of therapy, be it person-centred, cognitive-behavioural or otherwise.

As counselling psychology is a discipline that embraces a multiplicity (or what is often termed a plurality: Goss and Mearns, 1997) of therapeutic perspectives and approaches, it is important to clarify what is meant by the term 'person-centred counselling psychology', which constitutes the title of this book. Person-centred counselling psychology, in this regard, refers to the rightful place of person-centred therapy as an approach to psychological therapy that is embedded within the counselling psychology domain, a domain highlighting the *psychological* basis of therapeutic theory and practice. It does not, however, imply that it is possible to become a person-centred *counselling psychologist*. Such an identity would conflict with the pluralistic basis of counselling psychology as a discipline and thus be a contradiction in terms.

In addition to clarifying such definitions, it is also important to say a short word about terminology. Throughout the book I have attempted to represent the many different ways in which the person-centred approach is utilised by referring, interchangeably, to those applying it as 'counsellors', 'counselling psychologists', 'practitioners' and 'therapists'. In doing so I merely mean to avoid assuming a particular stance promoting any one of these identities over another. Although this book concerns person-centred therapy as a form of counselling psychology, not all readers will be counselling psychologists and hence many may not adhere to the philosophical stance on identity adopted within the counselling psychology domain. Furthermore, while counselling psychology emphasises no one approach as being 'right', person-centred therapy is not predicated in such terms and thus promotes like most other therapeutic approaches, its own theory and practice as most ideally suited to working with psychological distress. The tension between these views is not easily resolved and emerges from different philosophical standpoints on psychological knowledge. Although these standpoints will be explored in depth in Chapter 8, this tension highlights just one of the challenges faced by those wishing to work using a person-centred approach from a counselling psychology perspective.

Form and content

Any author attempting to explore person-centred therapy from a psychological perspective has available to them an infinite number of possible avenues for discussion and examination. The content of this book has therefore been guided by what I have found to be the key considerations in my own journey toward a clear appreciation of the complex relationship between person-centred therapy and the field of psychology. These are firstly the need to gain a clear understanding of the fundamentals of the theory and practice of person-centred therapy as contextualised within an appreciation of its historical development, secondly, the location of the approach within the key theoretical and practical arenas of contemporary counselling psychology, and thirdly, the identification of key processes and issues relevant to training and working as a person-centred practitioner, whether as a counselling psychologist or otherwise. These considerations provide the three different themes around which the book is organised.

The first four chapters of the book focus on person-centred therapy as an approach to counselling psychology, and explore its historical development (Chapter 1), theoretical propositions (Chapter 2) and, following on from these, its various methods of working. This latter task is conducted in two different ways: firstly via a theoretical outline of the procedures of the approach (Chapter 3) and secondly in two example 'case studies' written to demonstrate how the approach may actually work, 'in-action' (Chapter 4). Through the combination of these perspectives, it is intended that the reader is presented with a more rounded insight than theory alone can offer.

The second theme of the book broadens our focus to locate the approach within a contemporary counselling psychology context. This includes chapters exploring where person-centred therapy is situated philosophically and practically within the four main paradigms of counselling psychology (Chapter 5); its position within the contemporary mental health context and, in particular, working with severe psychological distress (Chapter 6); its standpoint on psychological research and the contemporary emphasis on the requirement for an 'evidence-base' (Chapter 7) for psychological practice; and finally its relationship to the critiques of the theory and practice of the contemporary psychology field made by those from a social constructionist or critical perspective (Chapter 8).

The book ends with a chapter (Chapter 9) examining some of the key issues relevant to anyone with a psychological background wishing to train in, or work using, person-centred therapy. This third theme is of vital importance to readers interested in deepening their exposure to the person-centred perspective, but also one that could provide sufficient material for a book in itself. Hence the chapter offers only a whistle-stop tour of relevant considerations and procedures, assuming interested readers will further avail themselves of the comprehensive training literature already available in the person-centred, counselling, and counselling psychology arenas.

So, now I have covered some basic 'scene-setting' we shall turn to Chapter 1 and commence our exploration of the history and development of the person-centred approach as a form of psychological therapy.

ONE   The History and Development of the Person-centred Approach

Introduction

The person-centred approach to counselling psychology has a long and complex history. Like any key movement in psychology, it emerged from a dynamic combination of historical circumstance with extraordinary human innovation. The circumstances were those of the USA in the early 20th century and the innovative characteristic of one man, Carl Rogers.

There has been much written about Rogers in terms of development of the person-centred therapy, often focusing on his background and personality (e.g. Thorne, 1992). Indeed, so closely identified is he with the theory and practice of the person-centred approach that many call the approach 'Rogerian' rather than use its fuller title. Yet, to understand person-centred counselling simply in terms of the work of one man is to do little justice to the diverse, and often radical, nature of the movement he brought into being. Moreover, it fails to account for the broader political circumstances and philosophical undercurrents that played a highly significant part in fuelling a drive toward a more *person-centred* form of psychology. Rogers himself disliked the term 'Rogerian', seeing it as inaccurate and overly constraining for those who wished to work in different ways to him but remain committed to the broad principles of the approach. Furthermore, he often acknowledged the role of history in helping germinate a method of psychological therapy that has become one of the most popular and influential in the Western world.

So what was it about this extraordinary man that led him to become one of the most dominant, but often unacknowledged figures in modern psychology?

Setting the scene for a new approach

Carl Rogers: a brief biography

Like many before him, Carl Rogers' journey into psychology was not straightforward. Born in 1902, Rogers spent much of his early life on a farm helping to raise crops and find ways of harnessing what he felt were the wonders of the natural world around him. So enthused was he by his early experiences he decided to enrol at the University of Wisconsin to study agricultural science. University life was a revelation, and Rogers found himself exposed to many new ideas, areas of study and people. He developed new passions and viewpoints, none more so than the discovery of a more compassionate, thoughtful version of the Christian faith under whose evangelical, moralising wing he had been raised. As his horizons broadened so did his perspectives, and he increasingly questioned his commitment to agriculture as his future vocation, wondering if life had other things to offer him than he had originally imagined. After a long period of contemplation, and subsequently change, Rogers ended up graduating with a degree in history. However that was not all he had gained during his time at university. He had also acquired a wife, marrying his childhood sweetheart, Helen Elliot, who'd been persuaded that he was more certain about his personal aspirations than he was about his future career!

Following his graduation, Rogers again changed course to train as a Minister of Religion, enrolling at the Union Theological Seminary in New York. He spent two years at the Union, a time which he never regretted, but one which convinced him that the constraints of religious doctrine were just too great for his evolving interests. He left just before qualifying, now greatly interested in psychology, a subject with which he had become well acquainted over two years of night classes. There seemed, to Rogers, a lot of overlap between the caring work of the applied psychologist and that of the Minister he had set out to become. Hence he decided to change direction once again, this time signing up for professional training in Clinical and Educational Psychology. Following a successful period as a Fellow at the Institute of Child Guidance and the completion of his doctoral research (developing a personality test for children), he secured his first formal post. It was 1928 and at last he was a professional psychologist working in the Child Study Department of the Rochester Society for the Prevention of Cruelty to Children. It was here he was to remain for the next 12 years.

Although the position at Rochester was by no means ideal, being both under-paid and professionally isolated, it provided an opportunity to work with a diverse range of children as well as with their parents. The practical difficulties of working with many children experiencing often unimaginable levels of social deprivation required a pragmatic approach, and Rogers did what he could in the circumstances around him. During this time he encountered a range of different ideas on how best to conduct psychological work, many of which called into question the 'advice-giving' models of the time. Added to these were his own therapeutic experiences which increasingly pointed toward an approach in which the client's needs and motivations were placed centre stage. He recounted one particular episode while at the Child Study Department that typified this learning (Rogers, 1961: pp.11–12), describing a conversation with one mother he worked with:

> The problem was clearly her early rejection of the boy, but over many interviews I could not help her to this insight ... Then she turned and asked 'do you ever take adults for counselling here?' When I replied in the affirmative she said 'well, I would like some' ... and began to pour out her despair about her marriage, her troubled relationship with her husband, her sense of failure and confusion, all very different from the sterile 'case history' she had given before. Real therapy began then, and ultimately it was very successful. This incident was one of a number which helped me to experience the fact that it is the client who knows what hurts, what directions to go, what problems are crucial and what experiences have been deeply buried. It began to occur to me that unless I had a need to demonstrate my own cleverness and learning I would do better to rely upon the client for the direction of movement in the process.

Practical experiences such as that recounted above profoundly influenced Rogers and, combined with his growing awareness of alternative psychological approaches to those in which he was trained, provided the basis for a new approach centred around the experiences of the client, and not the expertise of the therapist. His ideas were further cemented by the nature of American Psychology at that time, a discipline riven by professional rivalries but also filled with excitement at the thought of new possibilities ahead.

Psychology in 1920s and 1930s America

During Rogers' work in the Child Study Department, psychology was an enormously popular professional activity and psychologists worked in areas as diverse as improving performance in the workplace and assisting family functioning (Leahey, 1991). The focus of much psychological work at that time was often upon the application of the principles of natural science within a social context. This generally translated into the widespread application of standardised psychological 'tests' through which the human mind, and human behaviour, could be scientifically understood and managed. The utility of such tests had been fuelled by America's involvement in the First World War (1914–18), during which time psychologists had found themselves playing a pivotal role in selecting men to serve in the army. This role, and its many opportunities, had demonstrated the significant role psychology could play in matters of national importance, and highlighted the value of applying scientific principles to the realm of human behaviour.

The pre-eminence of psychological testing at that time was strongly informed by the principles of behaviourism, (e.g. Watson, 1917), which concerned itself entirely with observable (and measurable) manifestations of human activity. This approach was attractive in both its adherence to positivist, scientific methods (i.e. searching for general 'laws' of behaviour) which accorded the discipline its much sought after scientific status, as well as the possibilities it presented for addressing a wide range of social and individual problems. The behaviourist proposition that human activity could be understood (and managed) in terms of the scientific linking of particular, extrinsic *stimuli* (e.g. the encouragement of aggression in childhood) to certain behavioural *responses* (e.g. adult violence), seemed to offer a tremendous way forward in developing a scientifically reputable, as well as socially useful, psychological discipline. Its only real competitor at that time was the psychoanalytic approach, introduced to America in the late 19th and early 20th centuries through the writings of Sigmund Freud (e.g. 1938).

The psychoanalytic approach presented intriguing notions of an 'unconscious' mind riven with repressed desire and psychological conflict. These had quickly became popular among the rebellious American youth at the turn of the century, who had eagerly (mis) interpreted Freud's prioritising of the healthy expression of biological needs as indicating a link between a lack of sexual inhibition and good mental well-being! However, the biological basis of Freud's ideas had been quickly seized upon by the medical profession, alarmed at the rise in psychology in treating mental ill health, and psychoanalysis rapidly became a psychiatric (i.e. medical) method of treatment rather than a psychological one. Not to be outdone, a large number of psychologists, alerted by the evidence presented by Freud of his therapeutic successes, also began to practice using some of his proposed techniques and by the 1930s psychoanalysis was also a force to be reckoned with in psychological domains. Despite this, mainstream psychology was still driven by behaviourist thinking and the principles of changing behaviour through 'scientifically' managing the link between stimuli and responses, (principles still only demonstrated at that time in the laboratory with rats and pigeons). Such thinking fitted well with the era, one of progress and change embedded within a philosophy of 'modernism' highlighting the importance of human evolution through scientific means. This philosophy had a number of resonances in the USA of the early 20th century.

USA: 1900–40

Since its industrial revolution in the late 1800s, America had been in the thrall of a rapid urbanisation of its social and economic fabric. As industrialised production methods had taken hold, many people had found employment in the new, 'urban', environments, which rapidly generated a more diverse, permissive society to that of the traditional American farming heartlands. Such differences produced conflict, and moral issues came to the fore as the tight Victorian values of small town rural communities were eschewed by those revelling in new choices and city living. America's entry into the First World War (1914–18) provided further impetus to its growing industrial might and allowed for some distraction from the emerging social problems at home. However, this was short lived, and the problems of unrest in the new industrial workplaces (often due to the short-sighted imposition of 'scientific management' techniques promoting efficiency and profit at all costs), as well as in the new 'urban' society, soon emerged once again. The situation was not aided by an economy orientated around a rapidly changing manufacturing sector and almost entirely dependent upon a volatile stock market.

In 1929, the stock market crashed, propelling the nation and its citizens into an era now termed the 'Great Depression'. Unemployment became rampant and social welfare programmes (of which there were very few) seemed unable to help the many millions of people struggling to make ends meet. By 1933 the American people had had enough and grabbed, with both hands, the 'New Deal' offered to them by their new president, Franklin D. Roosevelt. This deal was to make some fundamental changes within America, healing the rifts of the past and generating a new national spirit of progress. In actual fact the New Deal was simply a massive programme of social regeneration enveloped in a climate of exploration and possibility (Barrett-Lennard, 1998).

Psychologists envisaged a clear role for themselves on the many welfare programmes to be put in place, but the conflict between behaviourist and psychoanalytic schools of thought generated competing solutions for many problems at hand. More importantly, however, was the fact that many of the tools provided by these approaches simply did not meet with the realities of psychological working in the poverty and deprivation of 1930s America. This raised a number of questions for psychology, as Kirschenbaum (1979: p.256) describes:

> A growing number of psychologists, therapists and other helping professionals were working daily with thousands of clients, in clinics, schools, consulting rooms, ministers' offices, homes and agencies. Psychoanalysis was clearly inappropriate in most of these circumstances. The learning principles derived from studying rats and pigeons seemed equally irrelevant. Work in behaviour therapy had not yet begun. Psychological tests and diagnoses were only a small part of the answer for most of the problems encountered. Where were all these non-analytic, non-laboratory-orientated professionals to turn?

The early development of a person-centred approach

During the period just prior to and during the Depression, as well as the subsequent implementation of the 'New Deal', Carl Rogers continued to work solidly in the Child Study Department. He was deeply affected by the desperate circumstances he saw around him, and eager to help the vast numbers of people he encountered in his clinical practice. Inevitably, however, he could not help but be caught up in the struggles between psychoanalytic and behaviourist methods of therapy, regularly encountering medical and psychology colleagues committed to one or other of these very different views. While the differences between such individuals, and the views they espoused often led him to feel he was 'functioning in two different worlds' where 'never the twain shall meet' (Rogers, 1961: p. 9), the conflicts thrown up between them were highly fruitful in allowing him to consider the merits of each while avoiding evangelising for either.

The influence of Otto Rank

One of the greatest influences on Rogers during this time was the work of Otto Rank. Rank was an Austrian psychoanalyst who had originally been one of Freud's 'inner circle', but who had started to move away from a Freudian psychoanalytic approach believing it paid too little attention to the autonomy or 'will' of the individual. Following the publication of his books (e.g. *Will Therapy* in 1936), Rank had challenged some key aspects of Freud's theory, proposing that harnessing the individual's 'will' was paramount in promoting healing. He also argued that the experience of a strong, positive relationship with a therapist was the primary means of enabling psychological growth within a client. This was in stark contrast to Freud's formulation of the relationship as primarily a vehicle for understanding the unconscious conflicts at the root of clients' difficulties.

Although he met Rank only once, in 1936, Rogers became familiar with his ideas through the work of his social work colleagues, Jessie Taft and Frederick Allen, both of whom were 'Rankian' in their approach (Merry, 1998). Taft (e.g. 1937) proved a strong influence on Rogers, particularly in terms of her emphasis on a positive therapeutic relationship over and above the use of particular psychological 'techniques', such as assessment procedures and advice giving. Moreover, her openness in transcribing entire therapy sessions allowed him to examine, in detail, the nature of her work and gain an understanding of her therapeutic procedures.

Box 1.1   Will therapy and the person-centred approach

Many aspects of Rank's 'Will therapy' were reflected in Rogers' initial ideas for a person-centred therapy (Kramer, 1995). Will therapy, often

(Continued)

(Continued)

termed 'relationship therapy' is a complex blend of ideas which Raskin (1948) simplified into the following terms;

- All people experience various conflicts linked to the dangers of living and the fear of dying. We are all, thus, ambivalent in life.
- Psychological distress or 'neurosis' is created by over-concentration on the ambivalences of living.
- The aim of therapy is the acceptance, by the individual, of their own uniqueness and self-reliance in the ambivalences that are experienced. This acceptance involves the freeing of their 'positive' will.
- The patient becomes the central figure in the therapeutic process, and is encouraged in becoming self-accepting and self-reliant through releasing the positive will. By implication, the therapist should avoid any actions, such as 'interpretation', which could inhibit the positive will and arouse the counter will.
- Self acceptance and self-reliance is realised through the experience of the positive will in the *present relationship* with the therapist, not through the explanation of the past.
- The ending of therapy is a symbol of all separations in life, hence it can represent the new 'birth' of the individual.

Behaviourism and other influences

While the work of Otto Rank provided a psychoanalytically informed background for Rogers' theoretical work, the scientific, empirical principles of the behaviourist paradigm also played their part in establishing the ground for a new perspective. Despite his interest in the therapeutic relationship, Rogers shared the desire of behaviourist psychologists to utilise the principles of natural science in understanding and shaping human behaviour. However, frustrated by their lack of clear method for doing so and wary of neglecting the experiences and viewpoints of his clients, he tentatively began to piece together an alternative perspective, derived from his broadening theoretical understandings as well as his *own practical experience* of psychological work.

Rogers' first book, *The Clinical Treatment of the Problem Child* (1939) introduced, for the first time, specifically person-centred ideas on the importance of the therapist's actions in relating to the client. For Rogers, a good psychologist possessed the following qualities: objectivity, a respect for the individual, an understanding of the self and, finally, psychological knowledge (Rogers, 1939). These propositions were further elaborated in a presentation given to students and faculty at the

University of Minnesota (by now he was Professor of Psychology at the University of Ohio). In this presentation, titled provocatively 'Newer Concepts in Psychotherapy', Rogers argued that *non-directivity* on behalf of the therapist was of paramount importance in facilitating therapeutic change. In contrast to much psychological practice of the time (which relied primarily on the knowledge of the psychologist to locate a solution to a client's problems), he proposed that practitioners should instead attend to the quality of their relationship with the client, listening rather than telling, and helping the client to reach their own conclusions.

Advocating a stance in which the psychologist did not, for example, give advice or use their expertise to determine solutions, represented a wholly new approach which, inevitably, was not welcomed by some (Thorne, 1992). However, it was received warmly by others, particularly those frustrated with the constraints of existing psychological methods and looking for a method of engaging more fully with the progressive social climate that surrounded them. Rogers had set the scene for a new approach that was to all intents and purposes, the first *person-centred* therapy, *non-directive* therapy.

Non-directive therapy

In continuing to develop his ideas on a non-directive therapeutic relationship, Rogers began flesh out his vision for how such a principle could be integrated into a more general therapeutic method. In 1942, he published his next book, *Counselling and Psychotherapy*, which described a therapeutic relationship that should be warm and caring, with a focus on the present rather than the past. The psychologist, in taking such an approach, would thus only be interested in listening to, and understanding, the client's experiencing (e.g. cognitions, emotions, bodily sensations etc.) at any given moment, and not in introducing his own ideas or suggestions. Although not referenced directly by Rogers, this orientation had much in common with the ideas of phenomenology (c.f. Husserl, 1977), an influential philosophical movement emphasising the importance of subjective experience in the 'here and now'.

In addition to describing the underlying principles of a non-directive therapeutic approach, Rogers also proposed some ways in which these could be translated into a *method of working*. Highlighted within this was the process of 'reflecting back' to the client aspects of their own experiencing (Rogers, 1942) In particular, he encouraged a focus upon a primary client's *feelings*, seeing these as the most intimate dimensions of *personal* experiencing. Hence the therapist was encouraged to repeat, or paraphrase (i.e. describe in different words) to the client what he or she had previously disclosed, focusing primarily upon its emotional dimension.

Box 1.2   An example of 'reflecting back'

Psychologist: So how may I be of help to you today?
Client: Well I don't really know why I am here. I made the appointment weeks ago and feel a bit silly now, as things haven't really got as bad I as I feared they would.
Psychologist: You feel silly 'cos, as it stands at this moment, things haven't gone the way you had feared and you don't know if they are bad enough for you to be here?
Client: Yes, well, I feel quite down but don't think I am falling apart in the way I thought I would be.
Psychologist: So you feel low but are just about holding yourself together?
Client: (becoming tearful) I think so.

For Rogers, such an 'expressive-responsive' dialogue (Barrett-Lennard, 1981) had two purposes. Firstly, it allowed the therapist to ensure that he understood the client's 'frame of reference' (i.e. their perceptions, attitudes and feelings) at any given moment by *directly checking* his understanding of it with the client herself (Brodley, 1996). This avoided any possible mis-interpretation which could lead the client to feel misunderstood or judged (hence diminishing the warm, caring quality of the relationship). Secondly, Rogers saw reflecting back as encouraging the client to attend more closely to how they felt (i.e. to check with themselves whether the therapist's reflection was correct). This had the effect of deepening personal experiencing, which in turn lead to increased self-understanding, self-acceptance and, as a result, personal autonomy. These two processes, the warm, understanding relationship and the deepening of personal experiencing were, according to Rogers, the key aspects associated with psychological growth and healing. He suggested no further techniques were required, nor proposed any role for specific directions or interpretations, stating (Rogers, 1942: pp.113–114):

> The counselling relationship is one in which warmth of acceptance and absence of any coercion or personal pressure on the part of the counsellor permits the maximum expression of feelings, attitudes and problems by the counsellee. The relationship is a well-structured one, with limits of time, of dependence and of aggressive action which apply particularly to the client, and limits of responsibility and of affection which the counsellor imposes upon himself. In this unique experience of complete emotional freedom within a well-defined framework the client is free to recognise and understand his impulses and patterns, positive and negative, as in no other relationship.

The non-directive method outlined by Rogers provided a radically different approach to psychological practice to the others available at that time. It attracted a great deal of interest and, in 1945, Rogers moved to the University of Chicago to further develop his ideas. This move allowed him considerable scope in attracting like-minded faculty and graduate students to a growing 'Counselling Centre Group', many of whom worked on applying non-directive ideas to a wide range of social and therapeutic contexts.

Developing a client-centred perspective (1945–64)

In the years following the publication of *Counselling and Psychotherapy* (Rogers, 1942), as well as praise, non-directive therapy also attracted considerable criticism. A number of psychologists saw the non-directive method of reflecting back as far too simplistic a method of working. The process of, what they thought to be, one of simply parroting words back to a client was hugely limiting and offered little to all but the most insightful of clients (Kirschenbaum, 1979). Of course, this interpretation of the approach was not at all what Rogers had suggested, for his proposition was a far more complex form of interaction whereby the therapist paid attention to the moment-by-moment experiences and perceptions of the client in the context of a warm, caring and supportive relationship (Merry, 1998). However, the criticism stung and in 1951 Rogers published *Client-Centred Therapy*. This book, drew on the findings of his now well-established scientific research programme, testing and refining the propositions of non-directive therapy, to address, head-on, many of the concerns raised about his ideas. Indeed, the title 'client-centred' was picked carefully, for it was seen as a term designed to shift the approach from the simplified, mechanistic formulations of *non-directive* therapy that had all too often characterised this method of working.

Client-centred therapy

Client-Centred Therapy (1951) allowed Rogers the scope to refine his focus and discuss the rationale for his method of psychological working. In doing so, he emphasised the role of *attitude* rather than behaviour in the therapeutic context. A psychologist's non-directivity, from this stance, was described as less of a mechanistic activity of reflecting back, and more about her attitude toward the client, one of respect and warmth accompanied by the desire for the client to make their own choices on the basis of their own experiences and needs. Techniques such as 'reflecting-back' were then discussed as possible ways of 'implementing' (Patterson, 2000) this attitude, rather than as methods in themselves. Rogers also highlighted the role of empathic understanding in such terms, arguing that this too was a central ingredient for a successful therapy.

As well as offering a comprehensive run-down of the practical basis of client-centred therapy, the volume also offered an opportunity for Rogers to describe a client-centred theory of personality development. This was of great importance, for as well as being criticised for having a limited therapeutic method, Rogers had also been criticised for failing to provide a detailed psychological analysis of personality and the causes of psychological disturbance as a grounding for his therapeutic procedures. The resulting chapter, 'A Theory of Personality and Behaviour' (Rogers, 1951) offered what he termed as 'nineteen propositions' to describe the development of personality from a client-centred perspective. Again drawing on the principles of empirical science, these propositions were organised along the lines of an empirical psychological inquiry, citing comprehensive psychological evidence for each in an if-then formulation.

Rogers' chapter on personality was generally seen as an important and insightful piece of work, and certainly provided much impetus for the growing status of the client-centred approach within the American psychological community (Evans, 1975). Indeed, the now eminent status of Rogers himself was formally confirmed in 1956 by the award of a Distinguished Scientific Contribution to him by the American Psychological Association.

Box 1.3   The scientific basis of client-centred theory

Despite its philosophy, terms and procedures being very different to behaviourist approaches to psychological therapy, Rogers' desire to situate his model of therapy within an empirical psychology framework was paramount during the evolution of his ideas. All of his initial suggestions on non-directive therapy were derived from practice and subsequently tested and refined using the techniques of empirical psychology to provide the basis for the theory of *Client-Centred Therapy* in 1951 (Rogers, 1951). Indeed, each of the 19 propositions constituting this theory were formulated in 'if-then' terms that allowed for further scientific examination and analysis. The influence of empirical psychology and the desire to find the causal relationships inherent in psychological distress and healing was central to Rogers' work, although it is often forgotten as a result of his therapeutic emphasis on the subjective meanings and experiences of the individual. We shall discuss the role of research in the development of the person-centred approach in Chapter 7.

Developing the client-centred approach

Following the publication of *Client-Centred Therapy*, Rogers and his associates at the Chicago Centre continued to expand their work. Research was a core activity and the range and focus of psychological studies into the client-centred approach continued to grow. In 1954, Rogers co-edited a book entitled *Psychotherapy and Personality Change* (Rogers and Dymond, 1954), in which a number of particular studies were presented. These mainly focused on the attributes and outcomes of the psychotherapeutic process and went far in providing an empirical basis for many of the propositions upon which the client-centred system was based. They also led Rogers to further develop his theory in two ways.

Firstly, in 1957, he produced a paper identifying for the first time six relational conditions that he viewed as necessary and sufficient (Rogers, 1957) for client-centred therapy to take place. These included familiar conditions such as empathy and warmth and acceptance (the latter two being combined into what he termed *unconditional positive regard*). Added to the mix, however, were new concepts such as *congruence* (where a counsellor is aware of his or her own feelings and experiences) and a therapeutic prerequisite that both counsellor and client are in psychological contact (Rogers, 1957). In actual fact, Rogers' most famous statement of his therapeutic approach was published subsequently, in a 1959 edited collection (Rogers, 1959), which had ironically been written before the 1957 paper, but subsequently held up in production. This 1959 chapter outlined the six necessary and sufficient conditions of therapy, albeit in an elaborated (and slightly different) form in the context of a comprehensive explanation of his theory of personality and motivation. Indeed, this chapter is still viewed today as the definitive statement of the theory and practice of client-centred therapy (Tudor and Merry, 2002).

Rogers' second theoretical development linked to the process of therapy and was spelt out by him in a presentation given to the American Psychological Association in 1957 when picking up his Distinguished Contribution award. This presentation contained a systematic description of client functioning throughout the process of psychological growth. Rogers' suggested seven stages, or distinguishable levels, of experiencing (c.f. Rogers, 1961) through which a client may pass in the process of becoming psychologically healthier; essentially moving from what Barrett-Lennard (1998) describes as 'a fixed, close, self-perpetuating mode of functioning to a state of fluid, open but integrated changing-ness' (pp.67). For many, the structured formulation of client process represented a real loss of innocence for the client-centred approach (Worsley, 2002), encouraging the development of therapeutic techniques and strategies to assist a client move from one stage of functioning to another. However, for Rogers, a scientific understanding of psychological change was simply another aspect of the attempt to understand what worked in psychological therapy and why.

A global approach

By the mid 1950s, and despite being at the forefront of client-centred activity, Rogers had decided to leave Chicago and return to the University of Wisconsin for a new role spanning both the departments of Psychology and Psychiatry. He saw this as a great opportunity to bring together the psychological and medical domains. However, the reality was much tougher than he imagined (Thorne, 1992) and he soon fell out with the rigid, dogmatic approach of many members of the faculty. Furthermore, his major research project on the application of client-centred therapy among schizophrenic persons (generally known as The Wisconsin Project) was difficult and provided little confirmatory evidence for the applicability of client-centred therapy to seriously disturbed individuals (McLeod, 2002). As a result, Rogers become some-what disillusioned and, when offered the chance to join the newly estab-lished Western Behavioural Sciences Institute (WBSI) in California, found the chance of a new start difficult to resist. He moved in 1963, soon after publishing his most successful and hugely influential book, *On Becoming a Person* (1961). Rather than a dreary academic tome, *On Becoming a Person* was a very personal and intimate book detailing the application of client-centred principles to all aspects of living, such as education, creativity and intimate relationships. It was the success of this book that made Rogers a household name and allowed him to contemplate, for the first time, a role in challenging some of the fundamental social deprivations that he had experienced in his early working life.

From client-centred to person-centred and beyond (1965–87)

In the years following his move to California, the client-centred approach evolved significantly, with a primary impetus being toward the broader application of its principles within a diverse range of ther-apeutic and welfare settings. Rogers himself was heavily involved in such moves and used his now celebrity status to encourage the grow-ing encounter group movement in the USA (see Box 1.4), as well as to push for the application of client-centred approaches to community and global concerns. This shift in emphasis, from a *client-centred psy-chotherapy* toward a more holistic *movement* founded on client-centred principles such as unconditional positive regard and empathy, was reflected in a change of name to the *person-centred* approach. The title *person-centred* was again picked deliberately, this time to denote the applicability of the approach to a wider range of contexts than simply to psychological therapy (as implied by the term *client*). Yet, despite this broadening of focus, the therapeutic aspect of the approach also remained important, and person-centred therapy exercised a continued influence on the growth of the humanistic psychology movement in which Rogers had been closely involved since the 1950s along with other psychologists such as Abe Maslow and Fritz Perls (Cain, 2001).

Rogers and the person-centred movement

Following his move from Wisconsin, Rogers quickly settled into his role within the Western Behavioural Science Institute (WBSI) in California. He found this new setting gave him the time to develop both personally and professionally, and spent much time applying person-centred principles to a wide range of social issues. In 1969, again frustrated by the institutional constraints of a university set-ting, he decided to form, with like-minded others, the Centre for Studies of the Person in La Jolla, California. This centre afforded the opportunity for a broad range of professionals from different areas of work to share experiences and interests in applying person-centred principles to a range of concerns. Moreover it provided Rogers with the basis (his chosen title was 'Resident Fellow') to continue his quest to apply his ideas in areas well beyond the traditional domain of psychology.

His work by the mid-1970s reflected this interest, with books and arti-cles published in areas such as education, marriage, society, encounter groups, and the helping professions. These broader concerns pre-sented some very different issues from those of academic psychology and Rogers become less interested in using the procedures of empiri-cal science to test his propositions, preferring instead to highlight the importance of experience and meaning in conceptualising problems and issues. For some, he went too far in this venture, (e.g. O'Hara, 1995) for he began to apply person-centred principles to general con-cerns without recourse to the empirical examination ordinarily neces-sary to justify such claims, an examination which would often have been hugely difficult in the limited terms provided by empirical psy-chology. Had the vibrant, conceptually sophisticated array of contem-porary qualitative research methods been available to him at that time, it is likely that these would have provided the alternative frame-work such work required. However, such methods were in their infancy and Rogers' work thus began to be seen, particularly within the discipline of psychology, as more rhetorical than scientific. This diminished both his credibility and standing, an outcome which also undermined person-centred therapy as a legitimate method of psychological working.

> **Box 1.4   Encounter groups**
>
> Due to Rogers' interest and central involvement in it, the person-centred approach is now often associated with the encounter group movement of the 1960s and 1970s. Encounter groups are small groups of individuals who do not know one another, but who agree to meet once or for a limited number of occasions with the purpose of communicating deeply and openly about themselves and their relationships in a safe, trusting environment. Encounter groups are facilitated by an individual whose job it is to encourage deep relating between members in a non-defensive manner as well as to maintain boundaries, such as time etc. Although they could be very profound, developmental experiences, encounter groups developed a reputation for excess, with some participants using them to express all manner of feelings without recourse to the usual constraints of social interaction and discussion. Hence they become, somewhat unfairly, synonymous with self-indulgence.

As the 1980s approached, Rogers became increasingly drawn into issues of world peace and global relations, publishing books and articles designed to set out his vision of the future in the terrible onslaught of nuclear proliferation and the on-going troubles in settings such as Northern Ireland (where he undertook community-building activities). Indeed, until his death in 1987, Rogers pursued political goals and was nominated, on the basis of his work toward world peace, for the Nobel Peace Prize. Unfortunately he died before learning of this nomination, leaving behind him a huge legacy of writing and research. Although his death represented a considerable loss, Cain (1993) points to the large number of his original terms (such as the 'self-concept') that are now part of general psychological discourse. This, in itself, is testament to his profound influence on the discipline of psychology, an influence which continues to this day.

The development of an experiential perspective

While Rogers was becoming interested in the social, rather than clinical, application of person-centred principles in the 1970s and 1980s, a number of his former colleagues and other associates were taking the person-centred approach in a very different direction. Following Rogers' discussion of psychological process and the seven stages of therapeutic change (Rogers, 1961), different ways of *enhancing* the capacity of clients to move through these toward greater well-being were being explored and developed. One of the most influential figures in this respect was Eugene Gendlin, a colleague of Rogers from Wisconsin. Gendlin's interest in facilitating change evolved from his involvement in the Wisconsin study of client-centred therapy among schizophrenic clients, and the struggles he noticed among such individuals to relate to their inner experiencing, such as their personal feelings (Gendlin, 1964). This led him to develop a method of facilitating a client's capacity to relate to, and understand, his or her felt experiencing, a method he termed *focusing* (Gendlin, 1978).

Focusing was initially outlined as a series of therapist provided procedures to assist a client attend more closely to how he *felt* in relation to a specific issue or topic. Rather than simply trust the relationship to provide this focus through the necessary and sufficient conditions, Gendlin argued it was useful for a client to be more actively directed to examine his 'felt sense' (Gendlin, 1996) through specific procedures introduced and guided by the therapist. The change in therapeutic emphasis proposed by Gendlin, from one relying solely on the relationship to one involving therapeutic direction of the process of therapy (but not the content of what the client experienced or talked about, unlike an approach involving advice giving or interpretation) represented a very significant break from the previous person-centred principle of not directing the client in any way.

A similar move was also advocated at around the same time by practitioners interested in identifying specific client processes in therapy (e.g. attempting to resolve internal conflicts) and in developing methods to address these (e.g. Rice, 1974). Although work in this area, now called process-experiential therapy, will be discussed in greater depth in Chapter 3, its development again represented a significant shift away from the principle of complete non-directivity toward a more active role for the therapist in providing possible techniques and methods to help a client move toward greater wellbeing. This role was predicated on a view, shared by Gendlin (e.g. Gendlin, 1964) that aiding a client to attend to, and work with, her personal experiencing more deeply would facilitate psychological change in accordance with the different levels of process described by Rogers. Hence, within this experiential domain, therapists used various techniques or methods designed to facilitate such personal experiencing. However in doing so, this perspective moved beyond what could be legitimately be described as person-centred in the terms set out by Rogers himself in his definitive, 1959 formulation of a non-directive, client-centred therapy. This is something that has been hugely controversial within the person-centred field.

A classical perspective

While moves toward experiential methods of working were embraced by some within the person-centred framework, many others remained committed to the original theory and practice of person-centred therapy outlined by Rogers in 1959. Those taking such a stance took great exception to the slippage advocated by the experiential perspective, particularly as it seemed to encourage moves toward an erosion of the unique principles and attributes of person-centred therapy as originally conceived (Swildens, 2002). These practitioners work in a *classical* person-centred way, with the term classical being used to denote their adherence to the classic theory and practice of client-centred therapy as set out by Rogers in 1959.

In 1990, Barbara T. Brodley presented a paper spelling out the concerns of many within the classical tradition of the person-centred community about the evolving direction toward experiential methods of working. Her paper, entitled Client-Centred Therapy – What it is? What it is Not?, argued for a more careful definition of what may legitimately be considered as person-centred and what may not be. She argued for a primary emphasis to be placed upon therapist non-directivity, suggesting that interventions involving the use of techniques (e.g. focusing) should *only* be employed when *explicitly* requested by a client or in circumstances when an awareness of a need that may be helped through techniques is *directly identified* by a client. This threw down a significant challenge to the experiential person-centred practitioners, many of whom could no longer define their work as *person-centred* in the terms thus set out. Brodley and others (e.g. Bozarth, 1996) within the classical tradition (also occasionally known as *literalist* person-centred therapy) view person-centred therapy as non-directive and any attempt to introduce direction into the approach as fundamentally flawed and to be resisted. However, as may be expected, such a viewpoint invokes considerable anger among those metaphorically cast out by her definition.

Person-centred counselling psychology into the new millennium

The events at a conference in 1988 bringing together practitioners from both classical and experiential perspectives was described by Thorne (1992) as akin to 'orthodoxy meeting heresy'. Certainly, during that meeting, and in the years following it, there was much heated discussion regarding what a person-centred approach could and should be and what it is not. Anger is often an effect of fear, and there is no doubting that both perspectives fear what the other represents; classical practitioners anxious to retain the core of person-centred therapy as originally conceived, experiential therapists nervous to ensure that the approach does not remain stuck in a past which has seen it marginalised by psychiatrists and other psychologists (e.g. Elliott, 2002).

In order to provide some coherence to the debate, various practitioners (e.g. Lietaer, 2002) have attempted to find some common ground between the perspectives by providing a core basis for defining the nature and basis of the person-centred approach in a contemporary context. Perhaps the most well-known of these attempts is that of Sanders (2000), who proposed a series of criteria to determine what person-centred therapy is, as well as what is not.

As well as a number of secondary principles, he identifies three primary criteria which any approach must possess to be legitimately termed person-centred. These are:

1.   A fundamental trust in the client's capacity to maximise their own potential.
2.   A recognition that the therapeutic conditions described by Rogers (1957) are *all* necessary for psychological change to occur (irrespective of whichever 'techniques' are employed).
3.   That a non-directive attitude must be present at least in terms of the *content* a client discloses (i.e. it is not acceptable for a therapist to attempt to determine what topics a client should think about or talk about)

These three criteria emphasise the significance of the therapeutic relationship as well as setting a clear boundary as to how any permissible direction towards a client may be employed – in using techniques or methods to assist a client attend to her difficulties (i.e. the *process* of therapy), but not to determine what these difficulties are, their cause, effects or solution (i.e. the *content* of therapy). In many ways, such a stance may be seen to take us back to some of Rogers' earliest ideas highlighting the importance of the client's own *views and experiences* and the avoidance of interpretation and advice-giving as part of the therapeutic endeavour. Hence they provide a welcome link between the past, present and future of the approach.

Other developments

As well as ongoing development of an experiential perspective (e.g. Greenberg et al., 1993) and the continued debate with those favouring more classical ways of working (Brodley, 2006) there are a number of other arenas of person-centred theory and practice which have evolved in recent years to provide practitioners with a range of new ideas and methods of working in the approach. For Sanders (2004), these developments represent the leading edges of the contemporary person-centred therapy, and provide much of the vibrancy and dynamism associated with a psychological perspective re-discovering its unique contribution to the field. For Sanders (2004: pp. 17–19), the leading edges of person-centred therapy are:

*   Pre-Therapy – an evolving form of person-centred therapy (e.g. Prouty et al., 2002) designed to help those with severe psychological disturbance (e.g. psychosis);

- Pluralistic self – theoretical advancements in person-centred theory to account for contemporary psychological understandings of the 'self' as a contextual entity composed of a number of different 'configurations' (e.g. Cooper, 1999);
- More than the actualising tendency – the development of person-centred theory to stress the importance of the social context in psychological change (Mearns and Thorne, 2000);
- A dialogical approach (e.g. Schmid, 2003) – a developing understanding of person-centred therapy as a co-created dialogue.
- Fragile and dissociated process – a form of person-centred theory and practice focused upon working with those commonly defined as having a 'personality disorder' or another severe form of psychological disturbance (e.g. Warner, 2000);
- Person-centred therapy as a fundamentally ethical activity – a theoretical exploration highlighting the ethical basis of person-centred therapy as a form of human relating (Schmid, 2001; Grant, 2004);
- Spirituality and the PCA – a growing body of work examining the relationship between person-centred therapy and various spiritual traditions and practices (e.g. Thorne, 2002; Moore, 2004).

In many ways this book could justifiably be filled by a detailed exploration of each of these exciting areas of work, examining their increasingly important contribution to the developing person-centred field. However, such a task would involve a neglect of so many important dimensions of the basis of the approach, both in terms of its development as a form of psychological therapy as well as the nature of its theory and practice when contextualised within a contemporary counselling psychology domain. Hence, while we shall touch upon many of these leading edge developments in our ongoing exploration, our priority is first and foremost the underpinning dimensions of person-centred therapy, and thus a broader elaboration of its theory, practice and context. It is to this task that we that we now turn, considering the person-centred theory of personality and individual difference in the following chapter.

Summary

- Carl Rogers developed the person-centred approach on the basis of his own therapeutic experiences, the theoretical ideas of the psychoanalyst Otto Rank, and the scientific principles of empirical psychology.
- The approach offered a contrast to dominant behaviourist and psychodynamic methods of working, and was first outlined formally in 1942.
- Although initially termed non-directive therapy, it was re-named client-centred therapy by Rogers in 1951.

- Client-centred therapy emphasises the importance of a warm, caring relationship between psychologist and client.
- In 1957 Rogers defined the six 'necessary and sufficient conditions' for therapeutic change to occur. These included the three so-called 'core-conditions' of empathy, congruence and unconditional positive regard. His 1959 paper is now seen as the definitive version of the theory and practice of person-centred therapy.
- The approach was re-named person-centred in the early 1970s to reflect its status as a series of principles applicable in many social contexts, rather than simply as an approach to psychological therapy.
- Carl Rogers died in 1987, just before learning of his nomination for the Nobel Peace Prize.
- Different interpretations of what person-centred therapy should involve have emerged over time. The two main schools of thought are the experiential and classical perspectives.
- Recent innovations in person-centred theory and practice, such as the development of 'pluralistic' models of self contribute to the approach's status as one of the most dynamic, vibrant areas within contemporary counselling psychology.

TWO   A Person-centred Theory of Personality and Individual Difference

Introduction

As we saw in the previous chapter, Carl Rogers first spelt out his person-centred theory of personality and motivation in 1951, in his book *Client-Centred Therapy*. The theory was based primarily on what he had seen happen, and work, in the therapeutic encounter. This was subsequently elaborated and understood both through scientific examination and a range of ideas derived from those around him (e.g. Otto Rank). In basing so many of his understandings on clinical practice, Rogers' theory was not a dry, academic approach revelling in philosophical complexity and metaphor. It was instead the stuff of the real world, a personality theory *based* on therapeutic practice, rather than the other way round, (e.g. behaviour therapy).

Although Rogers' initial theoretical writings in 1951 were somewhat tentative in approach, by 1959 his thinking had evolved and his subsequent definitive account (Rogers, 1959) was constructed in the confident terms of a scientific statement supported by an array of empirical findings. As may be expected of a psychologist grounded in the principles of natural science (Evans, 1975), this 1959 statement provided a clear, and testable, series of 'if-then' corollaries linking the assumed characteristics of the human infant to the subsequent development of a self with the potential for psychological well-being or breakdown. These theoretical propositions still form the bedrock of classical person-centred personality theory to this day.

In this chapter we will explore Rogers' person-centred approach to personality, focusing upon its view of the key dynamics relating to psychological functioning and distress. As with any personality theory, there are some fundamental concepts (or constructs) underpinning the theoretical ideas proposed. These require tentative exploration prior to examining how they link to the more general developmental themes. Our starting point is therefore the theoretical view (or model) of the person assumed by the person-centred perspective, and the three main constructs this proposes.

Model of the person

The actualising tendency

The most significant construct underpinning Rogers' theory of personality is that each human being has an inherent, biological tendency toward growth and development. This tendency is located at the level of the organism as a whole and is seen as the single, basic motivational force driving each human being toward the fulfilment of their unique potential (Merry, 1995). Rather than providing a pre-determined blueprint of what each person would become in ideal circumstances, as is often assumed (Bozarth and Brodley, 1991), the actualising tendency is defined as (Rogers, 1961: pp.351); a 'directional trend which is evident in all organic and human life – the urge to extend, expand, develop, mature, the tendency to express and activate all the capacities of the organism or the self'. It is a trend toward greater differentiation and autonomy, self-regulation and control (Rogers, 1961) in whatever circumstances that arise.

The concept of a growth-promoting, directional tendency is not unusual in psychological theories of personality, and Rogers shared many of his basic ideas with other humanistic theorists such as Maslow (1954), as well as those more psychoanalytically orientated (c.f. Rogers, 1987). Yet, the actualising tendency itself is an often misunderstood notion that can be seen to take a naively optimistic view of humanity and its basis (e.g. Wheeler, in Wheeler and MacLeod, 1995). By positing an integral tendency toward growth and enhancement, the presence of an actualising tendency is often assumed to imply a vision of human beings as essentially good, with bad or evil actions being a product of social conditioning. Yet, as Wilkins (2003) argues, very little is actually written within the person-centred tradition to align such moral judgements with an assumed directional tendency toward growth. Although the actualising tendency provides a trustworthy and constructive force prompting the organism to maximise its potentialities, this proposition does not carry with it any pejorative assessment of its inherent *goodness*. There is a difference, for Wilkins (2003) between such a moral evaluation, which is a social construct, and simply acknowledging an inherent tendency toward constructive growth (which may, in certain contexts, motivate actions and behaviours that, from other contexts, may seem extremely bad).

In recent years, the notion of an actualising tendency has become increasingly enmeshed with the idea of a creative force governing all living things within the universe. This universal, *formative tendency* (Rogers, 1980) has been highlighted by theorists in a diverse array of disciplines spanning from physics to philosophy (Ellingham, 2002). Certainly, a tendency toward organisation, complexity self-regulation and inter-relatedness may be seen as much in molecular biology (Zohar, 1990) as it is in human psychological functioning. For those in the person-centred tradition, placing trust in this tendency, as expressed within the individual, is absolutely central to clinical practice. It is the formative or actualising tendency that is seen as promoting growth and change in accordance with the unique life circumstances and potentialities of each individual. Hence it is the release or facilitation of this tendency that underpins the therapeutic practices advocated within the approach.

Organismic valuing

A related concept of great importance to person-centred personality theory is that of the human organism as a biological totality. Aligned with the actualising tendency is an ongoing, biologically-driven valuing process which allows each of us to assess experiences that are enhancing to, or maintaining for, our organismic needs and potentialities (Rogers, 1959). So, for example, we may crave food when we are hungry or we may experience anger when our desires are thwarted. Both of these experiences motivate us to the extent that their felt sensations (i.e. the craving of hunger or the feeling of anger) may be enacted (e.g. thinking 'I am hungry' and thus seeking food).

For a number of person-centred practitioners, organismic values are often seen as representing the *real* or *true* self (e.g. Van Kalmathout, 1998), for they are not a product of social conditioning, learned attributes or external influences. Moreover, despite not being an explicitly conscious activity, organismic valuing may constitute a considerable part of our experiencing. Moore (2004), for example, describes moving beyond the 'ego-bound practices of self-reflection' into a deeper, more intuitive process within which she encountered a deeply trustworthy, 'still small voice' (Gendlin, 1964), a consistent, felt and intuitive sensation that represented elements of existence beyond conscious perceptions, attitudes and beliefs. In many ways, this voice may be seen as more closely articulating organismic values, than the socially learned, reflective understandings associated with a conscious self.

The self

As well as the important role attributed to the organismic valuing, Rogers introduced a construct to describe the awareness of *who* we are along with our perceptions of the world of the world around us. This, he termed the *self* or self-concept, a construct heavily influenced by the personality theory of Snygg and Combs (1949) whose 'phenomenological' approach conflicted considerably with both behaviourist and psychoanalytic perspectives in emphasising *personal meaning* above all else (see Box 2.1).

Although initially proclaiming himself disinterested in the notion of self, describing it as a useless and pragmatically meaningless term, he became increasingly aware in his clinical practice of the important role of self-experiences to many of his clients. Many of the people he saw talked in terms of their self, using such phrases as the *real me* or my *true self* (c.f. Rogers, 1959). This observation provided the impetus for much theoretical reflection and the notion of the self was eventually introduced in 1947 to be integrated into a *self-theory* as part of the theoretical proposition on personality produced in 1951. In his subsequent 1959 formulation of person-centred theory, Rogers defined the self as:

> The organised, consistent conceptual gestalt composed of the characteristics of the 'I' or 'me' and the perceptions of the relationships of the 'I' or 'me' to others and to various aspects of life, together with the values attached to those perceptions. (1959, cited in Kirschenbaum and Henderson, 1990a: p.200)

In such terms, the self is viewed as the *subjective reality* of the individual, no less but no more. This is a highly radical formulation, for in defining the self simply in terms of perceptions, any possibility that unconscious processes lie *within* it are dismissed. The self is simply the sum total of the views an individual has about his or her-self and the surrounding world. In actual fact, the decision to eliminate any notions of the unconscious from the definition of the self was pragmatic rather than dogmatic. As we shall see later, Rogers did acknowledge the role of non-conscious influences on an individual's behaviour and experiencing (Coulson, 1995). However, in order to maintain a scientific basis to his theory, he was careful to avoid introducing anything that was untestable into it, preferring not to complicate matters with a theory of self positing an unconscious domain. The notion of the self as a phenomenological construct also allowed Rogers to maintain consistency with this therapeutic emphasis on the experiences and perceptions of the client. Any other aspects of the self could have called this into question.

Box 2.1   Snygg and Combs' phenomenological theory of personality

Donald Snygg and Arthur Combs were psychologists working in the USA in the 1940s and 1950s. In developing their theory of personality, they were particularly interested in what they termed the *phenomenal* field of the behaving organism, an idea based on the philsophical tradition of phenomenology (c.f. Husserl, 1977) which emphasised subjective meaning above all else. Snygg and Combs (1949) proposed that to truly understand an individual's behaviour, gaining an insight into this field was of utmost importance. All actions are meaningful to the

(Continued)

(Continued)

individual involved in them and thus must be seen in such terms. Yet these meanings are likely to differ in accordance with the different ways in which people perceive the world. Understanding any form of behaviour thus necessitates understanding the individual perceptions that motivate it. Snygg and Combs (1949) argued that psychological observers must therefore 'bracket-off' their own assumptions and interpretations, to rely entirely upon those relevant to the individual under observation. In such terms, understanding the subjective meaning associated with any behaviour was of primary significance in gaining a deep appreciation of it. This perspective contrasted strongly with the behaviourist emphasis on observable behaviour only as well as the psychoanalytic emphasis on unconscious conflicts and processes.

Although Rogers often used the term self, a somewhat confusing dimension to person-centred theory is that the terms self-concept and self-structure are also used frequently to denote individuals' perceptions of themselves and the world that surrounds them (Tudor and Merry, 2002). However, the emphasis given to different dimensions of experiencing often determine the use of a particular term and Rogers did briefly differentiate between these aspects (Rogers, 1951). The term 'self-concept' is generally used to refer to an individual's view of him- or herself (e.g. I am a happy, easygoing person). Contrastingly, the self-structure or self is a more global construct that denotes an individual's entire map of the world (Tolan, 2002). This map includes a person's views and beliefs about him- or herself (i.e. the self-concept), but also her perceptions and beliefs more generally. Thus the self-concept may be seen as a portion of the self-structure or self, although in practical terms, one that can be very difficult to clearly differentiate.

Rogers' initial formulation of the self has been explored and developed in many ways since its introduction within person-centred personality theory. A number of theorists have proposed amendments to the ideas outlined. Holdstock (1993), for example, has argued that the self is a relational construct (i.e. enmeshed within our relationships to other people and the world) rather than a demarcated, individualistic composite of perceptions and experiences. Others have focused on the dynamics within it, looking at how collections of perceptions can constitute a range of self-configurations (Mearns, 1999) or inner persons (Keil, 1996). This latter work is of considerable significance for it highlights a more plural view of the self-concept (i.e. as composed of a multiplicity of different possible elements or 'positions') rather than the single entity proposed by Rogers (1957), which has been strongly criticised by those (e.g. Sampson, 1989) from within a social constructionist framework (see Chapter 8). However, what remains central to the notion of the self within the now broad range of person-centred theorising is that it is seen as a *perceived self* (e.g. van Kalmathout, 1998), not any intra-psychic agent that regulates actions or influences actions in a manner that is beyond the conscious awareness of the individual.

The model of the person discussed so far has highlighted the three core constructs underpinning the person-centred approach to personality. It is the interaction between these elements that is seen to make up the personality of any given individual (Nelson-Jones, 2005), a process that may best be understood by charting their development from infancy.

Development of personality

Characteristics of the infant

In presenting his theory, Rogers (1959) described what he termed as the 'postulated characteristics of the human infant'. These are (in summary) that:

- He perceives his experience as reality.
- He has an inherent tendency toward actualising his organism.
- He interacts with his reality in terms of his basic actualising tendency.
- He engages in a basic organismic valuing process, valuing experience with reference to the actualising tendency as criterion.
- He behaves with adience (i.e. attention) toward positively valued experiences and with avoidance toward those negatively evaluated.

In the terms set out by this view, Rogers proposed that an infant's initial interactions with the world are regulated biologically, by an organismic valuing process in conjunction with the actualising tendency. Experiences only take place at a hormonal/physiological, motor (i.e. a readiness to react) and expressive (i.e. vocalisation, gestures, facial expressions etc.) level (Bierman-Ratjen, 1998), with no cognitive reflection or self-awareness present. However, although these are all internal experiences (i.e. within the infant) they often have an external manifestation, such as a facial expression, movement, or crying. Such behaviours, in turn, invoke responses from caregivers, who both give meaning to them (e.g. she's hungry) and relate accordingly (i.e. offering food).

As the baby develops, and through an ongoing relationship with caregivers, he or she begins to evolve a primitive awareness of self through the reflections provided by others. Hence, certain experiences become differentiated as self-experiences (Rogers, 1959), and thus the infant begins to conceptualise that it is *he* who is hungry, or who wants to sleep. The process of differentiation becomes increasingly sophisticated as the infant grows and before long, his self-experiences begin to become organised into a conceptual gestalt (i.e. whole) that constitutes the basis of an initial self-concept (i.e. his view of himself). This self-concept is not simply a list of various attributes (e.g. I get hungry, I like playing ball) but, as Cooper (1999: pp.54) explains, 'a patterned, coherent, integrated, organised gestalt ... the young boy does not experience him-self as a person who is "creative" plus "scared" plus "x"; rather he sees himself as "creative-scared-x" – as an interdependent, uniquely-constellated configuration of characteristics which cannot be broken down to its constituent parts'. This may seem a rather complex distinction but, at its core, is simply the idea that we come to see ourselves in a consistent way, with inter-related qualities, rather than as a series of particular characteristics that bear no relation to one another, or to those around us.

The regard complex and conditions of worth

While the developing self-concept of any child should, in an ideal world, map directly onto his or her organismic experiences (i.e. organismic values, such as anger, being acknowledged within the self-concept), this can be compromised by what Rogers (1959) viewed as the child's need for positive regard from others. This need arises from the actualising tendency, and may thus (simplistically) be seen as a biological drive toward maximising the nurturing felt from other peoples' warmth and acceptance.

   As the infant develops an increasingly differentiated capacity for self-experiencing, she begins to evaluate these experiences in terms of the extent to which they are received with positive regard by others (i.e. accepted and recognised by others in a manner that invokes warmth and nurturing). The nature of the messages received from others are of vital importance during this time. If caregivers are entirely empathic (i.e. understanding), warm and accepting, the infant's self-experiences are fully received and he or she gains a secure sense of all his organismic values (e.g. anger, sadness etc.) as being unconditionally positively regarded. However, should certain self-experiences be ignored or invoke a negative reaction, the infant begins to evaluate these accordingly. So, for example, he or she may realise that 'I am not liked when I get angry' or 'they like me when I am happy'. In associating certain self-experiences with positive regard, and others with no positive regard, the infant develops what Rogers (1959, cited in Kirschenbaum and Henderson, 1990a: p.209) terms a 'regard complex'. This may be defined as (1990b: p.209) 'all those self-experiences, together with their inter-relationships, which the individual discriminates as being related to the positive regard of a particular social other'.

   The emerging regard complex is hugely important, for it refers to the differentiated self-experiences which are received with positive regard by others. In order to maximise the level of positive regard received, the infant thus begins to recognise those self-experiences are positively regarded by those around him, and act in ways aligned to these. Hence, as well as developing an understanding of which self-experiences are worthy of reward by others and those which are not, the infant starts to shape his interactions with others in a manner designed to maximise the positive regard he receives. As a result, he increasingly orientates his attention toward positively regarded self-experiences, such as feelings of happiness and their associated behaviours, attending less to those that invoke less or no positive regard from others. Thus the infant's self-experiences become skewed towards those positively regarded by others, a process that has implications for how he evaluates his own experiences in turn.

As part of acquiring a regard complex, the infant begins to develop an evaluation of himself in terms of positive *self*-regard. In other words, he starts to view his own self-experiences in terms of the level of positive regard they have received from others. So, an infant may start to evaluate *himself* in positive terms when he, say, laughs and smiles. The expression of happiness, to him, is a good thing with which he feels comfortable as an aspect of himself. By contrast, the same infant may start to see his feelings of anger in negative terms, because he now *believes* this aspect of his self-experiencing is not one to be valued (through learning this is not positively regarded by others). Hence he feels uncomfortable with his anger, seeing it as an undesirable or unworthy quality.

For Rogers (1959), differentiating between self-experiences that are evaluated as worthy (associated with positive self-regard) and those evaluated as unworthy (not associated with positive self-regard) highlight the infant's acquisition of *conditions of worth*. Such conditions refer to the way that the infant has learned that his or her worth (manifested in the experience of positive self-regard) is conditional on particular characteristics being present, and others absent. Hence, her positive self-regard is *conditional*, and thus only accessed in relation to some self-experiences (e.g. being happy, quiet etc.) and not others.

As the infant's emerging self-concept becomes structured in terms of the regard complex, her need for positive regard of others becomes associated with the now internalised associations between particular self-experiences and positive self-regard. Hence, the *need* for the positive regard of others becomes associated with a *need* for positive *self-regard,* and she starts to seek out those experiences that she sees as providing positive *self-regard* while avoiding those not evaluated in such terms. Therefore the child begins to act and behave in ways that offer her a feeling of worth and internal reward ('I'll study hard because it makes me feel really good about myself'). Actions that do not offer such experiences (such as going out to play) are avoided because they are not associated with feelings of personal worth and value. So a child may get annoyed with herself for not concentrating hard enough ('why would I want to waste time playing?') rather than acknowledge this desire as one of importance. It is through this process that an infant's internalised conditions of worth begin to shape how she views herself and, accordingly how she interacts with the world. This shaping process is one that strongly informs how she will experience herself, and the world, in adulthood.

The notion of conditions of worth is a central concept in person-centred personality theory and is seen as pivotal to the nature of the self-concept as it evolves. As certain self-experiences do not invoke positive self-regard (hence contravening the child's *need* for positive self-regard), the child begins to selectively perceive herself in terms of those more comfortable associations that offer positive self-regard. Hence the self-concept becomes increasingly shaped around positively regarded self-experiences, with those other aspects of experiencing increasingly disowned as part of the self. In other words, the child starts to perceive herself (i.e. in terms of her self-concept) in terms of those self-experiences that she has learned to value, and begins to ignore those that she has learned not to. In effect, this introduces a split between those aspects of her organismic values which are acknowledged within the self and those which are not. Consequently, some experiences of the organism as a whole (e.g. organismic experiences such as anger etc.) may not be acknowledged as self-experiences (i.e. consciously acknowledged within the self-concept). These values although existing at an *organismic* level, thus become, to various degrees and in different ways, unconscious, a process which relies upon a mechanism defined as subception (Rogers, 1951).

Box 2.2   Attachment theory and the person-centred approach

There are a number of commonalities between the theory to personality development described by Rogers, and the processes of child development outlined by John Bowlby in his theory of attachment (Bierman-Ratjen, 1996). The most significant of these is perhaps the shared focus on the development of what Bowlby termed the infant's *inner working model* of herself and the expectations and likely behaviour of others (Bowlby, 1969). This model, formed in early infancy, influences her subsequent transactions with those around. Rogers conceptualised this process in terms of the formation of a self-concept containing internalised conditions of worth which, in conjunction with a need for positive self-regard, provide the basis for an infant's subsequent experiencing and behaviour. Bowlby, a psychiatrist and psychoanalyst, took a more differentiated approach, identifying

(Continued)

specific patterns of attachment that evolve during early interactions (e.g. secure, avoidant etc.). These are seen as playing a significant role in psychological disturbance manifest in later life, a view shared by Rogers (1959), who viewed the incongruence between the organismic valuing process or 'self' and the interpersonally acquired 'self-concept' as providing the seed for psychological difficulties encountered in adulthood.

Psychological defence and subception

For Rogers (1959), the split between what is experienced at an organismic level and what is acknowledged within the 'self-concept' is determined by psychological mechanisms he termed denial and distortion. Both these mechanisms prevent any organismic values contravening conditions of worth being *accurately perceived* within conscious awareness. Thus they may be seen as forms of psychological defence, with the term defence being used here to denote their function, which is to maintain the consistency and nature of the self-concept as it exists at any given moment. This takes place by preventing contradictory organismic values being acknowledged as self-experiences, thus protecting the individual from the psychological difficulties arising from a threat to his perceptions (or concept) of himself and his need for positive self-regard. These two processes of defence are defined as follows (Rogers, 1951):

- Denial – is when an experience felt at an organismic level is not perceived in any way at a conscious level. In other words, the organismic experience is not differentiated as a self-experience. An example of this is when, for instance, Jane's boredom in staying at home to look after her children is denied to awareness due to internalised conditions of worth relating to motherhood. In order to maintain positive self-regard, she is thus unable to acknowledge her organismic experiences, for she has a concept of self that does afford the possibility of feeling bored in her caring maternal role. Hence, when such organismic experiences are encountered, they are denied to awareness due to the threat that these would present to her view of herself as a caring mother.
- Distortion – is when experiences are perceived *inaccurately* to resolve the conflict they present to the self-concept. In terms of the previous example, the process of distortion may involve, rather than the denial of Jane's experience of boredom to awareness, its distortion into a welcome feeling of fatigue at being over-run by the children all day.

In discussing denial and distortion, Rogers (1951) explained how these processes operated by drawing on a study by McCleary and Lazarus (1949). This study suggested that all stimuli, and thus experiences, are evaluated by the organism *prior* to any reflective awareness of them, which, for Rogers (1951: pp.507) pointed to 'a process of "subception", a discriminating evaluative, physiological, organismic response to experience, which may precede the conscious perception of such experience'. Hence the process of subception provides a basic evaluation of the extent to which any organismic experience may present a threat to the self-concept *before* that experience is acknowledged consciously. Those experiences that do present a threat to the consistency of the existing self-concept are thus denied or distorted. This is not to say that such organismic experiences do not exist, merely that they are felt at an organismic level that is outwith conscious awareness.

Incongruence as a basis for psychological distress

As we have seen, the theory of personality proposed by Rogers envisages the existence of two different valuing systems operating within the individual: firstly that of the organism and secondly, as the infant grows up and into adulthood, that of the self (i.e. self-experiences). When the values are not in alignment, a state of *incongruence* occurs. Although some degree of incongruence between self-experiences and organismic valuing is almost inevitable, as the acquisition of at least some conditions of worth during childhood is highly probable, when the degree of incongruence between these becomes significant, the mechanisms of denial and distortion can begin to fail. This results in what Rogers (1951: p.248) terms a 'state of disorganisation' within the self, where the individual is forced to confront experiences that do not make sense in terms of his self-concept. Sometimes, the individual herself is able to integrate the previously denied or distorted experiences into her self-concept and a new equilibrium is found, thus reducing the incongruence and level of distress. However, when the incongruence is significant and the processes of denial and distortion repeatedly fall short in preventing threatening organismic experiences being acknowledged as self-experiences, the individual's entire concept of self becomes fractured and varying degrees of psychological distress ensue. These include difficulties such as anxiety and depression as well more severe forms of disturbance such as psychosis.

Although it is inevitable that all of us are incongruent to differing degrees, it is individuals who have encountered a large number of conditions of worth in their upbringing who are more likely to encounter the high degree of incongruence at the root of severe psychological problems. For such individuals, the self-concept is likely to be structured around a highly restrictive set of experiences (i.e. those associated with positive self-regard) resulting in a great many denied or distorted organismic experiences. These individuals were infants brought up in contexts offering either very little in the way of positive regard or circumstances in which the positive regard on offer was highly conditional. Hence they were significantly cut off from their organismic experiencing and have what Rogers (1959) terms as an external *locus of evaluation*. What this means is that they have had to make decisions almost entirely on the basis of external values (i.e. conditions of worth) rather than on the basis of the experiencing of the organism as a whole. Hence, when the processes of denial and distortion fail, the individual is left bereft of any coherent or consistent sense of self. Their entire self-concept, predicated exclusively on conditions of worth, is cast into doubt, often leading to significant personality fragmentation and distress.

Box 2.3   Example of psychological breakdown – Sara

Sara was a musician with a leading role in a well-known orchestra. She had grown up in a demanding family and her self-concept was strongly orientated around being a success in whatever she did. Sara was very driven and focused upon her career, often spending up to 16 hours a day rehearsing. Over the past year, Sara had begun to feel very down. She didn't understand why this was so, for she believed she was on the way to achieving her career goals and was fulfilling her lifetime ambitions within the music field. However, at the same time, she had also begun to experience many doubts as to the *point* of working so hard to the exclusion of so many other things. Although previously putting these doubts down to tiredness, they came to a head when she had been told by the conductor that she didn't seem to enjoy her work any more and that it might be better if she had some time off. Sara found this very distressing. It rang true but also made her wonder who she was if she wasn't the ambitious and successful musician she saw herself to be. It seemed as if her world was coming crashing down around her, and she endured a long depression feeling a failure and of little or no value.

Sara's experiences can be understood in terms of the incongruence between her self-concept (which revolved around conditions of worth regarding career success) and an organismic need for a more nurturing way of living. The incongruence between these valuing processes had hightened over the last year, perhaps due to her getting a bit older, and Sara's self-concept had a significant struggle maintaining its consistency in the face of organismic values prompting for a more

(Continued)

(Continued)

balanced existence. Her doubts about the job were regularly denied ('I am really happy in my job, I'm just tired') or distorted ('I do feel fed up, but that's a good thing – keeps me on my toes'). It was only when she came face to face with the clear evidence of her organismic experiencing, in terms of her conductor's awareness of her doubts, that she fully encountered the incongruence between these different values. It was this process that engendered the psychological 'breakdown' she experienced, resulting in her feelings of a loss of her self, of worthlessness and depression.

Alternative explanations of incongruence

Despite the emphasis placed by Rogers on the *developmental* basis of incongruence, other person-centred writers from within the experiential tradition (e.g. Purton, 2002) have argued that this theoretical perspective does not account for the many disturbances arising from events that are unconnected to the conditions of worth developed in childhood and subsequently evolved throughout life. For example, he points to Allen, a 15 year old whose terror of dogs was all embracing, but who had only been bitten recently and knew intellectually that few dogs were likely to attack him. Purton asks, in relation to Allen, how conditions of worth and the resultant incongruence could create such disturbance. Surely, he asks, it was something about the event of being bitten *recently* that was at the root of Allen's difficulties?

Although Worsley (2002) has argued that Rogers himself began to question the view that it is *only* introjected (i.e. learned) conditions of worth that produce incongruence, he acknowledges that questions such as those raised by Purton raise some significant issues for a person-centred theory of psychological disturbance. For Purton (2002), the solution to such concerns lies in the way experiences are *processed,* for sometimes organismic experiencing can become blocked (i.e. not accurately symbolised) for reasons unrelated to conditions of worth and thus remain as a bodily or emotional experience rather than a psychological one (e.g. Gendlin, 1996; Greenberg et al., 1996). As well as highlighting the role of processing in creating and maintaining disturbance, theory in this area has been further elaborated by Joseph (2004) in discussing Post-Traumatic Stress Disorder (PTSD).

In pointing to the commonalities in the processes of psychological breakdown (i.e. the disorganisation of self) as described by Rogers (1959) and the commonly understood experiences of Post-Traumatic Stress Disorder (PTSD), Joseph argues that out of the ordinary events present us with information that can often highlight the incongruence between self-experience and organismic experience. The reason for this, he argues, is that our self structure (including self-concept) often contains common distortions with regards to the nature of reality and human experiencing. He suggests (2004: p.106), for example:

> One aspect of self-structure in which there is a high degree of discrepancy between self and experience is in the denial to awareness of existential experiences, for example, that we are fragile, that the future is uncertain, and that life is unfair. Although many people will say they know these to be truths, when it comes to how they actually lead their lives, most go from day to day as if they were invulnerable ... what traumatic events do is to abruptly and obviously present them with experience that leads to a breakdown of these aspects of self-structure.

In this regard, Joseph is arguing that incongruence is not simply the product of learned conditions of worth, but also a functional process mediating the anxiety generated by the givens of everyday existence. Certainly, this would resonate with the ideas of a number of existential philosophers, such as Sartre (1956) or psychotherapists, such as van Deurzen (2002), who locate much psychological distress in the realities of human existence (e.g. the inevitability of death, feelings of loneliness etc.). However, as Cooper (2004) points out, such an approach is very different to the equation made by Rogers between mature forms of psychological development and high levels of congruence between self and organismic experience. In this respect, Joseph would seem to be calling into question some of the most fundamental propositions of person-centred theory of personality and its postulated possibility of living the good life.

Visions of the 'good life': the fully-functioning person

In detailing his theory of personality and proposing incongruence as the basis of all psychological breakdown, Rogers (1959) also provided a theory of what he described as the fully functioning person. This theory detailed the attributes of a *hypothetical* person whom he saw as the 'ultimate in the actualisation of the human organism' (1959, cited in Kirschenbaum and Henderson, 1990a: p.250). The nature of such a person was elaborated by Rogers, (1961), in a more detailed account of what he termed 'the good life'. So not only was there a description of psychological disorder and personality breakdown within person-centred personality theory, but also one of human potential and fulfilment. This emphasis on potential was important, for it resonated with Rogers' determination to avoid a deficit based model of human functioning and instead develop a method of working grounded in the potential for constructive growth and change toward an ultimate way of living.

In describing what he regarded as optimal human functioning, Rogers (1961) identified three broad attributes which, he proposed, characterised the experiencing and behaviour of *any fully functioning* individual. These are: a) openness to experience, b) living in an existential manner and, c) trust in organismic experiencing. Of course, few actual individuals possess these qualities in their ultimate form. The good life is more an ideal than a commonly realised state!

Openness to experience

The fully functioning person is entirely congruent and hence in direct conscious contact with the nature of all their experiencing at all times. No processes of psychological defence are necessary in such circumstances, and the individual owns all his organismic experiences, painful, anxious or otherwise. As part and parcel of this process, such a person holds herself in *unconditional* positive regard, and therefore is not attempting to satisfy any conditions of worth in her experiencing or behaviour. The upshot of this is a complete openness to all experience, positive or negative.

Living in an existential manner

With no need for psychological defensiveness, the fully functioning person is able to live each moment anew, engaging fully in the present rather than attempting to fit experience or behaviour to a schema orientated around a particular self-concept or view of life. Living in the *present,* rather than ruminating on the past or worrying about the future, is seen as part and parcel of a flowing, ever-changing self-experience.

Trust in organismic experiencing

The third attribute of the fully functioning person is her capacity to fully trust her organismic experience as a means of arriving at a decision regarding behaviour or action, rather than looking for external codes or structures to provide guidance. For Rogers, this meant the capacity to do what feels right in a given set of circumstances, trusting her inner reactions to find satisfactory ways of acting. As he suggests (Rogers, 1961: p.191):

> If they 'feel like' expressing anger they do so and find that this comes out satisfactorily, because they are equally alive to all of their other desires for affection, affiliation, and relationship...they realise how surprisingly trustworthy their inner reactions have been in bringing about satisfactory behaviour.

In detailing the attributes of a fully functioning person and their envisaged good life, Rogers stressed the *processes* of experiencing rather than a fixed range of characteristics or behaviours. This orientation is of great significance to the vision being presented. Rather than viewing the optimal state of human function as, say feeling or behaving in a specific way, he viewed it in terms of an *openness* to experience and fluidity. Hence, the fully functioning person is not seen as always happy, never sad or angry, but completely open to their moment by moment experiencing. As such, he proclaims, it is a life not for the 'faint hearted' (1961: p.196).

Box 2.4   The fully functioning person and Maslow's *self-actualised* individual

There are a number of similarities between the fully functioning person described by Rogers and the conception of a self-actualised individual first introduced by Maslow (1954). Both visions draw on the notion of the fulfilment of capability and potential (which, of course, is different for every person and dependent on other factors such as context, personality etc.) and present this as the ultimate goal of psychotherapy (Patterson, 2000). However, while the concepts may be similar, the term 'self-actualisation' has a very different meaning in person-centred theory to that used by Maslow, being concerned with the operation of the actualising tendency within the 'self-concept' *only* (Guthrie-Ford, 1991). Maslow's vision of self-actualisation refers to the fulfilment of the organism as a *whole*, not simply that of the self. Hence, while the underlying concepts are similar, the terminology is not and as such, a vision of a 'self-actualised' individual is not the same within the person-centred approach as the fully functioning person. Indeed, Rogers deliberately avoided using the term 'self-actualised' because of the confusion it would create.

In this chapter we have explored the fundamental ideas proposed by Rogers in relation to personality and motivation, as well as the explanation these provide as to the cause of psychological disturbance. The theory relies strongly on the notion of *incongruence,* and it is therefore of little surprise to learn that the theory of therapy also outlined by Rogers explores how, through therapeutic relating, a person-centred psychologist can assist a client to become increasingly *congruent* in his or her experiencing. However, this is not an easy process and in Chapter 3 we will explore some of the challenges a therapist (and client) may face in undertaking such work.

Summary

- Rogers first outlined his theory of personality and motivation in 1951, although the definitive statement of his ideas was published in 1959.
- Person-centred personality theory proposes that fundamental to all human endeavour is the actualising tendency, a biologically-based, pro-social motivating force serving to maintain and enhance the organism as an entity.
- During infancy, a child initially evaluates his experiences in terms of how they meet the needs of his organism as a whole. Through interactions with caregivers, he subsequently acquires a self-concept structured around the values he has learned from them. If these values associate some, but not all, aspects of his experiences with positive regard, he becomes only partially accepting of himself. His positive self-regard is conditional, and he has acquired conditions of worth.
- Due to the child's need for positive self-regard, he attends primarily to experiences that make him feel good about himself (i.e. those that offer him positive self-regard), neglecting those that do not. Those organismic experiences that do not offer positive self-regard gradually become disowned, and the child begins to no longer identify as his own, experiences that conflict with his conditions of worth.
- When organismic values and those of the self-concept conflict, a state of *incongruence* emerges. Due to the actualising tendency, the individual strives to maintain consistency of the 'self-concept' by unconsciously denying or distorting conflicting organismic experiences.
- When the processes of denial or distortion fail, in childhood or adulthood, the incongruence is experienced thus creating a state of psychological disturbance. Psychological difficulties are thus a product of incongruence.
- More recent work has highlighted the blocks to the processing of experience as an alternative to explanations citing introjected conditions of worth as the sole cause of incongruence.

THREE A Person-centred Theory of Psychological Therapy

Introduction

As we saw in the previous chapter, Rogers' (1959) theory of personality posited *incongruence* between organismic experiencing and the self-concept as the sole cause of all psychological disturbance. Following on from such a view, it is the reduction of incongruence that is associated with greater psychological well-being and, as such, provides the rationale for a person-centred approach to psychological therapy. In this chapter we shall explore the person-centred therapeutic approach, highlighting how it works to reduce incongruence in the ways initially described by Rogers (1957), as well as those subsequently developed by others within the framework (e.g. 'experiential' practitioners)

A theory of therapy

Since first outlining his ideas for psychotherapy in the early 1940s, Carl Rogers consistently highlighted the role of the relationship between client and counsellor as of primary significance in therapeutic practice. This was a stance that evolved from his own experiences of working as a psychologist, and informed by his awareness of a wide range of other psychological theories and approaches. Rogers saw an effective therapeutic relationship as denoted by the presence of a systematic series of counsellor attitudes in conjunction with certain factors primarily linked to the client. If each of these dimensions were in place, he argued it was *inevitable* that psychological growth would occur.

In 1957 he published a paper entitled 'The Necessary and Sufficient Conditions of Therapeutic Personality Change' in which he detailed six conditions which were 'necessary and sufficient' for psychological change to occur within a client. Rogers deliberately used the word *sufficient* to make it absolutely clear that these conditions, if met, were enough to produce change. Nothing else was needed. Indeed, he saw further techniques or methods drawing on the expertise of the therapist (such as advice-giving or interpretations) as an irrelevant sideshow.

This paper is now known as his *integrative statement* (Wilkins, 2003) because it was designed to be relevant to all psychotherapy and drew on research and analysis from a range of psychological approaches, not simply person-centred therapy. Hence, Rogers' (1957) proposition was that *any* relationship possessing the conditions he specified would produce psychological change within the client, irrespective of whichever psychological approach was employed. For him, psychoanalytic and behaviourist approaches would be equally effective if the relationship between client and therapist possessed the same qualities, and in the same measures, as those offered within a person-centred therapeutic context. What really mattered was the relationship a therapist had with his or her client, with psychological change *guaranteed* if this relationship met the following conditions (Rogers, 1957: p.96):

1. Two persons are in psychological contact.
2. The first, whom we shall term the client, is in a state of incongruence, being vulnerable or anxious.
3. The second person, whom we shall term the therapist, is congruent or integrated in the relationship.
4. The therapist experiences unconditional positive regard for the client.
5. The therapist experiences an empathic understanding of the client's internal frame of reference and endeavours to communicate this experience to the client.
6. The communication to the client of the therapist's empathic understanding and unconditional positive regard is to a minimal degree achieved.

Although there is some discussion over the precise terminology of the conditions as stated (c.f. Embleton-Tudor et al., 2004), the emphasis on relationship is clear. In general, the 6 conditions are considered as to have two basic components, those associated with the actions and experiences of the therapist (conditions 3, 4 and 5), and those linked to the client's experiences and capacity to engage in a therapeutic relationship. Conditions 3, 4 and 5, the so-called 'therapist conditions' (Barrett-Lennard, 1998) are often termed the *core conditions*, and are those most often referred to within other therapeutic orientations (e.g. Egan, 1998) as well as providing the focus for much research and analysis (e.g. Norcross, 2002). They are seen as *core* because they concern the conduct of the therapy by the therapist and are therefore often seen as the vehicle through which change is enabled. Each is seen to play a different, but equally important, part in facilitating a client to become more congruent.

The 'core' conditions

The core conditions of empathy and unconditional positive regard present a considerable challenge to the person-centred practitioner, for they are not formulated as skills to be acquired, but rather as personal attitudes or attributes 'experienced' by the therapist, as well as communicated to the client for therapy to be successful (this latter requirement is stated in condition 6). Congruence (condition 3) is somewhat different but again seen as a quality of the therapist, rather than an action or skill. This emphasis on personal attributes served to counteract any existing notions that person-centred therapy was simply a mechanistic process of non-directive repetition in the presence of warmth (as often simplistically understood). However, in placing the emphasis upon the therapist to *experience* particular qualities, and to *communicate* these in such a way that is, at the very least, minimally achieved (condition 6), Rogers highlighted the very personal nature of the therapeutic relationship he envisaged.

For Rogers, therapeutic work is an inherently *personal* task with its success wholly dependent on the capacity of the therapist to enter into an *experiential relationship* with a client, not to hide behind professional masks or intellectual expertise. This capacity is not acquired through formalised academic learning or by training to be a professional psychologist (although such knowledge is important to support such work), but through self-development and personal growth activities, such as group and personal therapy. Indeed, he later described this capacity, once developed, as a 'way of being' (Rogers, 1980), suggesting at times that the very 'presence' of another person offering these qualities is sufficient for psychological change to occur (Rogers, 1986).

Box 3.1   Non-directivity and the therapeutic relationship

Although often not stated directly, the principle of non-directivity is often seen to remain at the heart of Rogers' person-centred approach to therapy (e.g. Grant, 1990). It is enmeshed in the 6 conditions identified by Rogers in 1957, and in particular the conditions of therapist empathy and unconditional positive regard. In being committed to offering these attitudes, a person-centred counsellor does not attempt to take control of a client's experiencing by diagnosing particular psychological disorders or by instructing a client how best to deal with the problems he or she encounters. Instead, the client is viewed as the expert on his or her own life, and accordingly supported to exercise autonomy in making choices (Merry, 1999), As a result of this non-directive approach, the client is enabled to grow in accordance with his or her unique attributes, and fully trusted in this process by the counsellor. A commitment to non-directivity represents, at its most basic, a fundamental person-centred belief in the client's actualising tendency, or in other words her capacity to function as an autonomous, constructive and self-regarding being.

The notion of non-directivity is a highly controversial aspect of person-centred theory, with critics such as Kahn (1999) arguing that it renders a therapist passive in the face of all client desires or intents, as well as denying the inevitable impact of the counsellor's own views

(Continued)

(Continued)

and ideas on the counselling process itself. However, Mearns and Thorne (2000) propose that the whole question over non-directivity is misplaced, and that as in the 1940s the idea is often misinterpreted as a behaviour rather than an attitude or principle. Instead it is better seen, as Merry (1999) suggests as 'a general non-authoritarian attitude ... it refers also to the theory that the actualising tendency can be fostered in a relationship of particular qualities, and that whilst the general direction of that tendency is regarded as constructive and creative, its particular characteristics in any one person cannot be predicted, and should not be controlled or directed' (pp.75–76).

Empathy

Empathy is perhaps the most well-known of Rogers' therapeutic conditions, and is certainly the one which attracted the most attention in the early stages of the approach (Raskin, 1948, Patterson, 2000). The key characteristic of empathy is understanding another person's subjective reality as she experiences it at any given moment. This requires an orientation toward the client's 'frame of reference', a phenomenological term used to describe the particular issues, concerns and values that are relevant to that individual in that moment. It is thus an attitude through which the therapist strives to 'enter the client's private perceptual world and [become] thoroughly at home within it' (Rogers, 1980: p.142). In other words, empathy is the experience of trying to fully understand another person's world.

In contrast to sympathy, which involves a *sharing* of outlook or experience, empathy requires a 'bracketing' (Cooper, 2004) or setting aside, by the practitioner, of his own experiences, attitudes and ideas, with a focus, instead, on trying to understand how another person is feeling and thinking. From a therapist's point of view, an empathic attitude is a desire to understand a client's perceptual world *as if* it was his or her own (Rogers, 1959). The term 'as if' is important here, for it denotes that empathy is about deeply understanding a client's experiences while at the same time *not forgetting* that they reside within the client (McMillan, 1997). This recognition allows a counsellor to maintain the separation between his or her own experiences and those of another (Tolan, 2003), something which is of paramount importance to avoid confusion and misunderstanding.

Being empathic

The most common method of experiencing empathy is to listen to closely to what a client is saying, not only through words, but also through all forms of non-verbal and bodily communication. For Brodley (2001, p.18) the targets of empathic understanding are thus a 'client's perceptions, reactions, and feelings, and the ways in which the client as a self or person is an agency, *an actor*, and active force – a source of actions and reactions'.

Empathic understanding is only effective in person-centred terms if it is effectively communicated (condition 6) to a client, a process that ensures the client knows that the therapist understands how he feels as well as checks the extent to which the empathy expressed is accurate. There are a number of common mechanisms employed within person-centred therapy to achieve this. Perhaps the most familiar of these is reflecting back, or paraphrasing, a client's personal experiencing (which can include, thoughts, feelings and, indeed, motivations for future actions; Bohart & Greenberg, 1997). In order to ensure accuracy, however, any kind of empathic statement has within it the implied question 'is this how it is for you?' (Barrett-Lennard, 1998). Indeed, Rogers steered away from the use of the term 'reflection' in relation to empathy, preferring instead phrases such 'testing understandings' or 'checking perceptions'. These he argued, were more accurate descriptions of what was actually occurring in the moment by moment tracking of a client's frame of reference at any given moment (Rogers, 1986).

Box 3.2   Example of empathic reflection

C: I have been having a dreadful time recently, what with all the disruption at home and work. It just seems as if things couldn't get much worse.

T: So, it's been a terrible both at home and at work. It seems to be coming at you from all sides. Things couldn't get any more awful than they are at the moment?

C: Yes, I'm at my wits end (becoming tearful).

In this example, the client (C) describes a view of her situation, indicating that her recent 'dreadful' time is linked to 'disruption' at home and at work. Rather that ask for more details as to the nature of the disruption cited, or why it has had such an effect (as, perhaps, may be expected in normal conversation), the therapist (T) offers an *empathic reflection* of the client's experiences. This allows the client to experience the therapist's understanding of her feelings ('I'm at my wits end'), a process which deepens the extent to which she contacts her organismic experiencing (i.e. the feelings that invoke tearfulness).

Despite the emphasis on reflection, Bozarth (1984) has suggested the attitudinal basis of empathy within the person-centred framework allows for a far greater range of empathic responses than often acknowledged. He argues that the person-centred therapist should actively strive to develop what he terms as *idiosyncratic* modes of empathy which are (1984: p.75) 'not standardised responses but idiosyncratic to the persons and interactions between the persons in therapy sessions. Such modes are learned by therapists as they are allowed to affirm their personal power as therapists ... the equating of reflection with empathy has restricted the potency of therapists. The focus on empathy as a verbal clarification technique limits the intuitive functions of therapists'.

In suggesting the empathic attitude is idiosyncratic, Bozarth makes it clear that therapists must learn to use their intuitive experiencing as part of the empathy process, and hence employ methods such as metaphors, similes, questions, silences and personal reflections to relate their understanding to the client. Such methods, which may often be experienced as risky as they do not offer a certain outcome (Bozarth, 2001) and can evoke (Rice, 1974) an aspect of organismic experiencing not previously acknowledged. Indeed, for Cooper (2001) empathy is not simply a cognitive or affective process but also a bodily one involving physical sensations (such as feelings of nausea). Bodily sensations, when experienced by a therapist, may empathically resonate with a client's own bodily experiencing at a particular moment in time, thus providing an important vehicle for empathic understanding. Forms of physical posture and gesture that mimic, intentionally or otherwise, a client's bodily presentation may also be considered as inherent elements of a truly empathic relationship. Indeed, Cooper argues that there is much evidence to indicate such a mimetic process is what he terms 'an innate and instinctive human capability' (p.224). For the therapist, therefore, the issue is less of how to develop embodied methods of empathising and more how can such natural forms of relating be (2001: p.224) 'allowed to emerge' in the context of a therapeutic process.

The role of empathy in facilitating change

When situated within a person-centred therapeutic relationship, empathy is seen by some to play a curative role (Warner, 1996) in facilitating psychological growth. For Rogers (1959), this role links primarily to the act of clarifying and checking (i.e. reflecting back), a process which encourages a client to enter more deeply into his or her personal experiencing. As the therapist attempts to understand the client's inner world, her empathic responses serve to assist the client to contact (Warner, 1996) personal feelings, for example, to clarify the extent to which the therapist's description maps onto an aspect of organismic experiencing previously denied or distorted. As a result of this process, the client moves deeper into what is felt at an organismic level, perhaps for the first time recognising or conceptualising a particular experience (e.g. fear) that was not previously acknowledged within the self (i.e. something that I, as a person, feel). In doing this, she is potentially able to integrate these new felt experiences into her view of who she is (i.e. her self-concept). This process relieves the tension or anxiety produced by the incongruence between self and organismic experience, thus facilitating psychological change.

Over the years, many theorists have attempted to explicate in greater detail the role and nature of empathy as part of the therapeutic endeavour (Wilkins, 2003). Vanerschot (1993) has attempted to draw together a number of strands of such work in proposing a framework for understanding how empathy works to produce a number of *micro-processes* in the client. For Vanerschot, empathy works in three ways. Firstly, an empathic climate created by a therapist serves to foster self-acceptance and trust by the client through the experience of being understood and accepted by another. This works to counteract her lack of positive self-regard. Secondly, as discussed previously, the concrete empathic responses (e.g. reflecting a feeling) made by a therapist serve to enhance and facilitate a client's experiencing by assisting her to move further into her organismic experiencing (Brodley, 1996). Such responses may relate to aspects of a client's experience that are at the very edge (Gendlin, 1974) of her conscious awareness (i.e. poorly denied or distorted) and hence involve the therapist using responses such as exploratory questions (e.g. 'I wonder if there is something else other than anger in how you feel at the moment'), empathic guesses ('I guess you must feel pretty sad that she has left you') and experiential responses (e.g. 'I don't know why but I feel very tearful when you speak about your father'). Such responses are often termed 'deep' or 'advanced' empathy (Mearns and Thorne, 1999) to denote the way that they relate to an aspect of the client's experiencing that was not directly being addressed or acknowledged until that point.

Finally, all empathic responses to a client have a cognitive effect, assisting the client to also re-organise the meanings of the experiences being processed. This is the third element identified by Vanerschot (1993), and is a product of assisting the client to focus his or her attention on particular experiences, to recall information relating to an experience or to organise information in a more differentiated and elaborative manner. From such a perspective, the therapist may be seen as, Wexler (1974) suggests, a 'surrogate information processor', whose empathic responses facilitate a process of cognitive re-organisation and re-structuring.

Unconditional positive regard

Although empathy is seen by many as the primary, change-related dimension of person-centred therapy, unconditional positive regard has also been proposed by some (e.g. Bozarth, 1998; Wilkins, 2000) as the fundamental element of the relationship specified by Rogers (1957). In contrast to the long history enjoyed by empathy as part of Rogers' approach, the *concept* of unconditional positive regard did not emerge until the mid-late 1950s, having previously been referred to as acceptance, warmth, prizing and respect (Bozath, 2002). Indeed, the terms are still often used interchangeably, although for some (e.g. Purton, 1998) the differences in meaning between them introduces a conceptual confusion regarding what each actually involves.

For the majority of person-centred practitioners, unconditional positive regard, along with the various terms equated with it, simply refers to the experiencing and offering of a consistently accepting, non-judgemental and valuing attitude toward a client (Lietaer, 1984). For Brazier (1993) this may best be considered as a form of non-possessive 'love', a warm acceptance of the client as he is in any given moment, not judging, instructing or neglecting. The term 'unconditional' is thus used to denote this quality – nothing is required of a client for her to be viewed in a *positively regarding* manner.

Offering unconditional positive regard

Unconditional positive regard is perhaps the most challenging of all the conditions to meet and thus to offer. Indeed, in discussing how to experience and communicate it, the majority of training materials (e.g. Tolan, 2003) concentrate on what is *not* unconditional positive regard, rather than what it is! Despite this, offering unconditional positive regard often relies on listening and responding non-judgementally to whatever a client is experiencing at a given moment. Although this may imply a passive quality, unconditional positive regard is a more active, openly warm, valuing process. Indeed, Freier (2001) argues that the term *positive* is used deliberately to indicate the warm nature of the experience, rather than a cold form of passive acceptance indicating 'neutral passivity'. What this means, in practice, is that in offering unconditional positive regard, the counsellor actively strives to warmly value the client in all aspects of his or her experiencing. As Brodley and Schneider (2001: pp.156) suggest:

> Client-centred therapists consciously cultivate a capacity for unconditional acceptance towards clients regardless of the client's values, desires and behaviours. The UPR capacity involves the ability to maintain a warm, caring, compasionate attitude and to experience those feelings toward a client regardless of their flaws, crimes or moral differences from oneself.

Box 3.3   Is *unconditional* positive regard possible?

The idea of unconditional positive regard has been strongly criticised by various theorists (e.g. Masson, 1992) who argue that it requires a therapist to withhold any moral judgements on another individual's actions. This, they suggest is impossible as well as politically unacceptable. Certain forms of behaving (e.g. violence toward others) are wrong and should not be accepted. As someone's 'self' cannot be separated from her 'behaviour' (Purton, 1998), it is not possible to offer unconditional positive regard to an individual's inner experiences, while not condoning what they do. Hence, as Seager (2003: p.401) proposes, 'unconditional positive regard is impossible in any human relationship'.

For person-centred practitioners, such a view of unconditional positive regard fails to recognise a number of important aspects regarding its place within the person-centred therapy. Firstly, as with all the core conditions, it is not an experience that a therapist is viewed as able to have *all the time* when relating to a particular client. This misapprehension is perhaps a product of its name, which has an absolute, *either or* quality that does not reflect the flowing process of any relationship within which the conditions are upheld to different extents at different times (Rogers, 1957). Secondly, no act or experience is *inherently unacceptable*, and a therapist's capacity to offer unconditional positive regard is a product of his social, cultural and individual values. Thus the experiencing of unconditional positive regard is linked to a therapist's own moral standpoints. It is also enmeshed with the level of his own self-acceptance, for our capacity to unconditionally value another stems from our capacity to *understand*, and *accept*, ourselves in all of our flaws (Mearns and Thorne, 1999). Such understanding and self-acceptance enables us to experience a client in a non-defensive manner, and hence to look behind (Wilkins, 2000) an unacceptable behaviour or attribute to understand the psychological suffering or pain underlying it. Of course there are occasions in therapeutic relationships when this is not possible, for example, when a particular client is encountered who presents a particularly powerful challenge to the moral stance we uphold. For Wilkins (2000), within such circumstances we are able to recognise our limitations, which in turn allows us to find the most appropriate way of enabling that client to be transferred to a different therapist who, as a result of his or her own unique personality, may view the situation differently, or indeed may have the capacity to offer a greater level of unconditional positive regard. Thus, from such a standpoint, unconditional positive regard is not impossible, but dependent upon the match between therapist and client.

The role of unconditional positive regard in facilitating therapeutic change

Unconditional positive regard works, as part of the therapeutic relationship, by diminishing conditions of worth which are at the root of the incongruence between organismic experience and the self. As conditions of worth are acquired through a *conditionally valuing* relationship, unconditional positive regard is seen to stimulate the exact opposite, a climate of unconditional acceptance and warmth. It is the very *unconditionality* of this climate that promotes growth, for it enables the processes of psychological defence to be reversed. This reversal is simply a product of the degree of threat presented by conditions of worth being gradually eroded by the presence of an unconditionally warm and accepting other (Rogers, 1959).

The role of unconditional positive regard is enmeshed with the processes of empathy. In contacting denied or distorted organismic experiencing that is then unconditionally accepted and valued by a therapist who is empathically attuned, the client is able to feel fully accepted and thus develop a greater sense of positive self-regard. As Lietaer suggests (2001: p.105), unconditional positive regard thus produces 'a high level of safety which helps unfreeze blocked areas of experience and to allow painful emotions in a climate of holding ... self-acceptance, self-empathy and self-love are fostered'. When these are empathically received, the client is able to re-configure his or her self-concept to encompass greater levels of organismic experiencing, thus reducing the incongruence at the root of her distress.

Congruence

Like unconditional positive regard, the *concept* of congruence emerged in the 1950s and was first introduced in Rogers' personality theory (1951) to denote the state in which the self and organismic experiencing are aligned (i.e. the opposite of *incongruence*). It was subsequently identified as of relevance to therapy within Rogers' (1957) theory of the necessary and sufficient conditions of therapy. Congruence, as part of these conditions, is formulated as a state of being required of the *therapist* within the counselling relationship (i.e. 'the second person, whom we shall term the therapist, is *congruent* or integrated in the relationship' Rogers, 1957). By contrast, the client within such a relationship is *incongruent* ('the client, is in a state of incongruence, being vulnerable or anxious' (Rogers, 1957). He thus defined congruence in therapy as meaning:

> that the therapist is his actual self during his encounter with his client. Without facade, he openly has the feelings and attitudes that are flowing in him at the moment. This involves self-awareness; that is, the

therapist's feelings are available to him – to his awareness – and he is able to live them, to experience them, in the relationship, and to communicate them if they persist. (Rogers, 1966: p.185)

Congruence thus refers to the therapist's capacity to be aware of the full extent of her own organismic experiencing (unlike the client who is still *incongruent*). Although the term congruence was used interchangeably with other adjectives such as authentic and genuine, Rogers regarded the requirement for the therapist to be attuned to actual self as the most fundamental of all the three core conditions (Rogers and Sanford, 1984). He saw no role for professional façade nor the impersonal relating often associated with a lack of self-development (or incongruence) on behalf of the therapist.

Being congruent

The condition of therapist congruence is the least understood of all the core conditions and has been open to considerable misunderstanding and misinterpretation over the years (Wyatt, 2000). Although the meaning of congruence is not in doubt, being a state where a therapist is not subject to incongruence between self and organismic experiencing, there are a number of areas of debate surrounding what this actually involves in terms of therapeutic practice. Perhaps the most controversial of these is the extent to which a therapist communicates his or her inner organismic experiencing (e.g. feelings of anger, or sadness) to her client. This controversy stems right back to the work of Rogers, who viewed the expression of genuine feelings as part and parcel of *being* congruent within a therapeutic relationship (Rogers, 1959). Yet, for Lietaer (1993), a therapist's inner awareness of her ongoing experiencing must be differentiated from the outer expression of this experiencing. For him, these are two different things, and only when taken *together* represent the therapist's genuineness (or congruence) in the relationship. From such a standpoint, the congruent practitioner must be aware of these different elements and attend to each within the therapeutic encounter.

One of the key issues arising from the distinction between an awareness of organismic experiencing (e.g. feeling sad) and the expression of such experiencing is an important one, how each relates to the other, particularly in terms of what inner experiences to disclose, and how (e.g. Tudor and Worrall, 1994, Barrett-Lennard, 1998). It is one thing for a therapist to recognise and acknowledge within herself a particular experience with a client (e.g. 'Gosh, I feel so sad when she talks about her Mother'). It is a very different matter to determine when and how to express this experience to that client. Certainly, in discussing the expression of therapists' feelings and experiences in therapy with a client, Rogers (1966: p. 185) urged caution:

[congruence] does not mean that the therapist burdens his client with the overt expression of all his feelings, nor does it mean that the therapist discloses his total self to the client. It does mean, however, that the therapist denies to himself none of the feelings he is experiencing and that he is willing to experience, transparently, any persistent feelings that exist in the relationship and to let these be known to the client. It means avoiding the temptation to present a façade or hide behind a mask of professionalism, or to assume a confessional-professional attitude.

For Rogers, it is only *persistent* inner experiences that should be expressed to a client, nothing else. Such feelings may be either positive or negative, although both can be of vital importance in supporting the other core conditions (empathy and unconditional positive regard). For Rogers, it was far more important to admit to feeling, say, bored or frustrated, than attempt to *pretend* to a client that everything was OK.

Although the cautious expression of persistent personal feelings within a therapeutic relationship is advocated by the condition of congruence, this aspect of the approach presents a significant challenge to other therapeutic models in the counselling psychology or therapeutic field (Greenberg and Geller, 2001). Certainly the idea that professional psychologists or therapists express how they *personally feel* at times can seem a highly threatening prospect, particularly if it involves the admission of feelings that may imply weakness, confusion or vulnerability. These can seem so different to the distant, objective perspective that is often a part of a professional psychological activity. It can also open a psychologist up to charges of over-involvement and, potential inappropriateness.

Much concern over the potential expression of personal experiencing advocated by the condition of congruence stems from the way in which the disclosure of feelings by a therapist is often associated with an undisciplined process that Haugh (2001) calls the 'I felt it so I said it' syndrome. Yet, a therapist simply stating what he feels at any indiscriminate moment in time is certainly *not* what a person-centred approach advocates (Brodley, 1998), and a general rule of thumb in psychological therapy generally would be that saying less (not more) is to be valued.

The role of congruence in facilitating therapeutic change

For Rogers, congruence was the most important therapist condition due to the way that it *underpins* the experiencing of unconditional positive regard and empathy. Without congruent awareness of his own organismic experiencing, it is highly likely that a therapist's own experiences in relation to a client will be influenced by his own incongruence, and thus conditions of worth. This will inhibit his experiencing and communication of both empathy and unconditional positive regard in ways such as, a) his failure to recognise (and thus empathise with) a personally denied emotion that is being expressed by a client, b) his reaction (e.g. anger) to a client which is distorted into another feeling (such as excitement), and c) his judgemental feelings about aspects of a client's experiences (such as racist assumptions) due to his own conditions of worth regarding race.

By not being fully aware of his own organismic experiencing, the incongruent counsellor potentially makes life very difficult for herself and her client. This, for Mearns and Thorne (1999), highlights the importance of counsellor self-acceptance, as the more fully a practitioner can accept himself, the fewer conditions of worth that will inhibit the empathy and conditional positive regard he experiences in relation to his clients. Certainly, a counsellor who is highly congruent and self-accepting appears to practice what she preaches and her words and actions match up. Incongruence (or a lack of self-acceptance) has a different flavour, often manifesting in an inconsistency between what is being said and what is being expressed in other ways (e.g. tone, gesture, posture etc.). The reason for this is that the counsellor is, essentially, not fully aware of some of her own reactions (e.g. anger) which are being felt at an organismic level. These reactions that cannot necessarily be hidden from others can therefore be seen in unanticipated ways (Grafanaki, 2001) indicating, directly or otherwise to the client, that what is being said is not the whole picture. Such inconsistencies can have a considerable impact on a client's trust for the counsellor, potentially inhibiting a client's preparedness to experience her therapist's empathy and unconditional positive regard as fully as she may. In such circumstances the counsellor may not be seen as sufficiently trustworthy for her empathy and unconditional positive regard to be received.

The core conditions as a single condition?

Although it is possible to examine each of the core conditions in terms of their unique contribution to the process of person-centred therapy, it is misleading to consider any one of these as distinct from each of the others (Merry, 2004). The roles of empathy, congruence and unconditional positive regard are entirely interlinked within person-centred therapy, each supporting the others to invoke the climate of safety and understanding that is pivotal to reducing client incongruence. They make up part of a system that, from this perspective, is so interdependent it may better be considered as *one single condition* in itself. Certainly for Mearns and Cooper (2005), it is the *combination* of empathy, unconditional positive regard and congruence that allows a therapist to experience what they term 'relational depth' when with a client. This they describe as (2005: p.36):

> A feeling of profound contact and engagement with a client, in which one simultaneously experiences high and consistent levels of empathy and acceptance toward that Other, and relates to them in a highly transparent way. In this relationship, the client is experienced as acknowledging one's empathy, acceptance and congruence – either implicitly or explicitly – and is experienced as fully congruent in that moment.

Although, from such a perspective, it is possible to break down the experience of relational depth into the component parts of empathy, unconditional positive regard and congruence, Mearns and Cooper argue that these are in fact 'facets of a single variable: relational depth' (2005: p.36), rather than discrete variables in themselves. As a result, they emphasise the power of the core conditions as something that arises from the *integration* of these qualities into a particular way of being, rather than viewing each as something that may be assured independently of the others.

Despite the importance of the core conditions in the person-centred approach to therapy, it is also important to remember that three further attributes were also specified by Rogers (1957) as 'necessary and sufficient' for change to occur. These will be explored in the following section.

The conditions of psychological contact, client incongruence and therapist communication

As well as the conditions of empathy, congruence and unconditional positive regard, Rogers (1957) proposed that psychological change within the client was dependent upon, a) psychological contact between counsellor and client being established, b) the client being incongruent and experiencing anxiety or vulnerability and, c) the successful communication, even to a minimal degree, of the therapist's empathy and unconditional positive regard. Although these conditions are less concerned with the actions and attitudes of the therapist, they are instrumental in the *relationship* that is enacted between client and counsellor, and therefore of paramount importance in the therapeutic work undertaken. They are often termed the 'relationship conditions' (Sanders and Wyatt, 2001) because they refer to the *minimal requirements* any therapeutic relationship must meet in order for psychological change to occur (assuming the core conditions are also present).

Box 3.4   The case of the 'lost' conditions

Have three of the six conditions for therapy specified by Rogers been lost? Keith Tudor (2000) certainly thinks so. He argues that the way in which the person-centred theory of therapy is so often associated with the three *core* conditions has become a major problem for the approach, and part of the reason why the strong psychological basis of the theory is often neglected. He goes on to propose that the loss of the *non-core* conditions has lead to a significant dumbing down (2000) of the theory itself. Certainly, Rogers never termed any of the six conditions *core* nor specified that any was more important than others (as implied by the term *core* itself!). Such a view distorts the way in which each of the six conditions are essential for therapeutic change to occur, as well as the extent to which person-centred theory of therapy involves far more than simply a description of therapist's actions or attitudes.

Psychological contact

The first condition of therapy as defined by Rogers (1957) is that *two persons are in psychological contact*. For Rogers, this condition stipulated that an acknowledged *interaction* was required for successful therapy to take place. Certain aspects of contact were thus necessary, such as basic attentional and perceptual functioning, and the capacity to communicate with, as well as perceive, another person. Unless this pre-condition (Rogers, 1957) is met, and this is by no means guarantee, none of the other conditions can be fulfilled. Therapy, as a result, will most probably be ineffective.

On the basis of its apparent obviousness, psychological contact was, for many years, generally *assumed* within person-centred practice. Hence this condition became seen as the 'backing vocals' to the core conditions offered by the therapist (Sanders and Wyatt, 2001). However, theoretical work by person-centred practitioners such as Prouty et al. (2002) have highlighted a number of reasons why psychological contact *cannot* always be assumed. For example, highly disturbed clients with (psychotic) delusional experiencing or those with low-level functioning (e.g. people with advanced dementia) are often unable to establish full, relational contact with another person in a consistent manner. As a result, psychological contact is now often seen, not a dichotomous construct (i.e. being either present or not present – as implied by the wording of Rogers' condition 1), but as one that can *vary* in accordance with a client's level of psychological disturbance and cognitive functioning (Mearns, 1997).

Although some clients, by virtue of their disturbed psychological state, are what Prouty et al. (2002) term 'contact-impaired' to the extent that they are unable to engage in *any* therapeutic relationship (and thus require a process he terms 'pre-therapy'), others are more able to minimally establish contact with a therapist and vice versa. Such individuals often have considerable levels of incongruence and are liable to rigid processes of denial and distortion. Hence, psychological contact is often limited and therapy subject to considerable fluctuation in the degree to which contact is present or otherwise. The issue of psychological contact is an important area of work within the person-centred framework, and provides a framework allowing many of the severe psychological disturbances commonly associated with psychiatric (i.e. medical) definitions, such as personality disorders and psychoses, to be understood and addressed from a person-centred perspective. These will be explored in more depth in Chapter 5.

Communication

Condition 6 is often seen as the other side of the requirement to establish psychological contact. This condition (Rogers, 1957) states that, 'the communication to the client of the therapist's empathic understanding and unconditional positive regard is to a minimal degree, achieved'. Thus it is the client's capacity to *perceive* the communication of the therapist's empathy and unconditional positive regard that is stressed as also a necessity for therapeutic change to occur. Hence, as well as basic contact, the client must be able to experience the therapist's empathy and unconditional positive regard.

   Although the term 'minimally achieved' indicates that these qualities do not have to be perceived in significant terms (irrespective of the extent to which they are communicated by the therapist), the requirement is that they must be experienced to *some extent* as part of the therapeutic endeavour for psychological change to occur. For clients unable to establish *any* degree of psychological contact with a therapist, experiencing the counsellor's empathy and unconditional positive regard will be impossible and effective therapy is thus highly unlikely. Similarly, clients whose level of disturbance is high or cognitive functioning low will experience only minimal levels of the therapist's empathy and unconditional positive regard. In such circumstance it is probable that change will be slow and difficult.

Client incongruence

As well as stipulating that the therapist must be 'congruent or integrated' in the relationship, Rogers (1957) added a second criterion, condition 2, linked to the notion of incongruence. This states that 'the client is in a state of incongruence, being vulnerable or anxious', a condition which thus makes it necessary for the client to have a *need* for change, a need emerging from the uncomfortable experience of the vulnerability or anxiety (these are catch-all terms used to denote the experience of psychological distress) produced by incongruence. The notion of need is important, for the condition implies that, as a result of the experience of vulnerability or anxiety, the client is *aware* that he or she is encountering difficulties (Singh and Tudor, 1997). Embleton-Tudor et al. (2004) go on to argue that such awareness is, in essence, a self-identified sense of something being wrong which serves to motivate a decision to seek help. Hence, the condition may be seen as stipulating a client's *willingness* or *consent* to engage in the counselling process.

Of course there are situations where people are 'sent' to see a therapist, perhaps by an employer, parent or other senior figure. However, if the client in such circumstances does not experience themselves as anxious or vulnerable (such as in instances where the process of denial and distortion are working effectively to maintain the self-concept as it is) person-centred therapy is not guaranteed to produce change. A similar outcome is likely in individuals who are not significantly incongruent, and thus not anxious or vulnerable. Such individuals are seen to have sufficient positive *self-regard* and thus have no requirement (at that moment) for a therapist's empathy or unconditional positive regard. Although a therapeutic relationship may be helpful in talking through issues or concerns, further change is not certainly inevitable even if, indeed, it is possible.

Ways of person-centred working

In simply describing six 'necessary and sufficient' conditions for psychological change to occur, Rogers provided much potential for variability in how these processes would be enacted within the therapeutic context. As such, differences in therapeutic standpoint and practice were implicit within his original theory (which, in its 1957 presentation, was an integrative statement relevant to all forms of psychological intervention), and seen as something to be expected and celebrated rather than discouraged. Indeed, Rogers disliked the idea of the approach standing still, and was a strong advocate of innovation and change. Since the first presentation of theory of therapy, a number of different approaches to person-centred working have evolved, each taking a somewhat different slant on how best to facilitate change within a client. Indeed, for Warner (1999) there are now a number of different 'tribes' of the 'person-centred nation' that offer something different in terms of method of person-centred working.

One way of considering such 'tribes', as we explored in Chapter 1, is in terms of a general distinction between 'classical' and 'experiential' approaches. Hence we will briefly explore each of these domains as a means of mapping the key contemporary ways of working within person-centred therapy.

A classical approach

One of the most common ways of working among person-centred practitioners, particularly in the UK, is to employ a 'classical' approach which adheres to the terms of client-centred therapy detailed by Rogers in his papers published in 1957 and 1959. It is this 'classical' way of working that is detailed in the majority of skills development and practical texts associated with the a 'person-centred' approach to therapy. Merry (2004: p.43) proposes that a 'classical' approach to person-centred therapy has four central principles. In summary, these are:

1. A sole emphasis on the theory of actualisation as the motivation for growth.
2. A therapist's role as entirely that of a non-judgemental, empathic companion offering unconditional positive regard.
3. The therapist achieving a sufficiently high level of personal congruence to enable her to be fully self-aware and thus genuine.
4. The therapist fully trusting the client and thus maintaining a non-directive attitude in terms of the content and process of therapy.

Although each of these principles is significant, perhaps the most important element of 'classical' person-centred therapy, or at least the one that differentiates it from 'experiential' ways of working, is its fundamental emphasis on *non-directivity* on behalf of the therapist (Levitt, 2005). Classical person-centred therapy resists any form of direction in terms of both content (e.g. introducing ideas to talk about) or process (e.g. suggesting a focus on a particular aspect of experiencing). The client is fully trusted in his or her capacity for change (due to the presence of the actualising tendency, which is seen to motivate change when enabled to do so) and the role of the therapist is thus seen entirely as one of an empathic, non-judgemental companion. In essence then, the six conditions discussed previously remain both necessary *and* sufficient for change to occur.

Experiential approaches

There are a variety of different ideas and methods within the 'experiential', framework all of which share the same goal of classical person-centred therapy, namely to facilitate the client's processing of organismic experiencing and thus to reduce incongruence. Where these differ to 'classical' person-centred therapy is the way in which this goal is enacted, or as Lietaer (2002: p.1) states, the difference 'is to do with *how* a therapist tries to facilitate experiential self-exploration'. For 'experiential' practitioners, various strategies and techniques may be employed to assist a client contact (and process) previously denied and distorted organismic experiencing. Such strategies and techniques require a more active therapeutic stance, and therefore the therapist guides a client toward his organisimic experiencing in particular ways. Hence she sometimes 'directs' the therapeutic work, and in doing so, adopts a position of 'process-expert' in identifying an aspect of the client's experiential processing that may be assisted by a specific strategy or technique (Worsley, 2002). Although the relationship remains central in facilitating change, it is therefore not necessarily viewed as sufficient in itself. It is these aspects that differentiates experiential ways of working from classical person-centred therapy (Baker, 2004).

Eugene Gendlin and focusing

Without a doubt, the work of Eugene Gendlin has been hugely significant in the development of a experiential 'tribe' (Warner, 1999) within the person-centred framework. Gendlin was a philosophy student who, in 1953, became a colleague of Rogers at the University of Chicago with an interest in finding ways of assisting people to engage more fully with their own experiencing. Over time he evolved a method of working with what he termed the 'felt sense', devising a method, called *focusing*, as a means of contacting organismic experiencing at the 'edge' of conscious awareness' (Gendlin, 1978). Such experiencing was then allowed to 'unfold' from being simply a felt sense of *something* (Gendlin, 1996) to a more concrete conceptualisation of an experience or situation (e.g. the conscious acknowledgement of an organismic feeling of 'anger'). The process of focusing allows for psychological growth and a reduction of incongruence, as previously denied or distorted experiencing is conceptualised and integrated into awareness.

Although Gendlin's ideas have a complex philosophical slant, he provides a very straightforward method designed to aid the client to 'focus' on his own experiencing. This procedure (Gendlin, 1996) is taught to the client by the therapist and has six steps which *include*, a) clearing a 'space' (i.e. bringing attention to the bodily area in which we feel our emotions), b) identifying a 'felt-sense' in that moment, c) finding a handle for that sense (i.e. matching the physical felt quality with a way of representing it to ourselves) and, d) moving back and forth between handle and felt sense, noticing any shifts in either. Although this process has many technical aspects to it, in common with the 'classical' person-centred approach, Gendlin views the therapeutic relationship as of utmost importance in enabling a client to feel understood and valued in her experiencing. Moreover, the focusing procedure is client-directed in terms of content and always *offered* only as a possible method of working. It may therefore be seen to accord strongly with the fundamental respect outlined by Rogers as integral to a non-directive attitude (Purton, 2004a). However, unlike more 'classical' work, focusing involves the active 'direction' of a client toward felt aspects of his or her experiencing in accordance with the method outlined. Hence, the client is sometimes *not trusted* to determine how best to attend to and manage her experiences within the therapeutic encounter (and accordingly provided with techniques and methods for doing so), thus comprising the intention of the six conditions specified by Rogers (1959) as *necessary and sufficient* for change to occur. Indeed, focusing is now only one of a wide range of other techniques to facilitate experiencing by the client used by practitioners following Gendlin's ideas (c.f. Purton, 2004b).

Box 3.5   Key Differences between Classical and Experiential Approaches

Classical	Experiential
Six conditions of therapy seen as necessary and sufficient at all times	Six conditions of therapy seen as necessary but not always sufficient
Avoiding all direction of client's experiences or focus in therapy	Suggesting methods to help experiencing but *not* directing content of client's experiencing (i.e. through interpretations)
No additional therapeutic techniques utilised or taught to the client	Use of specific techniques to aid client contact organismic experiencing. Some techniques taught to the client

---

David Rennie's experiential approach

A psychologist who has done much to forge a middle ground between the work of Gendlin and that of Rogers is David Rennie, whose book *Person-Centred Counselling: an experiential approach* (1998) describes a method of working that highlights the role of reflexivity in the therapeutic endeavour. Reflexivity refers to the way that we are able to reflect on (i.e. be reflexive) our experiencing, as well as experience it, something Rennie feels is ignored by Rogers in his primary emphasis on empathising with a client's *experiencing* in the here and now. He argues reflexivity plays an important role in therapy as it allows the therapist to draw the client's attention to aspects of her experiencing of which she may not be consciously aware, and to enable reflection on these as part of the therapeutic process. Examples of such aspects may include, for example, ways in which the client uses language (e.g. common metaphors or words), aspects of non-verbal communication (e.g. clenched fists), aspects of 'meta-communication' (i.e. communication about communication) between client and therapist (e.g. the way a client implies to the therapist that he isn't good enough for her'). Rennie argues that a key role of the therapist is to 'direct' a client's attention to such aspects. In doing so, he views the reflection process itself as invoking further experiencing (e.g. recognising sadness exhibited non-verbally leading to a client consciously acknowledging that sadness) thus invoking psychological change.

Like Gendlin, Rennie (1998) views the role of therapist as going beyond that envisaged by 'classical' practitioners. In suggesting that the counsellor 'direct' the client toward particular aspects of her experiencing, he proposes therapists must assume the role of 'expert' at certain times in the therapy (e.g. by offering comments, observations and suggestions). Indeed, Rennie embraces this opportunity, arguing that such a role allows the therapist to 'model' to the client the capacity to make choices as an agential being (i.e. having agency to decide how to act, rather than 'being determined' and fixed). This, he sees, as vital to the therapeutic task. Many clients, he argues, do not see themselves as having choices and thus often need 'some help in dealing with themselves' (1998: p.81). One form of assistance is to highlight the client's capacity for agency or choice in all circumstances.

The process-experiential approach

By far the most controversial of all experiential approaches is that associated with the work of Leslie Greenberg, Laura Rice and Robert Elliot (e.g. Greenberg et al., 1993). Indeed, there is a very big question over the extent to which this work may be considered *person-centred* at all, for it does not share many of the ideas expressed by Rogers with regard to the nature and basis of personality change (Baker, 2004) and takes a highly technical stance on the therapeutic process thus diminishing the significance of the therapeutic relationship itself in facilitating change.

Greenberg et al. (1993), whose approach is now often known as Emotion-Focused Therapy, propose a complex theory of emotional processing (their focus is very much on emotion), arguing that we develop 'emotion schemes' throughout life that often do not match up to how we cognitively assess particular situations. So, for example, we may know we are safe in the dark, but still feel fear when the lights go out. The cause of such discrepancies they argue, are emotion schemes that are either maladaptive (i.e. no longer suitable for the situations being encountered) or those orientated around emotional experiences that were not processed fully or correctly when first formed. They identify a variety of formal techniques associated with making conscious the emotion schemes employed by a client, and where necessary, for re-processing the emotional experiences that originally gave rise to them. These techniques are arranged in relation to particular 'markers' linked to certain types of internal processes within the client. So, certain types of techniques are used in certain situations, such as 'two-chair' work (i.e. the client talking from two different two chairs alternatively, each representing a different 'part' of their self) when a client encounters internal conflict etc. The envisaged outcome of their work is what they term, the increased *mastery* (Greenberg et al., 1993) by a client over her emotional experiencing.

The work of Greenberg et al. has much in common with person-centred ideas on the role of incongruence in psychological disturbance (i.e. emotions often being unavailable to conscious awareness), and also highlights the significance of an empathic, non-judgemental relationship between therapist and client in the change process. However, it is certainly at the furthermost edge of person-centred work and for many (e.g. Brodley, 2006) may not be considered as a legitimately person-centered stand point in therapeutic terms.

New approaches – dialogical person-centred therapy

Although both 'classical' and 'experiential' approaches have evolved over what is, by now, a significant period of time, in recent years a new perspective on person-centred therapy has developed highlighting the importance of *relationship* at the core of the therapeutic encounter. However, unlike 'classical' or 'experiential' approaches to person-centred therapy, which give primacy to the *therapist*'s contribution and role within the therapy (e.g. in terms of 'attitudes' or 'techniques'; Sanders, 2004), a dialogical (often termed 'relational' or 'intersubjective') approach highlights the relationship that is created between client and counsellor, viewing this as a *co-created dialogue between two persons* rather than a series of therapeutic attributes offered to one by another (Barrett-Lennard, 2005). Hence it is not primarily concerned with maintaining a non-directional attitude (as in the 'classical' approach) or in facilitating change (as in the 'experiential' tradition), but instead with encountering the client in a deep, mutually experienced, way (Mearns and Cooper, 2006)

Prominent in developing this new perspective is Peter Schmid (e.g. Schmid, 2001), who argues that the fundamental basis of person-centred therapy is a dialogical encounter in which the differences between two human beings (i.e. therapist and client) provide the basis for deep, meaningful connection between them (Buber, 1958). From this, he argues, something new can emerge (Schmid 2004) as a result of the healing qualities of such an intimate, human-to-human experience (the lack of which, or its over-provision, is seen as the cause of all psychological distress).

The role of deep, interpersonal connection in therapeutic encounters is also highlighted by the concept of 'relational depth' (Mearns, 1997; Mearns and Cooper, 2005). As we discussed previously, this is a process involving the full *integration* of the core conditions into a mode of relating that offers the possibility of a meeting where (Mearns and Cooper: p.37) 'two people come together in a wholly genuine, open and engaged way' without psychological masks, roles or safety screens. To encounter a client at relational depth provides that individual with an experience of truly meeting another human being who is empathic, accepting and affirming in their 'presence' (Rogers, 1980), and one who is thus able to provide a depth of interpersonal connection that enables psychological healing to occur. Although this is, essentially, the same process as one defined by Rogers (i.e. the relationship itself providing a climate in which the actualising tendency enables growth to take place), it is one that emphasises to a far greater degree the importance of the *interpersonal connection* over its constituent parts (e.g. the counsellor's empathy). Such a connection can only ever be *co-created*, and thus is inherently dialogical (i.e. between two persons) in form and content. Yet, facilitating such a meeting is no easy task. For Mearns and Cooper (2005: pp.113–135), some ways that practitioners may attempt to do so are summarised as follows:

- Letting go of 'aims' and 'lusts' – allowing preconceived desires or intentions for the client to dissolve prior to the therapeutic encounter.
- Letting go of 'anticipations' – avoiding all expectations and assumptions about the client.
- Letting go of techniques – avoiding using techniques or methods, which may block the possibility of deep inter-personal relating.
- Listening, listening, listening – truly attending to what the client has to say at all levels of her being.
- Knocking on the door – inviting exploration of a client's lived experiencing.
- An openness to being affected by the client – a preparedness to be influenced by deep contact with another person.
- Minimising distractions – taking practical steps to ensure that the meeting is the primary concern, rather than the gas bill!
- Transparency – a preparedness to be open and honest about personal feelings, vulnerabilities and experiences, as well disclosing confusions and uncertainties about the therapeutic process itself.
- Working in the here and now – remaining present focused, and indeed using the therapeutic relationship to explore the processes potentially preventing the client from being intimate with others.

Although many of these may seem somewhat 'technical' in form, their intention is to facilitate something almost completely opposite, namely a deep, connected, person-to-person encounter of the kind rarely found within the psychological domain. It is this intent that, once again, demonstrates the unique place of a person-centred approach within the counselling psychology arena.

Summary

- The person-centred theory of therapy was formally outlined in detail by Carl Rogers in 1957, although it had been an integral part of his work until that point.
- Rogers argued that 6 conditions, if present within any therapeutic relationship, were *necessary and sufficient* to facilitate psychological change within a client.
- The 3 conditions linked to the activities of the therapist have become known as the core conditions. These are the experience of empathy and unconditional positive regard for the client, and the therapist being congruent in his or her own experiencing.
- Empathy is an attitude of understanding for a client's own experiencing or subjective 'frame of reference' at any given moment.
- Unconditional positive regard is an experience of non-judgemental value for the client.
- Congruence is a state of being in which the therapist is not subject to incongruent experiencing produced by conditions of worth. It is associated with high levels of self-acceptance.
- Three further conditions specified by Rogers linked to the potential for therapeutic relationship. These were psychological contact being established, the client being incongruent and the therapist's empathy and unconditional positive regard being perceived by the client.
- There are various ways of working within person-centred therapy. Classical practitioners follow the therapeutic processes outlined by Rogers, viewing the 6 conditions as necessary and sufficient for change to occur.
- Experiential practitioners view the 6 conditions as necessary but not always sufficient. They use different techniques or strategies to assist the client contact her organismic experiencing.
- In recent years a new 'dialogical' approach to person-centred therapy has emerged emphasising the importance of deep, person-to-person encounters that are co-created by counsellor and client.

FOUR   Facilitating a Process of Change: Person-centred Counselling Psychology in Action

Person-centred therapy and the process of change

In the previous few chapters we have explored different views on how person-centred theory accounts for the cause of psychological disturbance (incongruence), as well as examining the therapeutic conditions that it proposes as 'necessary and sufficient' for change to occur. However, the cause and effect relation between these factors may be further elaborated by an understanding of exactly what the process of change is like within a client. Rogers (1961) provides such an elaboration in his *Process Conception of Psychotherapy*. In this paper he describes how it is that people move from incongruence to congruence as a part of a therapeutic process. Yet working out precisely what he wanted to say in this respect was no easy matter, as he suggests, (Rogers, 1961: p.131):

> In trying to grasp and conceptualise the process of change, I was initially looking for elements which would mark or characterise change itself. I was thinking of change as an entity, and searching for its specific attributes. What gradually emerged in my understanding as I exposed myself to the raw material of change was a continuum of a different sort to that I had conceptualised before. Individuals move, I began to see, not from a fixity or homeostasis through change to a new fixity, though such a process is indeed possible. But the much more significant continuum is from fixity to changingness, from rigid structure to flow, from stasis to process.

For Rogers, the process of change is thus one involving a growing openness to all experiencing. It is not a move from one, fixed view to another, but instead from a fixity to a changingness. Hence, he talks of an increasing 'flow' of organismic experiencing. From such a perspective, any person engaging in therapy may be located at some point on a continuum between complete fixity (i.e. a wholly rigid method of experiencing) to complete changingness. All of this sounds somewhat complex, but is really a restatement of the observation that an increase in congruence is coupled with a reduction in psychological defensiveness (i.e. denial and distortion). Less defensiveness means, in effect, a greater capacity to be open to experiences, perceptions and viewpoints. At its logical extreme (complete changingness), such a state of being affords an ongoing capacity to engage in whatever experiences arise at a given moment, rather than attempt to fit these into a 'fixed' series of constructs about the self and the world. Hence the individual in such circumstances is constantly in a process of change.

The seven stages of change

In order to describe the continuum between the fixity and changingness, Rogers (1961) identified seven discrete stages of change within the client, each representing a step from incongruence to congruence. These are detailed as follows:

Stage one

A client views life in all or nothing terms, not seeing themselves as having any problems and thus blaming others for any difficulties that arise. All experience is gauged in terms of rigid viewpoints or ideas (e.g. 'I never get stressed or angry'). It is rare for a client at this stage to enter therapy voluntarily. He does not believe himself to require therapeutic assistance. He is wholly incongruent.

Stage two

Although some negative feelings might now be acknowledged, these are viewed in fixed terms (e.g. 'I am depressed') with little capacity for inner reflection or for taking personal responsibility for what is experienced. Contradictions in views or feelings may be expressed but often with little awareness of their contradictory nature. Again, at this stage, it is unlikely that a client will enter therapy voluntarily.

Stage three

By stage three a client is beginning to show some reflection on 'self', although mainly in terms of past feelings or experiences. Experiencing in the present is still tentative, and often externalised into the views of others ('I am well-known for being happy go lucky, but feel so down'), contradictory feelings or thoughts may be acknowledged. It is at this stage that most clients enter therapy, aware of their need for help.

Stage four

The client has an increased capacity to experience things in the here and now and is increasingly aware of uncomfortable (organismic) feelings. A greater level of questioning of 'self' is likely to occur, particularly in terms of existing viewpoints and constructs (e.g. the 'self-concept'). The validity of some of these viewpoints may be explored. Most therapeutic work takes place at this stage, and at stage 5.

Stage five

The client is increasingly able to 'own' her experiences, with a capacity to take responsibility for much of her experiencing. Previously held views may be critically appraised, a process which is accompanied by a greater ability to express experiencing in the present (e.g. by getting angry).

Stage six

By this stage a client is able to engage in moment-by-moment experiencing within the therapeutic encounter, expressing how he feels in a non-defensive way. There is greater freedom in what is explored. The client is now able to fully own his experiences. Hence what was once incongruent becomes congruent. A new 'self-concept' begins to emerge, one more closely aligned with the totality of organismic experiencing.

Stage seven

At stage seven the client is naturally engaging with her organismic experiencing, and no longer subject to processes of denial or distortion. There is a general looseness in feelings, which the client is able to accept in each moment. The client takes full personal responsibility for her experiences, good and bad, and has now become, what Rogers (1961: p.155) terms as 'a constantly changing flow of process'. The client is fully able to accept himself fully in each moment.

The process of change and person-centred practice

Although Rogers' work on the stages of psychological change is descriptive rather than proscriptive (i.e. not designed to *direct* therapeutic work with a client) it provides a useful framework for understanding the processes through which a client may go when engaging in effective therapy. As we have seen, paramount to this is the observation that change is not from one fixed state to another, but from a fixity in experiencing (i.e. rigid way of thinking/feeling) to a changingness (i.e. an openness to feelings and thoughts). Hence, effective therapy does not necessarily result in a client feeling 'good' about everything, but instead envisages that she is increasingly open to all her experiencing, able to accept it as a legitimate aspect of her personhood.

Clearly, not all clients move through all of the stages described by Rogers as part of every therapeutic process. It is extremely common for a client to enter, say, at stage three and finish counselling at stage four or five. Moreover, an individual's trajectory through the change process is not clear cut. Clients can appear to make little progress or indeed move backwards toward a greater rigidity as therapeutic work progresses. These outcomes may be understood as a product of incongruence, in terms of the 'self' working increasingly hard to maintain itself through the mechanisms of denial and distortion. As Mearns (1994) suggests, it is quite usual for the self-concept to 'strike back' when threatened by organismic experiencing.

Although much insight is given into the process of change by the stages defined by Rogers (1961), these can only go some way to enlightening what may happen during a person-centred therapeutic encounter. It therefore seems important to draw together the theory discussed thus far in the book with some examples of how person-centred therapy actually progresses or in other words, look at the person-centred approach 'in-action'.

Introduction to the case studies

The following two case studies explore how person-centred methods of working are employed to facilitate psychological change within a client. Rather than present the work from therapist or client perspective, the studies are written as narrative accounts in the third person. Although not unique in describing person-centred work (e.g. Bryant-Jefferies, 2005), this way of writing allows for a more efficient use of space than afforded by more common methods of therapeutic reporting (e.g. Bor and Watts, 2006). Furthermore, it accentuates the fictional basis of the work being described. None of the counsellors or clients described in these studies are 'real', in the sense that they are not based upon a specific person or amalgam of particular individuals. The same is true for the problems worked on and the outcomes described. Yet, the case studies do attempt to show just how person-centred practitioners may wish work with some typical therapeutic issues. As such, they offer an attempt to reach out to the 'realities' of person-centred therapy.

As we explored in Chapter 3, the person-centred approach encompasses a range of views on practice. These views can mainly be grouped into 'classical' and 'experiential' perspectives. The two case studies provided here are designed to illustrate how a counsellor generally aligned to each of these perspectives may approach the therapeutic task. Their methods of working are not discrete and the reader will notice much overlap between them. However, there are also some differences, particularly in terms of the techniques and strategies employed. If anything, these differences have been stressed to highlight where 'classical' and 'experiential' approaches diverge. Indeed, in the case of the latter, a range of experiential methods derived from different schools of experiential working (e.g. focusing, process-experiential) have been deployed to demonstrate their potential use within the therapy process. This does not mean to imply that all 'experiential' practitioners work in such an eclectic way; some prefer to remain strongly aligned to a particular 'experiential' standpoint (e.g. focusing).

An essential point to make prior to introducing the studies is that each explores only a small number of the issues relevant to person-centred therapy. Important personal factors such as gender differences, age, ethnicity, sexuality , disability etc. have not been discussed despite their importance in the development of any therapeutic relationship. Similarly, ethical and professional factors, such as the contracting process, have also been neglected. This is judicious and designed to enable a clear focus on the nature of the therapeutic work itself.

Finally, there is the issue of context. Person-centred therapy takes place in a huge variety of settings, each of which introduces a large number of important variables into the clinical work being undertaken. For example, counselling undertaken within a primary care setting (e.g. a GP surgery) may be limited to a certain number of sessions and conducted in a room set up for medical examination. A practitioner working in private practice may operate in an entirely different manner, with a dedicated counselling space and an entirely flexible approach to the number of sessions offered to the client (which is, of course, dependent upon the client's financial circumstances).

In the following two studies, the counselling work takes place, firstly, in an organisational context where the client has been referred to a workplace counselling agency, and secondly, within a private practice context. Although a study grounded in a primary care setting, such as an NHS Psychology Service, would be relevant to any reader wishing a professional career in Counselling Psychology, it has been omitted because of the complex range of factors commonly involved in conducting person-centred work in an NHS setting. Doing justice to these factors would require a far more detailed exploration than is possible here. However, this should not be taken to mean that person-centred therapy is not appropriate for working in applied healthcare domains such as the NHS, or indeed, with those with complex psychological needs, an issue that will be explored in more detail in Chapter 5.

Case Study 1   Bob's stress: a 'classical' person-centred approach

Bob's story

I am a 39-year-old married man with a 16-year-old daughter and 13-year-old son. I had a fairly happy childhood, going to university at 18 to study engineering. I got married quite young, at 22, to Lena and quickly became a father. I have worked at a large engineering company for the last 15 years and now have a demanding management

(Continued)

(Continued)

role. Up until recently I generally enjoyed my work and certainly had a happy home-life. However, a few months ago I started to feel very tired and stressed, hating what I was doing at work. I was struggling to cope, feeling very burned out and not at all interested in anything. I stopped being able to sleep at night and was having arguments with everyone. I wasn't 'me' anymore. In the end I walked out the office. I just couldn't take it anymore.

I saw my GP after that, and he signed me off work for a few weeks. At the same time I agreed with my manager that I would contact the Company's Employee Assistance Provider (EAP) to see a counsellor. EAP referred me to see Joanne. I didn't really know what to expect but felt I had to do something to get myself better.

Starting counselling

Joanne and Bob met for the first time on a Monday evening, at the counselling centre where Joanne was based. During their meeting Bob told her about his feelings of stress, loss of motivation and constant tiredness. He felt constantly 'on edge', regularly arguing with colleagues and family. Bob said this was unlike him, describing himself as generally 'easy going' and 'laid back'. He thought his change in mood may be a result of some pressures due to conflict at work. However, these were no greater than those to which he had become accustomed over the last 15 years. Hence he felt confused as to what was happening, why it was that it was that he felt so bad. Most recently, things had all come to a head when he had ended up shouting at a colleague. He had been off work since that time.

In meeting Bob, Joanne immediately noticed how he seemed to talk entirely about his job, saying very little about himself, his family or any other interests. Indeed, his 39th birthday had recently passed and he seemed non-plussed when asked how he felt about getting older. He didn't say much about his feelings generally, describing himself in terms of other's peoples views of him (e.g. 'I'm told I'm a good istener'). She also noticed her own feelings of fear (i.e. her congruence) when with him, but did not wish to make reference to these at such an early stage in their relationship.

After their first session, Bob and Joanne agreed a further 12 sessions. Bob had found the session strange, not being used to talking about himself and his life. He felt extremely uncomfortable at how much attention Joanne seemed to be paying to what he was saying, and would have liked to have been told things he could do to make things better. Whatever it was he would deal with it. He was a strong person, and couldn't understand why he felt so stressed-out.

(Continued)

Developing a relationship

Over the following few weeks Bob continued to find the counselling sessions frustrating. He often felt annoyed with Joanne because she didn't seem to want to give him advice or tell him how to improve how he felt. What he wanted was some very clear guidance from her on how best to address his stress, and ways of getting the 'old Bob' back. All Joanne seemed to do was to ask him how he felt and then repeat back what he said. Bob often found himself squirming at hearing Joanne's words, feeling a lot of pressure to think more deeply about his views and experiences. This was something he didn't like doing. It felt awkward and uncomfortable, as if he, himself, was somehow the problem.

Joanne too found those sessions a struggle, aware that Bob only seemed interested in hearing her views rather than exploring his own feelings or experiences. She recognised her annoyance at his lack of interest in talking responsibility for himself, and for becoming defensive when asked about his feelings. Joanne felt that she and Bob were finding it difficult to establish any rapport, and doubted the extent to which he was experiencing her empathy and unconditional positive regard.

Later that week Joanne explored her work with Bob with her clinical supervisor, Susan. She told Susan all about Bob's problems and his tendency to want practical 'solutions' from her all the time. She also owned up to feeling fearful when with him at times, although said she felt unsure as what it was that made her feel this way.

Susan listened intently to Joanne, noticing just how tense she seemed when talking about her work with Bob.

'You seem angry with Bob, Joanne'.

Joanne thought for a while, 'I don't feel angry, more annoyed with him'.

'What is that annoys you about him?'.

'Well, I suppose, er maybe I feel annoyed 'cos I feel useless, that I can't give him what he wants, a fix to all his problems. That scares me'.

Susan nodded, 'so you are questioning yourself, the worth of your work with him. You feel you are failing him'.

Joanne looked at the floor, 'yes, I suppose I do feel that'.

Following supervision, Joanne spent much time thinking about her relationship with Bob, in terms of the six 'necessary and sufficient' conditions of person-centred therapy. She realised that her feelings of uselessness when with him reminded her of painful experiences in her own past, feelings linked to not being 'good enough' as a counsellor. She wondered if these feelings about herself were being *distorted* into annoyance at Bob. This would suggest she had been insufficiently *congruent* in their relationship thus far, something to which she must attend.

(Continued)

Yet there was also the issue of *empathy* to consider. Susan had pointed out her feelings of fear with Bob, wondering if Joanne's feelings were an empathic response to Bob's experiences of being scared. This was not uncommon, thought Joanne, remembering the many times she had *felt* what a client was *feeling* during a particular moment in a session.

In the following session, Joanne decided to tell Bob about her feeling of fear when with him, preferring to be genuine with him rather than hide behind the professional mask of 'counsellor'. She was sure they were a mix of both her empathy for Bob and her own 'scars' from the past. However she wished to acknowledge them to him. She was aware they were affecting their relationship.

Joanne told Bob that she had noticed herself feeling a little scared in their previous sessions, wondering if this made any sense to him in terms of his own experiences during their work. Bob felt very taken aback at her question. It wasn't what he had expected at all. However, in digesting it he began to think about himself and his own feelings in the sessions. He often felt annoyed that Joanne wasn't telling him how to get better. However, he also was beginning to realise that she wasn't the problem. He felt terrified about what was happening to him, desperate for it to go away and for things to get back to normal. So, 'yes', he thought, 'yes. I feel scared as well. Scared about being here and scared about what is going to happen to me'.

Joanne and Bob worked on this feeling for a while, tentatively connecting it to far more in Bob's life than simply his experiences of counselling and his recent feelings of stress. He realised that he felt scared a lot, scared of not being 'good enough', scared of being seen as a 'failure'. This was a significant recognition, and he worked with Joanne on it over the remainder of the session. She tentatively asked him about what it felt like to feel as if he might 'fail'. For Bob, this was an awful prospect, like a 'gnawing' in the pit of his stomach, a feeling he had known for a long time yet hadn't been able to put a name to.

Joanne's disclosure of her feelings to Bob proved to be real turning point in their relationship. Bob felt he could relax a bit, seeing Joanne as someone he could trust to be really honest with him. He also found talking about his feelings of fear really liberating, having never really acknowledged them before, even to himself. Tentatively, he began to wonder why he felt so bad about himself.

Making progress

As their work progressed Bob began to tell Joanne more about *himself*, about his past, how he grew up in a very strict household with parents who were only interested in his academic 'success'; how

(Continued)

he met his wife, Lena at university and then soon married her. How he had then become a father and started on a career in his present company to be the success desired of him by his parents. Although he hated to say it, he felt bitter and angry that he had done so little in life other than follow a conventional path from school to university to marriage to work, doing what everyone else seemed to want from him rather than what he, himself, might have desired. Yet he felt scared of changing, of what people would think if he no longer held down a secure job, or was the friendly, 'doormat' for everyone to walk all over. Joanne noticed his increased awareness of how these ways of living no longer seemed to match what he felt himself to be. In many ways she felt he was telling her that he felt had lived a life for others, rather than himself. She tentatively tried to capture this in her empathic response to him, 'it's as if you don't feel you have ever 'owned' your life?'. Bob looked at her intently, 'owned isn't the right word, but yes it's something like that. I don't feel like, I suppose, I don't feel like it's really me who is living'. Joanne looked for a few moments at Bob as he reflected on his words.

'You don't feel, alive, as the person you are?'.

Bob took a deep breath and exhaled slowly.

'I suppose no, no sometimes I don't'.

Bob felt quite tearful after that session with Joanne, shocked at what he had said about himself and his life. He always knew deep down that he felt resentful at some of the sacrifices he had made but didn't realise just how profoundly they seemed to have affected him. Joanne's words, not 'owned your life' resounded as he thought about all the times he had stopped himself doing things he wanted to do what he felt he 'should' do. It wasn't as if he hadn't wanted to do things for others. He really loved Lena and the kids and wanted people to respect him. It was just that there had seemed so little time for anything else, anything he might have wanted. He was so scared of not being seen by others as the 'good employee' or 'supportive friend' that he always went for the safe option that denied him the opportunity to perhaps do things that he really wanted. He felt trapped by his need to live up to so many different people's expectations.

As the weeks passed, Bob and Joanne worked to explore Bob's feelings of not being able to live life as he may have wished to. Joanne paid careful attention to Bob's thoughts and experiences in the moment, empathising in a caring, non-judgmental manner with all that he expressed. They spoke widely about Bob's life, his youth, his upbringing and marriage to Lena, and his ongoing difficult relationship with his parents. They also looked at Bob's feelings about getting older, and how his 39th Birthday had raised many questions for him

(Continued)

as to what he had achieved in his life. This event had been very significant in highlighting to Bob the conflict between his fear of failing others and his desire to live more in line with his own values. His getting older thus seemed intertwined with a need for a different kind of living, one which seemed so far out of reach. He worried that he was running out of time.

Bob felt increasingly close to Joanne over this time, something which helped him feel at ease in talking about topics that were deeply painful for him, particularly those linked to his feelings of fear over failing his family by not being the 'perfect son, husband or father'. He became more emotional in sessions too and spent more time in silent reflection. Joanne also noticed a deepening of their relationship. However, she was careful to simply continue offering Bob the empathy and unconditional positive regard essential to helping him find his own way forward. She trusted Bob in his capacity to find his own direction and was happy to allow him the time to use the sessions in whatever way he felt he needed to. She was equally happy to agree to keep working with him after their initial 12 sessions were completed, respecting Bob's desire to continue coming. Of course they were both lucky in the fact that Bob's company were prepared to pay for his continued attendance.

On the day of their 14th session Bob arrived early, excited by something that had happened the previous weekend. He was now back at work part-time and managing to get by, although still finding it a great struggle.

'I met an old friend on Saturday and he started his own business last year. It's doing really well and it just made me wonder, er, wonder if that was something I could myself?'.

'You want to start your own business?'.

'Well, it's just an idea but I really fancy doing it. I want to start up my own company fixing computers. It's a risk but one I feel could really pay off'.

Joanne had never seen Bob look so enthused. Gone was the pallid, tense demeanour, now replaced by an energy and excitement which almost took her breath away. Bob eagerly stared back at her as she struggled to find the words to respond to him. It sounded a fine idea but she also felt cautious, aware that empathising too strongly with this 'new' Bob may diminish the other aspects of him upon which so much of their work had been conducted (i.e. his previous 'self-concept'). In the end, she found herself expressing surprise at the change she saw in him, a genuinely congruent response to the deeper shift in Bob she had observed. He smiled back at her, 'I feel

(Continued)

surprised too. I never thought I would even consider something like this but, I just can't believe how enthused I am by the idea'.

Joanne felt she had seen a part of Bob that he had only previously hinted at and, over the session, they worked solidly in exploring his ideas on self-employment. He wanted more freedom in how he worked, a chance to do new things and in different ways, to take more risks. However, by the following session, Bob's enthusiasm had waned and he expressed many doubts over what a change may involve; 'what if I fall flat on my face. I couldn't bear it', he said, doubting that his family would appreciate why he was walking away from a good job, even one that made him unhappy. He also felt scared of asking for the financial sacrifices Lena and the kids would have to make to support him.

'No' he said, 'it was just out of the question'. Yet, in saying those words, Bob winced.

'It seems as if part of you still does want to take a risk', said Joanne.

'Yes, I think part of me does'. He sighed. 'I just don't know what to think'.

As they worked, Joanne noticed how Bob often seemed to move between these two different viewpoints, or what Mearns (1999) has called 'self-configurations'. Firstly there was what he called 'selfless' Bob, concerned not to let anyone down and to keep things stable. Secondly there was 'restless' Bob, desperate to set out to do something that would enable him to feel more alive. Each seemed to want different things and each had different views on the best way forward. Rather take a stance in relation to either, Joanne paid careful attention to both, empathising with each of the different views expressed. She knew that to favour one over the other would diminish her unconditional positive regard, something which could potentially undermine their therapeutic relationship.

For Bob, working with his different views was a difficult process, and he often wished for Joanne to tell him what to do. Yet, he also know that if she did, it would simply be another opinion for him to live with, another expectation to attend to or 'let down'. What he needed, and he knew this deep down, was to make a decision for himself, perhaps for the first time in many years. Yet this was not something he could do lightly or quickly.

Ending

Although Bob was still finding things difficult, he returned to work full time just before his 16th session of counselling. Over time, he gradually began to feel much better, more able to cope. Indeed, getting back into the office every day reminded him of the many good things about his job, things which seemed once again to be

(Continued)

motivating him to work hard. He also felt less tired and stressed, and began to find himself leaving home in the mornings with a spring in his step.

During their 19th session, Bob asked Joanne whether it was time to end their counselling work. He felt so much better. At first, Joanne was a little taken aback to hear that Bob wanted to finish, and spent some time exploring with him why he no longer wanted to come. She knew that he was feeling more positive but was also aware of the conflict he still experienced with regards to his future. Yet, in reflecting on their progress she began to recognise all the ways in which Bob had changed. He was now so much more open to his feelings and experiences, 'owning' many of his doubts and fears. He was also more prepared to do more things for himself, such as booking a short walking holiday with a friend.

In discussing his decision to finish, Bob told her that starting a business wasn't the right thing to do at the moment. Yet, it was something he still wanted, perhaps for a few years time when his kids left home. Indeed, he said, 'by that time we'll have enough money to really give it a shot. At the moment, I think I can cope where I am, just knowing that I *will* be able to do something else in the future. In fact, I love the idea of enjoying what I have for the next few years while gradually planning to do something completely different!'.

Joanne looked at him as he spoke and smiled. She knew so much in him had changed. He seemed far more able to make a choice for himself and was no longer stuck in constantly trying to match up to what others want from him. He was more alive, more congruent, able to tell her what he wanted and act on his own values.

'It's lovely to hear you speaking so positively about yourself and your future'.

'It's just such a change for me. I feel alive again. I just feel I have some choice in what I do. I still feel scared about letting people down, but know deep down that I am not. I feel so much more laid back about things. Work has its place, but I have far more in my life now'.

'So you feel alive and open to the possibilities of life and have a plan for the future. That sounds great. Of course we can finish when you want. How many sessions shall we have before we finally call it a day?'.

Bob suggested they meet a couple more times, a number to which Joanne was happy to agree. During those sessions, they reviewed their work of the previous few months, noting just how different Bob was compared to when he had started. What was so important to him then, thought Joanne, seemed so much less so now. 'He seems more real, open to the possibilities in his life'. Although he was making no major changes, all sorts of small things seemed to be happening. Bob

(Continued)

also recognised how differently he was feeling about things. Indeed, he no longer wished to see the 'old' Bob again.

Joanne's final thoughts

I enjoyed working with Bob. He had so many concerns (conditions of worth?) linked to meeting the expectations of others. It was lovely to see him gradually becoming more aware of his own autonomy and capacity to take responsibility for his own feelings. He became so much more open and alive in becoming more congruent. Yet this was an internal process, one which allowed him to feel more in control, more able to choose. Although, at first, he wanted me to tell him what to do, he became more confident in making his own choices and assessing things for himself. Yet, all I did was offer him what I could in a relationship with him, my empathy, congruence and unconditional positive regard. It wasn't easy at times but I think it was worth it. I still marvel at the power of the actualising tendency in promoting growth. It's a nice thought to think that this power is within everyone.

Case study 2   Sara's depression: an experiential approach

Sara's story

I am a 19-year-old student, presently working in a nightclub, which I hate, and live in a bedsit by myself. I had quite a difficult childhood and am an only child. My parents split up when I was 9, and my mum got quite badly into drugs. My dad just left and I haven't seen him since. When I was 16 I left home and moved into my boyfriend's digs. I left when he wanted us to get a flat together. I couldn't handle the fact that he wanted us to commit to one another. I eventually left him a note saying that I was leaving him. My aunt let me stay with her for a few months after that and I started college. In many ways it was great but I started to drink a lot, smoking dope all day and going out all night. The college chucked me out. After that I argued a lot with my aunt. Eventually I walked out on her too and lived on the streets for a while. I felt so angry with everything and everyone.

I feel I have ruined my life and don't know what to do. I'm stuck in a job and house which I hate, have no real relationship with any of my family and feel as if I have nowhere to turn. I sit around a lot, feeling depressed and wanting things to change. But I just don't seem to be

(Continued)

able to motivate myself to do anything. A friend suggested I see a counsellor. I didn't like the idea at first. The more I thought about it the more it seemed a possible way of changing things. I decided to contact Paul after seeing his advert for counselling psychology services in a local paper. There was something about him that I liked. He offered (heavily!) reduced fees for those on low incomes so I emailed him to ask for an appointment.

Starting counselling

Sara's first session with Paul went well. She found him easy to talk to and told him a lot about her difficulties in motivating herself. Although he listened intently, empathising with her concerns, Paul also asked some questions, about what she thought her problems were and what she wanted from the counselling process. Sara answered as best she could, although often felt unsure as to what to say about herself. She just wanted someone to help her find a way of changing things, but wasn't sure what changes to make or, indeed, what it was she really wanted in life. She felt angry at how difficult life was for her.

Paul found Sara very talkative in the first session, but also detached and withdrawn. She talked about her feelings in an objective, almost cold manner. He wondered if this was as an aspect of her incongruence, recognising the extent to which she seemed to deny any deep emotional experiences. Paul also wondered a bit about her past. Although she had hinted at some difficulties from around the time her parents split up, Sara was very hazy about that period, describing it as 'in the past' and as something she had 'dealt with'. However, he noticed that she became very tense when mentioning her mother. He felt this was one to watch.

Over the first few sessions, Paul and Sara got to know one another. Paul spent a lot of time listening to Sara talk about her situation and her frustration at not being able to motivate herself to do things. He was very focused on communicating his empathy and unconditional positive regard to her, and, as the sessions progressed, Sara seemed to relax a little, reflecting more deeply upon how she felt. One common issue for her was the confusion she experienced over who she was and what she wanted in life. Sara found this confusion very difficult to describe, it was a vague sense but one which paralysed her. For Paul, Sara's difficulty in describing how it was suggested it was an aspect of her organismic experiencing at the 'edge' of her conscious awareness. He wondered if it might be explored using a *focusing* procedure. He tentatively described this process to Sara, asking if it was something she wished to do. Sara thought it sounded a really good

(Continued)

idea, trusting Paul enough by that point to try what he suggested. He was very careful not to 'push' Sara into saying yes. It was her choice after all.

Focusing

At the start of the next session Paul talked Sara through the focusing procedure, just to be clear that she was happy with what they would do. He then asked her to relax into her chair and 'clear a space', allowing herself to become aware of whatever sensations she felt in her body. Sara felt a few things, but most clear to her was that familiar, vague sense of confusion which she chose to work on. Paul encouraged her to feel this sense as vividly as she could, trying to find a word or image that best represented it (its handle). Sara described it in very vivid terms, as an icy rock sitting inside her chest and weighing her down. Paul encouraged her to try to keep feeling the 'icy rock' for a few minutes, asking her questions about it. He tried to reflect back the language Sara herself employed in her responses, ensuring that he remained very empathic and non-judgmental toward what she described. Indeed, he reflected back word-for-word much of what she said.

As they focused on it Sara felt her confusion become more intense, describing the icy rock as becoming filled with piercing icicles. She felt her body stiffen, as if she was in danger. She said the word, 'danger', and felt her body tighten still further. Paul repeated this back, 'danger', noticing the change in her bodily posture. After a while he asked Sara if she felt OK to carry on. Sara opened her eyes, having had enough. She felt quite shaken at what she had experienced, a sense of being threatened. Paul warmly encouraged Sara to 'welcome' what she had learned – it was an important part of her, and one which they would return to in following sessions.

Paul and Sara continued to use the focusing procedure each time they met. As they worked, Sara experienced a number of different 'shifts' in her experiencing. She gradually began to connect the 'icy rock' to a fear of allowing herself to be happy. Her confusion thus seemed a way of stopping herself doing anything that could achieve this. As she said to Paul, 'It's as if I've become so scared of being hurt that I am too scared to even try anymore'. This shift was hugely significant for Sara, and she felt tears begin to roll down her cheeks. She began to sob as memories of the past came flowing back. Paul empathised with Sara's sadness. The words 'you feel so cold, so stuck under that rock' came to his lips, a deeply evocative empathic response. Sara nodded, feeling shaky and upset, remembering how long it had been since she had felt happy.

Box. 4.1   Mapping the process of change

In reading these case studies, to what extent to you think Rogers' (1967) ideas on the process of psychological change are helpful? Tudor and Merry (2002) suggest that Rogers' 7 stages of change are characterised by themes such as:

- Feelings becoming increasingly identified, owned and accepted
- A growing level of internal communication, such as awareness of internal experiencing
- Changing cognitive structures from rigid views and perceptions to looser, more fluid ways of thinking
- Problems being increasingly acknowledged, owned and dealt with responsibly
- Ways of relating to others becoming increasingly close

Can you see ways in which the two clients are changing in such terms? What stages described by Rogers do you think Bob and Sara move through during their counselling work?

(Continued)

In the weeks following that session Sara found herself feeling very emotional. She burst into tears for even the smallest thing and spent lots of time daydreaming, remembering her past, happy times as a young girl with her mum and dad, times with friends when she used to really laugh. She enjoyed looking back but felt consumed with sadness when remembering all the things that she no longer had. Sara felt very depressed and very stuck.

Identifying a process

By their 19th session Paul noticed a change in Sara's approach to their work. She had begun to turn up late for their meetings and seemed very agitated in talking about her feelings. Although not wishing to make something out of nothing, Paul noted his own congruent feeling of anxiety and decided to ask Sara about how she was finding things.

Although she found it awkward to say, Sara told Paul that she wished to stop their counselling work. Despite the valuable things they had achieved, she felt things were not improving and worried they may even be getting worse.

Paul empathised with Sara's worries, 'so you feel so frustrated, at our lack of success and fear we are making things worse'.

Sara nodded, 'I am just sick of things going nowhere and here I am again, worse than when I started'.

'You sound really angry'.

'I am angry, totally and completely angry'.

(Continued)

'totally and completely angry'.

'Yes, sickenly angry'.

'Sickenly angry?'.

'I feel sick talking about it, even thinking about it. And I want it to stop'.

'You just want it to go away'.

'Yes, I do. I want it to go away'.

Paul waited for a moment or two.

'And stopping coming to see me will do that?'.

'Yes'.

Sara stared at Paul, fists clenched, a familiar tightening in her chest. She didn't want to stop seeing him but couldn't see any other way. Paul held her gaze, trying to convey his understanding of her struggle, and his care for her in it. He decided to speak, tentatively identifying a process that Sara seemed to experience time and time again.

'You know that anger so well, Sara. Something makes me wonder if stopping our sessions really will take it away?'.

Sara slumped in her chair, feeling tearful and drained. She knew that what she was feeling was about far more than her sessions with Paul. She felt angry with him because she felt so scared that he would eventually give up on her.

Paul and Sara spent a long time discussing the process of her desire to leave counselling. It was an important process, one which seemed to resonate a theme running though much of her life. In talking it through, Sara realised just how angry she felt at Paul because she felt scared that he was getting fed up with her. In effect, she was terrified of him letting her down by stopping their work, so she decided to get in first, to leave the process before it became too important. This was a common way she had of dealing with things, blaming others when things got difficult to avoid the pain of losing something of value to her. She recognised that stopping coming to see Paul would not solve anything, like walking out on her aunt hadn't made it better. Once again she would simply be turning her fear against herself and her own wellbeing. She still needed Paul's understanding and care, and he assured her that his regard for her was *unconditional*. He wasn't planning to stop their work or reject her. What he wanted was to understand how badly she felt and to find ways of helping in this. One thing he suggested in this regard was that they work more on Sara's process of leaving things that were important to her, really looking at how what it was about and how she could find other ways of coping.

Over the following sessions they explored the patterns of feeling and behaving that Sara often found herself caught up in. Sara said

(Continued)

she hated 'taking responsibility' for herself, gradually linking this to a feeling that she had never 'grown up'. She still felt like a child, constantly waiting for terrible things to happen. Sara spoke a lot about her mum and dad in these sessions, describing how unfair it was she felt that she had been deprived of a normal childhood. She blamed them both for walking out on her, for letting her down, yet felt 'numb' when talking about how she felt. She didn't know where to begin in making sense of it all.

Working on the past – a two-chair dialogue

Although he spent much of his time empathising with Sara's feeling of numbness about the past, Paul acknowledged just how stuck Sara seemed to be in coming to terms with her upbringing, a 'stuckness' that seemed to stop her feeling able to 'grow up'. The particular difficulties she had in relation to her parents seemed of great importance, and Paul wondered if finding a way of enabling her to have a dialogue with them may help her to find a way of processing her deep feelings about them. Sara felt nervous about this suggestion, concerned that working with her feelings about the past might be extremely painful. But she thought Paul was right. She needed to find a way of coming to terms with her feelings about what had happened to her.

Paul's tentative suggestion was to use a two-chair technique, in which Sara imagined her mum or dad sitting in another chair listening to what she was saying to them. She was then able to move into that other chair, and speak back to 'herself', trying to explain how things were for them and why they had acted as they did or do.

Sara worked firstly with her dad, telling him how she felt at his leaving them, and how she blamed him for not being able to stick around. As she did this she seemed to well up with feelings, imagining him sitting opposite her listening to what she was saying.

'You make me sick, you coward', she told him, 'leaving me to pick up all the mess' cos you couldn't be bothered. I was only 9'. Paul encouraged her speak as candidly as she could, actively assisting her to express how she really felt. After Sara indicated enough had been said, he suggested she swap places and try to answer back as her father. At first Sara didn't know what to say, but Paul gently encouraged her to keep going and she gradually started to speak, 'I feel so sad for letting you down, I was just too weak to stay with you. I hate myself for leaving you but I just couldn't stay with your mum anymore, and you were too young for me to take with me. I know it was wrong and I still miss you'.

Sara continued with this dialogue for much of the session, moving between the chairs as the conversation unfolded. As this took place

(Continued)

she became increasingly aware not only of her anger, but also of her grief, fear and, indeed, compassion. Over the following weeks she repeated the exercise, returning to speak with her dad as well as her mum and others in her life. It was a draining process and she found herself exhausted at the end of each session. However, as time went on, she began to feel she was making some progress. Her work with Paul slowly took on a different shape involving occasional two-chair work, focusing and more general exploration of her feelings.

Ending counselling

Sara had been working with Paul for around 15 months when she first began to wonder if it was time to stop coming to see him. In a previous session she had been startled by the realisation that her 'icy rock' was no longer solid, but seemed to have melted a little. She linked this process to the presence of 'a warm, gentle sun in the sky', an image that she had first encountered during a focusing session a few weeks previously. Although she still felt scared and down a lot of the time, these experiences just didn't seem to have their previous energy. Moreover, Sara now felt a greater degree of compassion for others, as well as care for herself. Paul, too, felt that the time had come for their work draw to a close. He could see Sara was at last finding her own feet and beginning to see a future for herself. Indeed, she had taken responsibility by applying for college and was busy working on her portfolio of art. She'd also made contact again with her aunt, who'd been delighted to rekindle their relationship.

It took around 10 weeks for Sara and Paul to work toward a final session. Paul felt it important for Sara to be able to determine when exactly she was to stop coming. He wanted her to make the decision, not him. Sara felt relieved at being able to control how they brought their work to a conclusion. It was a big thing for her to not have Paul around as a support. At the end, and despite telling him how much she appreciated their time together, she decided to give him one of her paintings. It was of a beautiful sunrise over a lush green valley, thawing out after a long winter. This, she said, was what she had begin to see for her future and thus what she wanted him to know.

Paul's final thoughts

I found my work with Sara extremely rewarding. In many ways the essential ingredients in our work were the conditions of empathy, unconditional positive regard and congruence. Without these, I don't

(Continued)

think Sara would have felt sufficiently trusting of, and understood by, me to enable her to move into a far more flowing, open way of relating to herself and others. In the context of this relationship, what was extremely important for us was to identify the 'process' she often utilised of 'rejecting' others due to her fears of getting hurt. In identifying this, and talking about it (meta-communication) Sara was able to become far more aware of what she did and thus able to challenge it. Furthermore, our use of focusing and two-chair techniques allowed Sara to become far more congruent with her own experiencing, and to work through feelings about the past.

Sara became increasingly congruent as we worked, and during our last sessions seemed more at ease with herself. As last she saw a future.

Summary

- In 1961 Carl Rogers presented a paper titled 'A Process Conception of Psychotherapy', which identified 7 stages through which a client may pass in the process of undertaking psychotherapy. This built on a presentatian given 4 years previously.
- The stages chart a move from rigidity and defensiveness (incongruence) to looseness and openness to all experiencing (congruence).
- In a case study on Bob we explored how Joanne used a classical method of person-centred working to facilitate change.
- Bob moved from feeling 'stressed' about work to increasingly identifying feelings of fear and anger regarding himself and his future.
- Over the course of the therapeutic process, Bob increasingly 'owned' how he felt and become more aware of his conditions of worth. He developed stronger internal locus of evaluation.
- In a case study on Sara we examined how Paul employed an experiential method of person-centred work to facilitate change.
- In working with Sara, Paul paid careful attention of maintaining the 6 'necessary and sufficient conditions of person-centred therapy', while also employing techniques such as focusing, two-chair work and meta-communication.
- Sara became increasingly able to experience feelings about the past that she had previously denied or distorted, and became more aware of patterns of relating that prevented her making changes.

FIVE The Person-centred Approach and the Four Paradigms of Counselling Psychology

Introduction

As we discussed in the Introduction, counselling psychology encompasses a broad range of approaches to psychological therapy situated within, or between, four overarching paradigms – humanistic, existential-phenomenological, cognitive-behavioural and psychodynamic – each of which may be seen to constitute a series of general assumptions about human personality, the causes and nature of psychological distress, and the role of therapy in addressing it.

In this chapter we shall consider the relationship between the person-centred approach and each of these four paradigms, focusing on how person-centred therapy relates to their core assumptions as well as the therapeutic theories and practices they encompass. The chapter represents nothing more than a snapshot of such relationships, and is thus a generalised account rather than a comprehensive overview. Furthermore, the limited extent to which we are able to explore the complexities of each paradigm means that the chapter cannot purport to provide a detailed analysis of these, but instead offer only a basic summary of each. Such an outcome is not ideal, but an inevitable product of our focus being person-centred therapy rather than counselling psychology per se. Any reader wishing a more comprehensive understanding of the therapeutic paradigms presented here, or indeed the therapeutic approaches they encompass, is advised to consult more complete accounts, such as those contained in Woolfe. et al. (2003). Our exploration will instead attempt to summarise the place of the person-centred approach within its counselling psychology context, which is an important undertaking in terms of our goal to explore person-centred therapy from a psychological perspective. Our starting point for this is the humanistic paradigm, and the relationship of the person-centred approach to it.

The humanistic paradigm

The humanistic paradigm emerged in the USA during the 1950s and 1960s, and rapidly become known as the 'third force' (Bugenthal, 1964) in psychology due to its philosophical differences with behaviourist and psychodynamic standpoints, the first and second forces respectively. In many ways, humanistic psychology was a reaction to these two forces, rejecting the Freudian emphasis on destructive, unconscious urges and the over-simplified, laboratory based analyses provided by behaviourism. For Bugenthal (1964), the humanistic paradigm evolved on the basis of five fundamental postulates (or principles). These are:

1. Human beings, as human, supersede the sum of their parts. They cannot be reduced to components or isolated elements.
2. Human beings have their existence in a uniquely human context, as well as in a cosmic and ecological setting.
3. Human beings are aware, and also aware of being aware – i.e., they are conscious. Human consciousness always includes an awareness of oneself in the context of other people.
4. Human beings have some choice, and thus responsibility.
5. Human beings are intentional and goal-orientated. They are aware that they cause future events and seek meaning, value and creativity.

While each of these postulates highlights a specific aspect of humanistic thinking, they also hint at an underlying philosophy encompassing a small number of core themes. For example, the proposition that human beings are something more than the *sum of their parts* (i.e. cannot be reduced to components) reflects the theme of holism, a standpoint stressing the importance of viewing people as *unique* and comprised of a complex range of living systems rather than a narrow range of psychological dimensions (or 'variables') that may be scientifically measured (Warmoth, 1998). From a holistic perspective, people are viewed as complex individual beings with histories, personal values and creativity, not simply psychological 'objects' amenable to scientific study (Seeman, 2001).

A second underlying theme is that of choice. Individuals are seen as active and constructive agents in their lives and trusted as such to meet their unique needs and desires. Along with choice comes personal responsibility. As Cain (2001: pp.4–5) suggests, the humanistic paradigm thus assumes people to be:

> self-aware and free to choose how they will live and responsible for the choices that they make. Although a variety of factors make people's choices difficult and sometimes risky, in most instances they experience choice and

agency within their capacity. One of the main endeavours of humanistic therapists is to strengthen clients' beliefs that they can be the authors of their own lives.

A third theme of the humanistic paradigm is that of recognising human potential. The paradigm promotes an optimistic stance, viewing people as striving toward meaningful growth and evolution wherever possible. This theme is reflected in the concept of 'actualisation', an idea proposing an intrinsic human motivation toward constructive growth and change (Maslow, 1954). Although this motivation is seen in different ways by the various approaches contained within the paradigm, it reflects an optimistic and positive view of humanity.

Relationship to the person-centred approach

Concepts and philosophy

In examining the basic dimensions of the humanistic paradigm it is abundantly clear that its core themes and the philosophical standpoint of the person-centred approach are strongly intertwined (Macleod, 2003a). Indeed, Carl Rogers was so strongly associated with the development of the humanistic paradigm that he is universally acknowledged as one of its founders (e.g. Cain, 2001). As a result, many dimensions of the person-centred approach reflect humanistic ideas and concerns. One example of this is the emphasis placed on the role of choice and the promotion of an internal locus of evaluation. Another is the focus on potentiality rather than deficit (Patterson, 2000), and the familiar concept of the individual as striving toward positive growth as a result of a biologically given 'actualising tendency' (Rogers, 1951); a concept similar to, but not the same as the 'self-actualising' individual proposed by Maslow (1954) (See box 2.4, Chapter 2).

Therapeutic approach

While the person-centred approach may be situated at the heart of the humanistic paradigm in terms of concepts and philosophy, its 'classical' approach to psychological therapy may be seen as somewhat different to the other main humanistic therapies (Wilkins, 2003). Like humanistic approaches such as Gestalt Therapy (Perls et al., 1951), Transactional Analysis (Berne, 1968) and Psychosynthesis (Assiogoli, 1965), 'classical' person-centred therapy promotes themes such as autonomy, growth and human potential. However, it does so in a manner that accords primary emphasis to the therapeutic relationship, which is seen as 'necessary and sufficient' (Rogers, 1957) to facilitate change. Such a stance places full trust in the client's actualising tendency within such a relationship and there is no need for further techniques or information provided by a therapist. It is this view that contrasts with the approach taken by other humanistic therapies, as Mearns and Thorne (2000: p.27) argue:

> although the approach was always positioned 'thus' [as a humanistic therapy], it does not in fact have much in common with the other established humanistic therapies. The governing feature of person-centred therapy (PCT) is not its humanistic orientation, but its forsaking of mystique and other powerful behaviours of therapists. In this regard, many humanistic therapies are as different from PCT as psychoanalysis.

The proposition that other 'humanistic' therapies advocate a more mystical, power-laden therapeutic stance relates to the way that they rely on various techniques or strategies designed to facilitate change rather than simply *trusting* the client's own resources (i.e. actualising tendency) as sufficient to motivate constructive growth. Such techniques and strategies are seen as mystical or 'powerful' behaviours because they situate the therapist as the *expert*, whose concepts and ideas are viewed as of greater significance in enabling change than the perceptions and experiences of the client alone. The client is thus viewed as the consumer of the therapist's interventions, a process which, from a 'classical' person-centred perspective, undermines her capacity to experience freedom and autonomy in the relationship. Furthermore, the client is not necessarily party to the purposes or intentions of the therapist thus further reducing her power within the therapeutic encounter (Natiello, 1990).

A particular example of a humanistic approach taking such a stance is gestalt therapy (e.g. Parlett and Hemming, 2002). Like the person-centred approach, gestalt therapy sees self-awareness as key to promoting psychological growth, and person-centred theory shares much with gestalt psychology (which underpins gestalt theory and practice) in emphasising what Rogers (1951: pp.4) describes as 'its emphasis on wholeness, and inter-relatedness of the cluster of phenomena we think of as the individual'. Yet, in contrast to 'classical' person-centred therapy, the gestalt approach seeks to facilitate change by actively promoting client experiencing, doing so by use of various techniques designed to encourage a client to attend to aspects of her experiencing of which she is unaware, such as drawing her attention toward a seemingly contradictory non-verbal behaviour such as clenching a fist (Parlett and Hemming, 2002). This way of working involves the therapist deciding what aspects of a client's experiences or actions to identify, and following this up by using a range of experimental techniques (such as encouraging her to imagine what the clenched fist would like to do) designed to further heighten her experiencing in the present.

Added to its differences with 'classical' person-centred therapy is the fact that gestalt therapists do not attempt to offer '*unconditional* positive regard' (O' Leary, 1997) nor attend primarily to empathising with a client's 'frame of reference'. Instead (gentle) challenge and experimentation are viewed as a necessary aspect of assisting a client become more fully aware and self-supporting. Hence the nature of the therapeutic relationship within gestalt therapy is different from 'classical' person-centred therapy, with gestalt therapists viewing a strong, supportive and empathic bond as vital, but insufficient, in itself, to enable change (Yontef, 1998).

Although humanistic therapies such as this may have little in common with 'classical' person-centred practice, they share more with person-centred therapists employing 'experiential' methods. Indeed, the 'process-experiential' approach advocated by Greenberg and colleagues (Greenberg et al., 1993), is actually an amalgam of 'classical' person- centred therapy with gestalt therapy (Baker, 2004), albeit one which stresses to a far greater degree the conditions of empathy and unconditional positive regard over traditional gestalt-style exploration and experimentation. As a result, while 'classical' person-centred therapy may be strongly differentiated from other main 'humanistic therapies, 'experiential' approaches share more common ground with these and may thus be more readily viewed as 'humanistic' in therapeutic orientation.

Box 5.1.   Person-centred therapy and power

One of the key dimensions differentiating person-centred therapy, and in particular the 'classical' tradition, from other forms of humanistic therapy is its emphasis on the relationship as 'necessary and sufficient' (Rogers, 1957) to facilitate change within the client. In doing so it promotes a greater sharing of power (e.g. in terms of the client, and not the therapist, determining the focus and content of therapy) than many other therapeutic standpoints, humanistic or otherwise. It is this commitment to eschewing 'expert' therapeutic stances by avoiding the imposition of techniques and agendas that differentiates 'classical' person-centred therapy from almost all other therapeutic approaches and paradigms in counselling psychology (Natiello, 2001).

The existential-phenomenological paradigm

The second paradigm of counselling psychology we shall consider in terms of its relationship to the person-centred approach is the existential-phenomenological paradigm. In many ways, strongly differentiating between this paradigm and humanistic psychology creates a false dichotomy. There is a great deal of conceptual overlap between them due to the significant influence of *existential philosophy* on both (Yalom, 1980: Embleton-Tudor et al., 2004).

Existential philosophy is a European philosophical tradition of the 19th and 20th centuries (van Deurzen, 2002) that attempts to *describe* what it is like to be human, mainly in terms of the challenges, opportunities and dilemmas this affords. It charts the fundamental aspects of our 'being' in the world (van Deurzen, 2002) and does so by highlighting the following dimensions (summarized from Cooper, 2004):

1. Existence as unique – we are all unique beings, and thus not 'reducible' to general psychological mechanisms or attributes.
2. Existence as a process, not a thing – we are constantly creating and re-creating who we are throughout our life, hence our existence is not a fixed entity but a fluid one.
3. Existence as freely choosing – we are all fundamentally and unavoidably free to make choices about everything (in the context of the practical constraints we encounter).
4. Existence as future and meaning-orientated – we are orientated toward future goals rather than simply living in the 'present', and we attend to what we feel is meaningful rather than what is pointless.
5. Existence as limited – we all face many fundamental limitations (often termed 'givens') on our existence, such as death.
6. Existence as in-the-world – we are inextricably connected to the physical world around us, rather than separate or 'independent' beings who are in some way separable from the context within which we live.
7. Existence as with others – our existence is inherently enmeshed with that of other people and the social world around us.
8. Existence as embodied – we are all embodied beings and hence have physiological and emotional dimensions to our being in the world.
9. The tragedy of existence – the very nature of existence offers the inevitability of tragedy, such as physical and emotional suffering, hopelessness and despair;
10. The choice between authenticity and in authenticity – existence is suffering and we are faced with a choice whether to face up to this and accept the realities of life (living authentically) or pretend that they do not exist and deny them (living inauthentically).

Many of these dimensions make familiar reading due to their influence on humanistic psychology, such as those highlighting human uniqueness and choice. However, there are a number of others, highlighting the constraints, challenges and tragedies of human existence which also feature prominently within the existential-phenomenological paradigm. These are explored in terms of the common existential 'realities' shared by all (such as the inevitability of death) as well as the ways in which each one of us *interprets* the meaning of our existence at any given moment in time (Spinelli, 2003). This latter interest derives from the tradition of phenomenology, founded as a method of 'inquiry' (essentially an early research method) by the philosopher Edmund Husserl (e.g. 1977) in the early 20th century, and which constituted an important element in the initial formulation of much existential philosophy.

Phenomenology proposes that human beings make sense of events and experiences (i.e. phenomena) by giving *meaning* to them. Unlike the motivation of natural science (and empirical psychology) to objectively explain events, phenomenology is concerned with only *describing* the unique, subjective meanings through which we interpret things, attempting to do so by a method of metaphorically, 'bracketing' (Spinelli, 1989) all prior assumptions to gain a true, bias-free appreciation how any person makes sense of a phenomenon at a given moment. Phenomenology thus adopts an *existential* focus exploring 'the human condition as it manifests in lived experiencing' (Spinelli, 2003: pp.180), doing so in a manner that is only interested in describing, rather than explaining, the meanings it reveals. Indeed, this view challenges the very possibility of a single 'objective' reality that may be measured and explained, highlighting the different meanings given to any event by different individuals. It is the relationship between these individual meanings and the shared existential realities which we all have to come to terms with that constitutes the focus of much existential-phenomenological theory and practice.

Since the 1950s, a number of approaches have evolved that attempt to apply existential-phenomenological ideas to the therapeutic domain (c.f. Cooper, 2003). What these have in common is a recognition of the existential dilemmas at the heart of human 'being', and a belief that, in some way or another, these are implicated in any psychological distress encountered. Existential-phenomenological approaches undertake therapy with the aim of enabling people to, a) become more honest with themselves about the realities of their existence, b) understand themselves and the meanings through which they make sense of their lived experiences, and c) create more meaningful ways of living within the limitations and constraints they encounter (van Deurzen, 2002). These principles are enacted in different ways by the various approaches that have evolved, all of which emphasise the role of a deep, respectful and interested approach to the client's subjective truths whatever they may be, at any given moment.

Relationship to the person-centred approach

Concepts and philosophy

The person-centred approach shares many fundamental concepts with the existential-phenomenological paradigm. A particular example of this is the emphasis it accords to the individual's 'frame of reference', a phenomenological concept that refers to the subjective perceptions (and meanings) of the individual at any given moment. (Stumm, 2005). For Rogers (1959) prioritising a client's frame of reference is essential if that person's 'lived experiences' are to be deeply appreciated and understood, an emphasis that resonates with the existential-phenomenological desire to explore and respect personal meanings.

Another area of overlap between the two is the emphasis on individual autonomy and choice. The cultivation of personal freedom is at the heart of both existential-phenomenological and person-centred philosophies, albeit in the context of an acknowledging the challenges such autonomy involves. For example, Sartre (1956), an existential philosopher whose work is strongly influential within the existential-phenomenological paradigm, stresses the freedom at the centre of all human existence, describing the angst tied up with acknowledging the choice of living 'authentically' (i.e. in a manner fully accepting the existential dilemmas of living). Similarly, Rogers (1961) highlights the challenges of living in a 'fully functioning' manner, whereby personal autonomy and self-awareness brings with it the challenges of living in process, aware of all personal experiencing, both positive and negative, in each moment.

Despite such commonalities, the stress placed within the existential-phenomenological paradigm on the constraints, dilemmas and challenges of human existence (e.g. Yalom, 1980) contrasts with the strongly optimistic stance of the person-centred approach and its humanistic emphasis on human potential, growth and autonomy (Cain, 2001). Certainly, many existential-phenomenological practitioners do not share the person-centred view of people as possessing a biologically given 'actualising tendency' motivating only *constructive* growth and change. Instead, they highlight the many violent and aggressive acts committed within the world, arguing that these demonstrate an inherent human potential for destructiveness and evil; an issue explored in long correspondence between Carl Rogers and Rollo May (see box 5.2). Linked to this more circumspect view is the attention given to the tragic dimensions of human existence. These may be seen to highlight a case for pessimism, not optimism, as Cooper (2004: p.104) suggests,

From an existential standpoint life has an unavoidably tragic element to it, that we come into the world eager and keen to make something of ourselves, discover that we will one day turn to dust and realise that, in the short time we have available, there are so many possibilities that we must reject ... Such a sense of tragedy, then, contrasts somewhat with the more optimistic and hopeful client-centred perspective which hypothesises that a 'good life' is attainable if we can experience the necessary and sufficient conditions.

Box. 5.2   Does the person-centred approach account for evil?

In discussing the question of evil, one of the foremost existential-phenomenological therapists of the 20th century, Rollo May had a long running debate with Carl Rogers on whether or not the person-centred approach accounted for human destructiveness and 'evil' in its optimistic view of the person (e.g. Rogers, 1961). For May (1982, cited in Kirschenbaum and Henderson, 1990b), human beings possess what he terms a Diamonic force, a biological motivation toward asserting themselves and their perpetuation. This force results in both constructive and destructive urges. May argues that the latter aspect is ignored by person-centred concepts stressing only constructive growth and human potential. Hence, he argued, person-centred theory offers a 'seductive and enticing picture' (p.242), but one which is somewhat innocent and naive.

Carl Rogers (1982, cited in Kirschenbaum and Henderson, 1990b) responded to this accusation by questioning the idea of an inevitable destructiveness within humanity, arguing there was little evidence to suggest that human beings have an *innate* tendency toward destructiveness. Instead, he suggested (pp.253–254) 'if the elements making for growth are present, the actualising tendency develops in positive ways. In the human these elements for growth are not only proper nutrition etc., but a climate of psychological attitudes'. Hence, destructiveness or evil is not ruled out, but seen as emerging from a context of inadequate nurturing rather than a direct manifestation of inherent destructive impulses. From such a view, human beings will only become destructive when the climate within which they have been brought up, or continue to live, is in some way inadequate to their needs.

Therapeutic approach

The existential-phenomenological framework contains a number of different therapeutic standpoints, each of which highlights the existential dimension of psychological distress. These span from 'Logotherapy' (Frankl, 1984), where missing existential meanings are seen as at the root of psychological difficulties and thus actively created in the therapeutic encounter (i.e. finding a purpose for life) to Deseinsanalysis (e.g. Boss, 1979), which views an individual's 'closedness' to the world (e.g. never experiencing beauty) as the cause of psychological problems, with a consequent focus on promoting a greater 'openness' within the client.

The approach that has most in common with person-centred therapy is contained within the 'British School' of existential-phenomenological therapy (e.g. van Deurzen, 2002), and that of Ernesto Spinelli.

Spinelli (1989) proposes a strongly *phenomenological* standpoint focused on understanding a client's perceptions, a process which, for him, involves three aspects; firstly, the therapist 'bracketing off' his own views and assumptions to listen intently to the meanings relevant to the client, secondly, the therapist avoiding any interpretation or explanation of these to the client, and instead only describing back to the client what he or she has said, and finally, the therapist paying equal attention to, or 'horizontalising' each aspect of what is being said by the client, not attending to some things over others. This listening method is embedded within a commitment to deeply respecting and fully accepting what a client has to say (i.e. *her truths*) as well as what he terms 'intersubjectivity' (Spinelli, 2001), a recognition that people are inherently inter-related and thus that their meanings and practices of the client have implications for others. Such a recognition translates, therapeutically, into encouraging the client to consider how his experiences and actions may effect those around him and vice versa, as well as using the therapeutic relationship itself as a mechanism enabling an exploration of how the client experiences and behaves in the relationships he conducts (Spinelli, 2001). It is through this process that a client's existential meanings are explored and new possibilities examined.

Clearly there are many similarities between the phenomenological listening outlined by Spinelli and the methods of 'classical' person-centred therapy. For example, the desire to attend closely to what the client is saying and to 'describe' (i.e. reflect back) rather than interpret or explain is similar to the person-centred emphasis on empathic listening and responding. Similarly, the importance of the therapist 'bracketing off' his own assumptions and relating in a deeply respectful manner accord with a person-centred emphasis on the client's 'frame of reference' and the avoidance of judgement in a manner akin to 'unconditional positive regard' (c.f. Rogers, 1957). Yet the approaches diverge when Spinelli talks of introducing a clear intersubjective 'agenda' for the therapy. This 'therapist-driven' (i.e. seen as important by the therapist rather than, necessarily, the client) perspective contrasts with the 'classical' person-centred emphasis on following the client's moment-by-moment experiencing with an inherent trust in her actualising tendency to promote growth (e.g. Bozarth and Brodley, 1991). Yet, this aspect of Spinelli's work does have something in common with a number of 'experiential' approaches (e.g. Rennie, 1998), in terms of encouraging the client to reflect on how she experiences and acts in the therapeutic relationship. However, such commonalities should not be overstated. Spinelli's approach, due to its phenomenological emphasis, is far closer to 'classical' person-centred therapy than most 'experiential' approaches using techniques and strategies to facilitate change within the client (e.g. Greenberg et al., 1996).

In contrast to the work of Spinelli (1994, 2001), the other main existential-phenomenological approaches share far less ground with the person-centred approach due to their more explicit focus on the promotion of existential themes and explanations to clients. Therapeutic approaches such as existential-humanist (e.g. Yalom, 1980) emphasise, for example, themes such as the inevitability of death and the exclusion of 'opposites' (i.e. un-chosen possibilities) in guiding a client toward an examination of the dilemmas these afford as well as their impact upon her 'lived experiences'. This examination is designed to deepen a client's understanding of his choices in relation to these as well as his way of 'being' in the world. However, in actively introducing and promoting such a focus, the approaches take a very different stance to both 'classical' and 'experiential' person-centred therapy, providing a clear agenda for the *content* and *focus* of the therapeutic work being undertaken and relying, to a far lesser degree, on the therapeutic relationship, and conditions such as empathy and unconditional positive regard, to facilitate change.

Box. 5.3   Is 'classical' person-centred therapy a phenomenological approach?

As we have seen, 'classical' person-centred therapy may be differentiated from humanistic therapies (as well as other counselling psychology approaches) due to its sole emphasis on understanding a client's 'frame of reference' in the context of a relationship meeting the 6 'necessary and sufficient' conditions (Rogers, 1957). This focus on understanding, describing and accepting the client's meanings or 'truths' has much in common with the principles of phenomenological inquiry (Husserl, 1977). As such, it may be argued that 'classical' person-centred therapy is actually a phenomenological approach best situated within the existential-phenomenological paradigm, a point supported by Spinelli (1989) who terms 'classical' person-centred therapy as 'clinical phenomenology'. Hence, while person-centred *theory* is undoubtedly humanistic in character, the 'classical' approach to *therapy* may be more readily accommodated within a phenomenological framework (Worsley, 2002). Do you think this creates a tension for the approach and its 'humanistic' tradition?

The psychodynamic paradigm

So far we have explored the relationship of the person-centred approach to the two paradigms in counselling psychology with which it has most in common. We now turn our attention to its relationship with its more distant cousins, the psychodynamic and cognitive behavioural paradigms, focusing firstly on its relationship to psychodynamic theory and practice.

The psychodynamic paradigm encompasses a diverse array of theoretical and practical standpoints united by a focus on the inner dynamics of the mind (as in the term *psycho*-dynamic) as well as their effects on experiencing and behaviour (Jacobs, 2005). Such is the diversity of psychodynamic approaches, for example those influenced by Jung (e.g. 1963), Klein (e.g. 1957) and Freud (e.g. 1938), that any summary can only provide a generalised caricature containing the most fundamental of assumptions. However, from such a simplified standpoint the psychodynamic paradigm may be seen as promoting the following propositions (based on Thomas, 1996: pp.286–294):

1. *Human behaviour and consciousness are largely determined by unconscious motives* – perhaps the most distinctive feature of psychodynamic approaches is that they view the majority of our intentions, desires, fears and assumptions as unavailable to conscious awareness until such time that they are (only ever partially) revealed to us, such as through therapy with a trained psychodynamic practitioner.
2. *Consciousness and internal versions of the world are systematically distorted so as to avoid emotional pain and anxiety* – contained within the unconscious is considerable psychic torment resulting from inner conflict, often linked to the interactions between our desires, motivations and feelings and our experiences as social beings. Various mechanisms of psychological defence are seen to protect us from this torment, such as *denial* of socially unacceptable feelings or desires (Stevens, 1983).
3. *Internal versions of the world form very early in life and are emotionally charged constructions* – much emphasis is placed upon childhood experiences, such as our relationships with the people around us and the consequent assumptions we came to about the social world and our place within it. As Thomas suggests (1996: p.291), 'it is the minutiae of the responsiveness, overall feeling tone, emotional states, power relations (and internal worlds) of other people, especially mothers and fathers or other early carers, that are by far the most important environmental influences of the shaping on infants' internal words and their developing versions of psychic reality'. This psychic reality is strongly emotional, for young children do not have the sophisticated conceptual and thinking capabilities of adults, and are thus unable to reflect on their emotional experiences. Life, at this age, is therefore entirely emotional, and conflicts experienced during this time are highly emotionally charged. This charge remains into adulthood at an unconscious level.

4. *Individuals' own idiosyncratic meaning systems, constructions, memories, fantasies, unconscious phantasies and dreams are the raw data of psychodynamic theories and clinical practice* – the focus is very much on individual meanings rather than more general psychological processes or behaviours. Each person is seen as unique in terms of her own inner world, and the focus of psychodynamic approaches is subjective experiencing, albeit in terms of unconscious defence mechanisms and the inner processes they mask.

On the basis of such assumptions, psychodynamic approaches to therapy employ a catalogue of therapeutic practices designed to increase a client's awareness of his unconscious desires, impulses, feelings and conflicts (Burton and Davey, 2003). Bringing such material into conscious awareness enables their emotional and behavioural consequences to be examined and 'worked through' (Lemma, 1997) in turn affording greater choice and functionality in living.

Relationship to the person-centred approach

Concepts and philosophy

The person-centred approach shares an uneasy relationship with many of the concepts and assumptions integral to the psychodynamic paradigm. One of the primary areas of contention relates to their respective views of the 'person', with psychodynamic approaches assuming an individual governed by an unconscious containing, in part, 'anti-social, selfish, destructive and aggressive – desires (Lemma, 1997). By contrast, the person-centred approach adopts a more optimistic, positive view of people, stressing our essentially constructive, *pro-social* nature as manifest in the 'actualising tendency'. Despite this difference, both views emerge historically from a shared understanding of the role of both biology and the environment in 'personality' development. Although psychodynamic approaches diverge significantly over the importance of biological drives, the ideas of their founding father, Sigmund Freud – who argued that biologically given instincts (the 'id') interact with environmental factors, such as the relationships with caregivers (the 'super-ego') to form adult 'character structure' or 'ego' (Zeigler, 2002) – promote a similar interaction to that proposed by person-centred theory, where the biological *organism* (and actualising tendency) is seen as interacting with socially acquired conditions of worth (Rogers, 1951) to produce the 'self-concept'.

Another area of common ground between the psychodynamic paradigm and the person-centred approach is the shared assumption of an unconscious dimension to human experiencing (Wheeler and Mcleod,

1995), an assumption which, within the latter, is embedded within the concept of *incongruence* (Ellingham, 1999) between self and organism. This disjuncture is seen to have the potential to generate huge anxiety which is seen, in common with psychodynamic understandings, as masked from conscious awareness by processes of psychological defence (Owen, 1999).

The person-centred approach assumes two mechanisms of psychological defence, denial and distortion, both of which serve to maintain the 'self' from the anxiety and threat generated by contradictory organismic experiencing. By contrast, psychodynamic approaches have identified around 42 (Burton and Davey, 2003), organising these into a hierarchy linked to the stage of childhood development during which they are believed to emerge (e.g. Perry, 1993).

Different forms of defence (e.g. such as those termed repression, projection and denial) in adulthood are considered as more or less 'mature', in terms of the developmental stage to which they relate (i.e. the developmental stage of the infant at the time of the experiences that gave rise to them). It is the least mature forms of defence (i.e. those associated with the earliest stages of child development) that are viewed as the most problematic and thus most highly associated with serious mental health problems such as psychosis (Burton and Davey, 2003). Indeed, psychodynamic approaches use the different kinds of defences displayed by a client to 'diagnose' the kind of psychological difficulties he or she is contending with, a process which now supports the various categories of mental illness identified by medical doctors (psychiatrists) as well as the therapeutic work undertaken by practitioners. For example an individual may be seen to have a 'narcissistic' personality disorder, a diagnosis based on a psychodynamic conceptualisation of a personality orientated around a range of psychological defences to produce a grandiose view of self and consequent diminishing of the importance of others (e.g. Johnson, 1994)

Psychological defences are viewed in a very different way within the person-centred approach. While both denial and distortion are seen emerge in conjunction with the acquisition of conditions of worth during childhood, these are not ordered hierarchically nor used in any way to inform the therapeutic work conducted. This reflects the lack of importance accorded to 'unconscious' processes within the person-centred framework with its sole focus on the client's experiences and perceptions in the present moment (Mearns and Thorne, 2000). Any therapeutic analysis of the content of the client's 'unconscious', in terms of particular feelings, motivations or conflicts, from a person-centred perspective, is seen as both irrelevant and unnecessary, despite its centrality within the psychodynamic paradigm. Indeed, there is significant disagreement between the two as to the very necessity of psychological defences in effective human functioning.

While psychodynamic approaches view psychological defences as functional and thus part and parcel of healthy and effective living (i.e. protecting the individual from excessive anxiety), person-centred therapy views *non-defensive* experiencing (i.e. becoming fully congruent) as both possible and ideal, enabling what Rogers (1961) termed the 'the good life'. Hence person-centred therapy assumes previously denied or distorted organismic experiencing can become a full part of conscious awareness, in contrast to psychodynamic approaches which assume the inevitability of a significant and ongoing unconscious dimension to life. From a psychodynamic view, psychological change is thus associated with the *adaptation* of unhealthy defences (i.e. challenging those which are dysfunctional or 'immature'; Jacobs, 2005), rather than their elimination.

Therapeutic approach

There is considerable disagreement between therapeutic approaches within the psychodynamic paradigm and the person-centred approach in terms of the nature of psychological therapy and its role in enabling change within the client. From a psychodynamic perspective, psychological change is a product of increased conscious awareness of previously unconscious impulses, motivations and defences. This outcome is viewed as best enacted through the direct analytic input of the therapist, whose primary role is to guide the client toward a greater degree of awareness by offering 'interpretations' of her actions and experiences in terms of the unconscious processes motivating them.

Due to the emphasis on the developmental basis of psychological difficulties, psychodynamic interpretations orientate around the links between past and present, highlighting, for example, how present day adult relationships are informed by childhood experiences. The therapeutic focus is thus very much on what Jacobs (2005) terms 'the presenting past', a focus which allows previously unconscious material (feelings, motivations and related forms of psychological defence etc.) to be brought into conscious awareness and attended to.

Person-centred therapy, by contrast, adopts a very different therapeutic focus, exploring the client's perceptions and experiences in the *present moment*, with no agenda to encourage an exploration of how these link to the past unless wished by the client. Indeed, understanding childhood experiences is not seen as necessarily relevant to the process of change, which is instead viewed as a product of deepened experiencing of organismic feelings in the *present* (Davy and Cross, 2004). Furthermore, rather than viewing therapy as a process reliant on the 'interpretations' provided by a therapist, the emphasis within the person-centred approach is on trusting the client to contact her own organismic experiencing within the context of a supportive, facilitative therapeutic relationship. Neither 'classical' and 'experiential' traditions see a place for any therapist-derived interpretations of 'unconscious' processes, preferring instead to *work collaboratively with* the client to become more fully congruent in her experiencing. Although techniques may be suggested to assist this process (i.e. by those within the 'experiential' tradition) these are only ever facilitative and designed to aid the client draw his own conclusions. Interpretations are wholly unacceptable, undermining the client's autonomy and prioritising the therapist's expertise. As McLeod, in Wheeler and McLeod (1995: p.286) suggests, rather than being the 'expert', 'As a person-centred counsellor I always want to be following the client, half a step behind, rather than "knowing" the answer to the puzzle'.

Another, but related, difference between psychodynamic and person-centred therapeutic approaches is the type of relationship that is envisaged between client and therapist. Although an empathic, or close emotional relationship is emphasised by some psychodynamic standpoints (Mitchell, 2000), a more detached, opaque therapeutic stance is often encouraged to enable the client to 'transfer' unconscious feelings from the past onto his therapist (who, accordingly, discloses as little as possible about herself to avoid confusing things). This process, known as 'transference', is hugely important within the psychodynamic paradigm for it is seen as a core technique through which to identify the unconscious motivations and feelings within the client as they are enacted within the therapeutic relationship. The therapeutic relationship is thus seen as of great significance, for it is assumed that within it – as an ongoing, regular and intimate interaction – the client begins to repeat, unconsciously, patterns from the past linked to unconscious feelings, desires and motivations (Freeman, 1999). For example, a client feeling scared of her therapist's judgements may be 'transferring' experiences of an authoritarian and castigating mother onto this relationship. In bringing these unconscious feelings into conscious awareness, the therapist is able to assist the client work them through and change their influence on her life.

From a person-centred perspective, the concept of transference is problematic because it detracts from the primacy of the actual, adult-to-adult, relationship between therapist and client, a process which may be seen to 'infantilize' the client by undermining the legitimacy of her feelings in the moment (Rogers, 1987). In viewing the client's relationship with the therapist as, in part, a re-enactment of the past, the actual dynamic between them is distorted to the extent that the therapist is viewed primarily as a 'blank screen' upon which the client may 'transfer' feelings from the past rather than an actual person whose behaviour and methods of relating have real consequences within the relationship (Owen, 1999). This potentially provides the therapist with more power in the relationship with the client, for she is potentially able to define a client's feelings as transference from the past rather than a *legitimate* response in the present. By contrast to this, within the person-centred framework it is the 'real' relationship between therapist and client that is accorded primary significance. Practitioners aim toward being as genuine (or congruent) as possible in relating, trusting the client and viewing her as an autonomous participant with legitimate motivations, experiences and choices in the present relationship (Brodley, 1997b). Indeed, they take a highly personal, actively warm, and unconditionally valuing stance – often termed 'prizing' by Rogers (1951) – in contrast to the more detached, impersonal style traditionally associated with much psychodynamic practice.[1] Hence, the power relationship between the two may be seen to be different, with the person-centred therapist working toward a collaborative, equal therapeutic relationship between two persons in contrast to the traditional psychodynamic interaction between practioner and 'patient'.

Box 5.4   Is transference a fiction?

In a now famous article, a well know person-centred practitioner, John Schlien (1984: p.23), argued that 'transference is a fiction, invented and maintained by the therapist to protect himself from the consequences of his own behaviour'. This strong proposition expresses Schlien's concern at how the concept of transference enables a psychodynamic therapist to remain unaccountable in the relationship, able to avoid his own legitimate feelings/behaviours and those of the client by viewing these as re-enactments of the client's past. It is an invented 'fiction' because, as Schlien argues, it suits psychodynamic practitioners to remain impervious to the dynamics of the 'real' relationship with a client, as such a relationship may raise personally threatening issues; such as how to deal with a client's actual dislike for him. In accordance with humanistic principles, he proposes instead that it is this 'real' relationship between client and counsellor that is of therapeutic significance; a relationship masked by what he terms the 'transference neurosis' prioritising things from the client's past which emerge from in the mind of the therapist (as analytical interpretations) rather than from client directly.

Of course Schlien's view has its detractors, even among those within the person-centred community. Lietaer (1993), for example, states (pp.35–36): 'Yes John, there is transference … in client-centred therapy [*sic*] too, the client repeats his past with the therapist …' However Lietaer (1993) goes on to suggest that this can be worked through in the 'here and now' context of an actual healthy relationship, rather than used, as in psychodynamic therapy, as a vehicle for interpreting unconscious feelings from the past.

While there is little doubt that person-centred therapeutic practices differ substantially to those advocated within the psychodynamic paradigm, it is all too easy to see them as fundamentally oppositional and thus as having little or nothing in common (Geller and Gould, 1996). This is not the case, for the two do share some general similarities in approach, such as that they both operate mainly through talking, that they both take an exploratory stance with the aim of helping the client increase self-awareness and develop understanding, that they both emphasise, albeit in different ways, the relationship as central to the therapeutic encounter, and that they both demand a high level of self-awareness and personal development on behalf of the therapist (Wheeler and McLeod, 1995: p.284). Hence, while the psychodynamic paradigm and the person-centred approach do not agree on many aspects of how therapy should be conducted, there are also many areas of cross-over and commonality, a point best illustrated by recalling the considerable influence of Otto Rank, the psychoanalytic psychotherapist, on many key aspects of person-centred theory and practice. Indeed, recent dialogues between prominent therapists from both traditions (e.g. Mearns and Jacobs, 2003) also highlight the significant extent to which mature therapeutic practice in either approach is actually more similar in process and style to such practice in the other than is often assumed.

The cognitive-behavioural paradigm

The final paradigm of counselling psychology we shall consider in terms of its relationship to the person-centred approach is the cognitive-behavioural paradigm. This paradigm is one of the most well-known within the field of psychology and is a product of two different psychological traditions, namely behaviorism (e.g. Skinner, 1953) and cognitive psychology (e.g. Neisser, 1967).

Although there are a large number of different therapeutic approaches within the cognitive behavioural framework, (Scott and Dryden, 2003), two of the most well-known are rational emotive behaviour therapy (REBT) (e.g. Ellis, 1994) and cognitive therapy (often now simply called, confusingly, cognitive behaviour therapy: Beck, 1995). Both of these approaches highlight the inter-relationship between cognition, emotions, physiology and behaviour (Scott and Dryden, 2003) in creating and maintaining psychological problems while at the same time highlighting the faulty or 'maladaptive' thinking patterns at their hub.

Rational-emotive behaviour therapy proposes that there are two types of distorted thinking which create psychological difficulties; ego disturbance where the individual evaluates herself in an irrational or unrealistic manner, and discomfort disturbance, where an irrational expectation that life must be comfortable at all times prevents a client functioning in an effective way (Ellis, 2004). Therapy focuses on challenging all these 'irrational' beliefs preventing any individual achieving his basic goals and purposes as well as those inconsistent with 'reality' (Dryden, 2002).

The cognitive (behaviour) therapy of Beck (e.g. 1967) takes a similar therapeutic stance, albeit one highlighting a wider range of maladaptive cognitions. Distorted thinking is seen to operate at three different levels, organised hierarchically; firstly that of the 'automatic thoughts' used to make sense of everyday situations, (e.g. 'he doesn't like me'), secondly, the more general assumptions and rules underpinning for living ('I must be liked by everyone to be a success'), and finally, the deep, core beliefs seen to be the basis of psychological disturbance (e.g. 'I am a failure as a person'). Each of these levels are viewed as linked to one another, with 'automatic thoughts' arising from rules/assumptions and their corresponding core belief.

In common with REBT, cognitive (behaviour) therapy generally (but not exclusively) views psychological change as a product of modifying, or more effectively managing, distorted thinking and its effects (Moorey, 2002). This is supplemented in both by interventions at behavioural, physiological and emotional levels designed to support the cognitive changes being enacted. These interventions may include relaxation techniques and behaviour modifications such as confronting previously feared situations (Scott and Dryden, 2003). It is also not uncommon for behavioural interventions to take precedence over cognitive work (a stance derived from the tradition's behaviourist underpinning) in the treatment of specific difficulties (e.g. obsessive-compulsve disorder).

Relationship to the person-centred approach

Concepts and philosophy

As may be expected from their diverse theoretical ancestry, the concepts and philosophy of person-centred therapy and the cognitive-behavioural paradigm differ substantially. A particular example of this difference lies in their respective views of psychological disturbance and its causation.

The person-centred approach proposes incongruence as the basis of all psychological difficulties, viewing the tension between the *experiences* of the organism as a whole, and those acknowledged within the 'self', as the cause of psychological dysfunction (Rogers, 1959). By contrast, cognitive-behavioural approaches emphasise the primary role of *cognition* in psychological disturbance (Scott and Dryden, 2003), highlighting the role of dysfunctional or maladaptive thinking patterns in creating emotional, physiological and behavioural difficulties. As these patterns may be corrected through the acquisition of more effective thinking skills (Person, 1989), the cognitive-behavioural view is thus of the client as a *learner* (Clarkson, 1996), and change a product of the client *being educated* to think (and behave) in a less dysfunctional, and more realistic way. This is in contrast to the person-centred view of the individual as *already possessing* the inner resources for constructive growth (the actualising tendency), which render her both trustworthy and capable of change within a facilitative climate.

Such a climate is seen within the 'classical' person-centred approach as the 6 'necessary and sufficient' conditions specified by Rogers (1957). Yet, while the presence of the conditions of empathy, unconditional positive regard and congruence are also seen as important within the cognitive behavioural paradigm, they are not viewed as 'sufficient' to enable change within a client, as Gilbert (1992: p.13), suggests:

> Cognitive counsellors doubt that the qualities of accurate empathy, positive regard and genuineness are, by themselves, sufficient to produce change. Education into the way an individual thinks about events and labels or puts him/herself down is crucial for change. But cognitive counsellors do believe that these qualities are necessary ingredients of a helping relationship.

Another conceptual difference between person-centred therapy and cognitive-behavioural approaches follows from their understanding of psychological disturbance (Zeigler, 2002). If psychological difficulties are understood in terms of distorted thinking, it is possible to link specific, identifiable psychological 'disorders' to particular patterns of thinking, and as a result employ diagnostic techniques and pre-determined, interventions designed to alleviate them. Cognitive-behavioural approaches are thus 'disorder-specific' (e.g. Palmer and Dryden, 1995), in that they differentiate between different psychological disorders, and often intervene in a manner 'targeting' the specific cognitive and/or behavioural components associated with each. In recent years this method of working has become increasingly enmeshed with the practices of medicine whereby particular psychological 'illnesses' are diagnosed and their symptoms treated in a specific (structured) way, such as focusing specifically on the perceived 'threat' causing anxiety and attending to the often unrealistic (cognitive) appraisal of evidence at its root (Padesky and Greenberger, 1995). An approach like this strongly contrasts with the person-centred perspective and its emphasis on client autonomy and self-direction, although as we shall explore in Chapter 6, specific client 'processes' may be identified (e.g. Warner, 2000) from an 'experiential', person-centred standpoint.

> **Box. 5.5   The person-centred approach and the medicalisation of psychological distress**
>
> In contrast to many of the therapeutic approaches within the different paradigms we have explored, the person-centred approach does not undertake practices or provide explanations which support a 'medicalised' view of psychological distress. (Joseph and Worsley, 2005). A 'medicalised' view is one that views such distress as something that may be diagnosed in accordance with medical classifications of mental disorders, and treated using specific interventions targeted solely on these in order to alleviate symptoms. The identification of particular psychological defences within the psychodynamic paradigm accords with a medicalised view because this process supports the classifications of different kinds of mental disorders by providing explanations for these in terms of their primary causes and effects (as well as their likely response to psychodynamic treatment). Approaches within the cognitive-behavioural paradigm adopt a similar stance, albeit one using CBT methods to focus specifically on alleviating symptoms and improving functioning in relation to the particular psychological difficulty being encountered. The person-centred approach does not share either of these views, refusing to view clients in medicalised terms; as people with diagnosable 'disorders' that may be 'treated'. Instead, the focus is on relating to the client as a whole person, trusting that she has the necessary resources to enhance her own well-being when provided with the right conditions to do so (i.e. an effective therapeutic relationship), facilitated or otherwise by the use of 'experiential' techniques.

Despite their differences, there are also numbers of areas of conceptual agreements between the person-centred and cognitive-behavioural standpoints, none more so than their shared emphasis on the capacity of clients to become more 'flexible and confident to practise and develop ... 'potentialities' (Mearns and Thorne, 2000: p.34). Both person-centred therapy and cognitive-behavioural approaches view the individual in terms of what he *may be* (i.e. able to think more realistically, able to become 'congruent') and hence adopt a positive, optimistic perspective. Similar to this is their shared phenomenological basis. In emphasising the *personal meanings* at the core of all psychological distress, cognitive-behavioural approaches accord with the person-centred emphasis on individual perceptions and thus attend to the unique meanings of events to every individual in the *present* rather than their links to the past, unlike, say, psychodynamic approaches (Zimring, 1974).

Recent developments indicate still further scope for shared perspectives. A particular example of this is the evolution of 'mindfulness' based cognitive therapy (e.g. Teasdale, 1999), a Buddhist-inspired approach stressing ongoing awareness (and acceptance) of thinking (and feeling) patterns. This has a number of similarities to Rogers' (1961) 'process-conception', and his model of the self as an ongoing 'flow' of experiencing. It also shares much in common with more contemporary work exploring person-centred thinking from a Buddhist perspective (e.g. Moore, 2004). Another area growing synergy between the approaches is the increasing awareness of the importance of the therapeutic relationship between client and therapist within the cognitive-behavioural domain (e.g. Giovalolias, 2004).

Therapeutic approach

Cognitive-behavioural approaches draw on a whole range of techniques designed to *teach* a client cognitive-behavioural ideas (e.g. on the link between thoughts and feelings) and methods (e.g. how to challenge 'thoughts' or use breathing techniques to combat panic). These are underpinned by inquisitive forms of questioning (e.g. 'if you did get embarrassed and turn red, what do you think would happen then') designed to elicit and progressively elaborate the thinking patterns at the root of the problem, and identify the problematic cognitions to 'target' (e.g. 'what is the evidence that your boss would sack you for being weak if she saw you turning red?'). While practitioners vary with regards to how they balance teaching and questioning activities within sessions, they generally introduce information, explanations and ideas into the therapy and as such situate themselves in a position of 'expertise' over the client.

Box 5.6   Can person-centred therapy be integrated with therapeutic approaches from other paradigms?

Although a number of approaches have developed which attempt to integrate person-centred therapy with therapeutic approaches from other paradigms, (e.g. Egan, 1998), these generally take what is termed a *technical eclectic* stance (Norcross and Newman, 1992) drawing on different therapeutic techniques for different ends, such as applying various cognitive-behavioural techniques while at the same time employing many aspects of person-centred therapeutic relating (e.g. offering the 'core' conditions etc.) to establish an effective working bond. However, this stance arises from a commitment to what Grant (1990) terms, *instrumental* non-directivity, where the person-centred relationship is seen as a *technique* (or instrument), like any other, that may be used to support change.

(Continued)

If person-centred therapy is primarily viewed as a set of attitudes held by the therapist (Rogers, 1957), the relationship these enact cannot be seen as a technique, for it is instead an ethical commitment to a particular 'way of being' with a client. In 'classical' person-centred therapy this, as a matter of *principle*, is non-directive (in terms of the therapist not being prepared to assume an expert stance in directing the client toward particular ideas or techniques). Hence integrating such an approach with, say, a cognitive-behavioural standpoint is impossible. These perspectives are fundamentally different with regards to therapist behaviour and process of change (Hollanders, 2000). However, clearly such a stance is compromised if 'experiential' approaches are considered, for many of these draw on methods and techniques offered by the therapist and designed to facilitate change.

As we have seen, the development of 'experiential' standpoints has been highly controversial within the person-centred framework, for they more readily accommodate the integration of methods from other therapeutic approaches (such as gestalt therapy) from within the humanistic paradigm. Yet, to be defined as person-centred requires, in all fundamental formulations of the approach (e.g. Schmid, 2003) a commitment to not introducing *content* into therapeutic work and therefore avoiding, as much as possible, an 'expert' stance over the terms of the client's experiencing. This is unlike most approaches in the existential (e.g. introducing 'existential' concerns), psychodynamic (i.e. through 'interpretations') and cognitive-behavioural (i.e. through 'teaching' a client cognitive-behavioural ideas and methods) paradigms. Hence, generally speakling, integrating person-centred centred therapy with therapeutic approaches from other paradigms raises some significant philosophical, as well as practical, dilemmas for the person-centred practitioner.

Despite the many philsophical and pragmatic difficulties presented arising from the notion of integration, recent theoretical work has highlighted the extent to which it may be possible to conceive of a different grounding for integrating person-centred therapy with therapeutic approaches from different paradigms. Gergen (1991), for example, argues from a social constructionist perspective that it is no longer possible to argue that any one paradigm or therapeutic approach offers the moral 'truth' over the other. Hence, he argues, there is spacc for a multiplicity of ways of working, a stance often termed *pluralism* (Samuels, 1997) and within which the possibility of new, more integrated perspectives may emerge. Such a move would require a new philosophical grounding for person-centred therapy, but is a possibility increasingly highlighted by social constructionist critiques of existing assumptions within the psychological domain, assumptions of direct relevance to the theory and practice of person-centred therapy. This critique, as it applies to the person-centred approach, will be explored in Chapter 8.

The person-centred approach takes a very different stance, rejecting the idea that a client requires to learn more effective thinking skills in order to alleviate distress. Practitioners within the tradition work instead toward establishing a facilitative relationship within which the client is viewed as already possessing the resources to enable change. Person-centred therapists do not adopt a directive or teaching role (although some 'experiential' methods involve the therapist teaching the client the techniques involved), assuming that it is the client who is best able to know what is wrong, and what direction to take things in making things better. Indeed, from a person-centred point of view, encouraging a client to attend to, and challenge, 'maladaptive' cognitions may be seen, like the use of 'interpretations' in psychodynamic practice, to 'suppress the individual's growth process' (Bohart, 1982: p.248), undermining her internal locus of evaluation and capacity to contact her own, organismic experiencing.

As well as differing in terms of therapeutic focus, a further area of divergence between person-centred therapy and cognitive-behavioural approaches lies in the formal organisation of each therapy session. As well as an emphasis on targeting specific problems or 'disorders', the emphasis within cognitive-behavioural methods is on therapeutic 'efficiency' (Ellis, 2004). Therapy is thus designed to be as minimally invasive as possible (i.e. in terms of number of sessions as well as their regularity) to prevent dependency on the therapist (Dryden, 2002) as well as to emphasise the primary importance of the client learning for himself how to identify and change faulty thinking and associated behaviours.

To promote efficiency, cognitive-behavioural practitioners generally adopt an organised approach to the conduct of therapy, with sessions highly structured to ensure that little time is wasted on material that is irrelevant to the problems being addressed. A typical session structure involves the following aspects (Blackburn and Davidson, 1995):

1. Review client's present state – clients first have the opportunity to explain what, if anything, has changed since the last meeting (an issue that may mean some revision is required in terms of the types of problem being addressed in the therapy).
2. Set agenda – an 'agenda' for the session is negotiated and agreed, defining the specific problem/s to be worked and the goals it is designed to achieve.
3. Review homework assignment(s) – a review of the client's activities since the previous session is conducted to examine how he got on completing the tasks he had agreed, tasks that were designed to support his learning outwith the session.
4. Target problem – focus therapeutic work on an agreed specific problem, undertaking activities and techniques designed to identify and address the difficulty being worked on.

5. Negotiate homework assignment(s) – determine what tasks the client will work on to support his learning, such as identifying unrealistic thoughts and evaluating the evidence for and against them to arrive at a more realistic conclusion.
6. Session feedback – review the actual session itself with a view to enhancing future work.

An approach such as this differs substantially to the usual process of person-centred therapy, which avoids the imposition, by the therapist, of a formal structure on the sessions and instead enables the client to determine what to focus upon as the session progresses. Although for some clients an unstructured approach can be challenging and frustrating (Bozarth, 1993), the client is trusted to know 'what hurts' (Rogers, 1951) and seen as able to judge what aspects of her experiencing to attend to as a result as each session evolves. From a person-centred perspective, the very nature of therapy means that its process cannot, and should not, be planned for at the outset, for previously denied or distorted organismic experiencing may be contacted at any point. This may, in turn, influence the subsequent focus of the session. For a therapist to police a pre-agreed 'agenda' may thus inhibit a client's capacity to contact his experiencing as it unfolds (i.e. deepens), something which would be viewed as significantly detrimental to the therapeutic process (Rennie, 1998).

Another dimension of the cognitive-behavioural approach to therapy which does not accord with person-centred understandings is that of 'homework'. Homework is an important aspect of cognitive-behavioural approaches, designed to help a client challenge his old beliefs by 'testing' these against reality through experimentation, such as undertaking activities in a manner supporting the realistic thinking being practised. From a person-centred perspective, however, there is little need to agree specific 'homework' tasks with clients, for all individuals are seen as fundamentally trustworthy, and able to determine how best to meet their goals at any given moment. Furthermore, the approach views incongruence, rather than maladaptive thinking, as the cause of psychological distress. Hence, the technical requirement to rectify particular symptoms, aided by 'homework' is seen as irrelevant.

Summary

- The person-centred approach is strongly associated with the humanistic paradigm, known as the 'third force' in psychology.
- The approach promotes key humanistic concepts such as human potential, autonomy and choice.

- Classical person-centred therapy is very different to other humanistic forms of therapy due to its sole emphasis on the therapeutic relationship and the client's actualising tendency to motivate change. No therapist provided techniques or strategies are seen as necessary, unlike in other humanistic therapies such as the gestalt approach.
- The person-centred approach is strongly influenced by existential philosophy and has much in common with the existential-phenomenological paradigm.
- Classical person-centred therapy has been called 'clinical phenomenology' due to its similarity to phenomenological ideas. As a result, some theorists view 'classical' person-centred therapy as a phenomenological therapeutic standpoint, despite the humanistic basis of its underlying theory.
- The person-centred approach has many differences with the psychodynamic paradigm despite sharing the view that there is an 'unconscious' dimension to experiencing.
- Person-centred and psychodynamic approaches to therapy differ due to their respective emphasis on the present and the links between the present and the past.
- The person-centred approach does not agree with cognitive-behavioural propositions that psychological disturbance is caused by faulty or maladaptive thinking. Instead, it views incongruence as the sole basis of all psychological difficulties.
- Cognitive-behavioural approaches take a structured therapeutic approach, teaching a client new methods of thinking and behaving to encourage well-being. Person-centred therapy, by contrast, views the client as already possessing the resources to enable growth and change.

Note

1 It is important to note here that psychodynamic approaches vary considerably in therapeutic stance, and the more 'relational' perspective emphasising a positive, genuine relationship between practitioner and patient is becoming increasingly popular (e.g. Stern, 1986). See Mitchell (2000) for a review of this 'relational turn'.

SIX Person-centred Therapy and Contemporary Practice in Mental Health: Working with Distress

Introduction

In the previous chapter we explored how the person-centred approach relates to the four paradigms in counselling psychology. We now turn our attention to the context of psychological provision in the UK to examine where person-centred therapy is situated within it. Although there is a diverse range of services offering psychological therapy to individuals (e.g. voluntary agencies, charities, private practitioners etc.) most commonly those with psychological difficulties are supported within healthcare contexts, such as those of the National Health Service. In this chapter we shall explore the ways in which psychological distress is attended in the contemporary healthcare arena, highlighting the extent to which this context is informed by a medical standpoint viewing psychological difficulties as 'disorders' which require treatment. Such a stance is highly problematic from a person-centred perspective, and we will explore some of the key reasons for this, investigating prominent person-centred objections to the 'medicalisation' of psychological difficulties and their associated 'treatments'. We will also examine some of the alternative, person-centred, understandings and practices pertaining to severe psychological disturbance. These offer a radical alternative to many of the methods commonly employed from more medicalised standpoints and thus again point to the alternative perspectives offered by the person-centred framework.

A medical model of 'distress'

While methods of attending to psychological distress have a long and complex history (e.g. Bentall, 2004), it is medicine that currently provides the framework for how psychological difficulties are understood and addressed in the Western world (Tudor, 1996). This medical framework provides a particular view on the nature, causes and treatment of psychological difficulties, a view which assumes, as Sanders (2006: p.26) suggests, that;

> the best way of thinking and talking about human mental distress … [is] to think and talk in terms of 'illness' and 'health', or if we prefer, 'normality' and 'abnormality' … Since mental health is a medical condition, we need a psychopathology and system of classifying symptoms, and by association, treatments (diagnosis).

From a medical perspective, psychological difficulties are illnesses (often termed 'psychopathologies' or 'disorders') which may be diagnosed and treated like any other. Such a process relies on an underlying classificatory scheme identifying the different kinds of psychological or mental illnesses that exist (Sommerbeck, 2003). Although there are a number of different classificatory schemes, one of the best-known is *The Diagnostic and Statistical Manual* (APA, 1994, 2000) published by the American Psychiatric Association. This manual is designed to provide an up-to-date categorisation of all disorders and their diagnostic symptoms (i.e. reported by the client) and signs (i.e. behaviours observed by the practitioner), as there are no biological tests that can confirm or otherwise the presence of a non-organic mental illness. These disorders change over time as psychiatrists (medical doctors specialising in treating mental illness) refine and elaborate their views on what types of mental illness exist and how these may be identified. Hence the 106 types of mental disorder identified by the American Psychiatric Association in the DSM 1 in 1951, are now superceded by the 347 described in the 1994 version of the DSM IV (APA, 1994) a manual now so well known in the USA that it has even featured in the comedy programme *Frasier* without further explanation or description (Bentall, 2004). Typical examples of the mental disorders identified in the DSM IV include depression, anxiety, obsessive-compulsive disorder, borderline personality disorder and psychosis (APA, 1994).

Diagnostic manuals (such as the DSM IV) are widely used within the field of mental health to enable practitioners to diagnose what particular disorder an individual has. This diagnosis is generally made as part of an assessment process, where a psychiatrist, psychologist or other relevant individual examines the psychological state of the client using various mechanisms, such as open questions, observation of verbal and non-verbal behaviour, psychometric tests, asking for verbal reports of particular symptoms (e.g. feeling depressed) etc. Like biological medicine, a diagnosis is followed by a treatment or 'care' plan detailing what interventions are necessary to improve mental well-being. As mental illness is seen by the medical profession as having a strong biological component (Breggin, 1993), a common form of treatment is pharmacological and psychiatry uses a vast array of drugs designed to treat the different illnesses diagnosed (e.g. anti-depressants such as Prozac). Psychological therapy is also often employed, either as an adjunct or as an alternative to medication, and it is the provision of this that constitutes the primary task of psychologists working within healthcare settings.

A medicalised 'psychology'

While Counselling Psychology, as a discipline, adopts an engaged but wary perspective on the diagnosis and treatment of specific psychological disorders (Golsworthy, 2004), the area of psychology that dominates the clinical arena (Clinical Psychology) has traditionally aligned itself strongly with a medicalised approach (Proctor, 2005a). Clinical Psychologists play a central role in the assessment, diagnosis and treatment of individuals with psychological difficulties within the healthcare domain, and a whole area of psychological research, abnormal psychology, has emerged to support it, as Lazarus and Colman (1995: p.14) explain:

> Abnormal psychology is devoted to the study of mental, emotional and behavioural aberrations. It is the branch of psychology concerned with research into the classification, causation, diagnosis prevention and treatment of psychological disorders or psychopathology. ... The essence of abnormal psychology is its emphasis on research into abnormal behaviour and its endeavour to classify the wide range of mental and emotional aberrations into coherent categories, and to understand them. Abnormal psychology serves as a backdrop or guide to clinical practice.

Abnormal psychology provides a theoretical framework for Clinical Psychology practice, promoting psychological understandings of, and ways of working with, a range of different mental disorders (Sanders, 2005). Both psychodynamic and cognitive-behavioural paradigms are implicated in these, often providing their conceptual basis and underlying rationale. However, it is the cognitive-behavioural framework that is presently dominant within both abnormal and clinical psychology (Proctor, 2005a) due to its nature as a disorder-specific, symptom-focused and efficient manner of psychological working as well as its close relationship with the empirical basis of contemporary Western psychology.

Box 6.1   Should we use the term patient or client?

For psychologists working within medicalised settings, the term *patient* is generally the norm when referring to individuals receiving 'treatment' of one sort or another. Yet, the term 'patient' is highly

(Continued)

(Continued)

controversial, for it carries with it number of connotations linked to how the person being treated is seen, and the power he or she has in relation to the diagnosis and treatment of his or her difficulties. For many, calling an individual a *patient* is depersonalising, reducing the entirety of a person to the status of a particular pathology or disorder (e.g. anxiety). Moreover, it implies passivity in the relation to the treatment being received. For Rogers (1942) the strong relationship between the term 'patient' and the principles and practices of medicine rendered it inappropriate as a way of referring to individuals experiencing psychological difficulties or distress. Instead, he preferred the term *client,* which inferred that the individual being treated was, in effect, directing the course and nature of his or her therapy. Moreover, the term *client* suggests a more equitable relationship of power and expertise between the counsellor and the individual with whom he or she is working, in contrast to the medicalised understandings informing much psychological work. Hence *client*-centred therapy (now *person*-centred therapy) was preferred over all other options.

Medicalised distress: a person-centred perspective

It would not be an exaggeration to say the person-centred approach, particularly the 'classical' tradition, takes one of the most radical stances within psychology toward the medicalisation of psychological distress, rejecting many of the fundamental terms and processes associated with it (e.g. Bozarth and Motomasa, 2005). For person-centred practitioners, objections to medicalised approaches crystallise around the process of diagnosis, an activity viewed as highly problematic for a number of reasons.

In diagnosing a particular 'disorder' (e.g. anxiety disorder), the practitioner *defines* an individual experiencing psychological distress in terms of a single classification rather than viewing her as a whole being with specific needs, experiences and resources. This results in a client being *reduced* to a generalised classification or diagnostic category, undermining her autonomy and status as a unique human being. Furthermore, it situates the psychological distress being encountered as central to her identity. This not only detracts from the entirety of her lived experiences, but also emphasises her *deficiency* (i.e. her illness or 'disorder) rather than her resourcefulness and potential. A diagnostic standpoint thus adopts a *deficiency* rather than *potentiality* model, in contrast to the person-centred emphasis on the individual's actualising tendency and inherent potential for creative growth and change (Mearns, 2004). As a result, Irving Yalom (1989. p.185), an existential psychotherapist and psychiatrist, argues:

> I marvel that anyone can take diagnosis seriously, that it can ever be considered more than a simple cluster of symptoms and behavioural traits...Even the most liberal system of psychiatric nomenclature does violence to the being of another. If we relate to people believing we can categorise them, we will neither identify nor nurture the parts, the vital parts of the other that transcends category. The enabling relationship always assumes the other is never fully knowable.

As well as a conceptual objection to *reducing* a person through diagnosis, Yalom hints at a practical question in asking the extent to which an accurate diagnosis is *possible* bearing in mind the many 'unknowable' dimensions of another person. Such an argument reflects the way that the many signs and symptoms of psychological distress frequently indicate a variety of possible difficulties and thus do not enable clear-cut classification of any underlying pathology (Boy et al., 1989). Added to this is the subjective basis of the diagnosis process itself. A number of theorists have demonstrated that diagnostic categories, such as those within the DSM IV, are not reliable in statistical terms due to their low levels of inter-rater reliability (Bentall, 2004).

As well as highlighting the subjective nature of a diagnostic process within the psychological domain, person-centred practitioners further challenge the extent to which such a method detracts from the client's perceptions and experiencing. As an approach spanning the humanistic and existential-phenomenological paradigms, person-centred therapy prioritises the client's own meanings and frame of reference over those of any external party. Such a view is very different to a medicalised approach in which an expert practitioner (psychologist, psychiatrist etc.) determines what is wrong (i.e. a particular disorder), and accordingly decides what to treat. In this latter way of working, the views and knowledge of an expert clinician are accorded greater power and significance than those of the patient (Natiello, 2001) which reduces the client's autonomy as well as undermining the development of an internalised locus of evaluation.

Although person-centred theory (Rogers, 1957) does provide a diagnosis for psychological distress, i.e. *all* psychological difficulties as caused by incongruence, it is the *client's diagnosis* of his experiences that is seen to matter, as Rogers, (1951,22 pp.222–3) suggests:

> Therapy is basically the experiencing of the inadequacies in old ways of perceiving, the experiencing of new and more accurate perceptions, and the recognition of significant relationships between perceptions. In a very meaningful way, therapy *is* diagnosis, and this diagnosis is a process which goes on in the experience of the client, rather than in the intellect of the clinician.

Hence, externally derived classifications are seen as irrelevant, or even dangerous in detracting attention from the client's perceptions (Merry and Brodley, 2002).

A further objection to diagnosis, from a person-centred perspective, is linked to its underlying function of differentiating between disorders to enable treatment to be determined. Inherent in this activity is the assumption that different types of psychological difficulty require different forms of intervention. In many instances these are composed of various medications supplemented by the specific psychological interventions indicated by research studies to be effective in working with that specific disorder. However, from a person-centred perspective, identifying different psychological treatments is unnecessary, for there is only one way of enabling psychological change; facilitating a client's own actualising tendency by means of therapeutic relationship meeting the six conditions specified by Rogers (1957), a process supported, within the 'experiential' tradition, by various techniques or methods. As this relationship is seen as embodying the same elements irrespective of the problems or difficulties of the client, person-centred therapists see no need for differentiated methods of working. Diagnosis thus has no pragmatic purpose, for all treatment is the same; not symptom or problem-centred but *relationship*-centred (Mearns, 2004).

Clearly, as we explored in Chapter 4, a therapeutic relationship meeting the 6 conditions may be difficult or indeed impossible to establish due to the requirement for psychological contact not being met. For significantly disturbed individuals (e.g. those with psychotic experiencing), it may therefore be the case that person-centred therapy (or indeed psychological therapy of any kind) cannot take place and an alternative intervention is needed instead. Within the person-centred framework, such an intervention is termed *pre-therapy*, a method of working with contact-impaired individuals (e.g. Prouty, 1994) which we shall explore later in the chapter.

Box 6.2   Can diagnosis sometimes help?

Although very critical of many features of psychiatric and psychological approaches to mental health, Rachel Freeth, a person-centred counsellor as well as psychiatrist (Freeth, 2004) argues that some patients find a 'diagnosis' helpful in the process of trying to make sense of their feelings and experiences. Freeth argues that, on occasion, a diagnosis can help a person come to terms with what is happening to them, perhaps allowing them to feel less guilty over the cause of their difficulties or to understand that they are not entirely to blame for what is happening (i.e. by showing that their disorder is not

(Continued)

uncommon and, in tandem with current psychiatric thinking, has a likely biological component). Alternatively, Rowan, (1998) argues that diagnosis can have many negative effects for the client in terms of the stigma and social consequences of being 'labelled' mentally ill. Indeed, they suggest that these consequences can include that they become self-fulfilling prophecies, in that the person begins to be related to by others in terms of his diagnosis rather than his personality, such as viewing someone as being a *depressive*.

Do you think a diagnosis is a help or hindrance to someone experiencing psychological difficulties?

An insufficient basis for psychological working?

Although the person-centred approach offers a strong critique of medicalised approaches to psychological distress, its radical perspective has had a number of consequences over the years. By far the most significant of these is the evolution of a corresponding critique of the person-centred approach as a model of therapy which is inadequate for working with those with significant or severe psychological difficulties. This critique is based on the view that person-centred therapy is not underpinned by a sufficiently elaborate theoretical understanding of the different types of psychological disorder to enable therapists to work effectively with them. In conceptualising all forms of psychological distress as incongruence, person-centred theory is seen as too lightweight to fully prepare practitioners to meet the range of complex needs presented by those with significant distress (Cain, 1993).

Linked to such arguments are concerns regarding the approach's disavowal of 'disorder-specific' (Schmid, 2004) diagnoses, and the refusal of a number of person-centred practitioners to undertake 'assessment' procedures prior to commencing work with a client. Within a medicalised psychological framework, assessment of every patient is undertaken prior to therapeutic work as a means of diagnosing the specific disorder presented, and for determining how best to treat it. However, as assessment is for the purposes of diagnosing a specific disorder and in developing what is termed a psychological formulation (see Box 6.3) of a client's difficulties on the basis of which treatment is decided, from a person-centred perspective (e.g. Bozarth, 1998) it is seen as unnecessary. Yet in refusing to undertake any explicit diagnostic procedure, the person-centred practitioner may be seen as neglecting to ensure that the client receives the best form of treatment for her needs, which may or may not be person-centred or any psychological therapy (depending on the type of difficulties identified and the research evidence regarding their effective treatment). Hence practitioners working in such a manner may be seen as acting naively and even recklessly, potentially failing in their obligations to their clients (c.f. Wilkins, 2005a). This is a particular concern for counselling psychologists whose training, professional identity and common working environments (e.g. in the NHS) require a significant degree of engagement with assessment procedures, albeit in a manner that is highly sensitive to the client's subjective experiences as well as the dynamic of power in the relationship between practitioner and client (Strawbridge and Woolfe, 2003). As a result, the issue of assessment and diagnosis raises a number of significant philosophical and practical tensions for counselling psychologists when working using a person-centred approach.

Box 6.3 Psychological formulation and person-centred therapy

An important concept in psychological approaches to distress within healthcare setttings is that of psychological formulation. (e.g. McMahon) This formulation elaborates, from a psychological perspective, a diagnosis by providing what Kang et al. (2005: p.289) define as the 'predisposing, precipitating and perpetuating factors of these [diagnosed] problems as well as the relationship between these factors within the patient'. Hence a psychological formulation requires the development of a psychological understanding of the client in terms of the factors causing and perpetuating her difficulties, as well as a prediction for how these may impact as therapy continues (Sperry et al., 2000). Thus it supports psychological 'treatment' by providing greater insight than a diagnosis alone, providing a 'blueprint' for appropriate therapeutic goals (Persons, 2006) in conjuction with evidence-supported treatment protocols.

From a person-centred perspective, a psychological formulation (which is central in both cognitive behavioural and psychodynamic methods of working) is highly problematic, for it is inherently diagnostic in prioritising therapists' knowledge and expertise over that of the client. It is a process which, although often conducted as mutually as possible, draws heavily on psychological theory in understanding a client's difficulties, thus detracting from the client's own experiencing and perceptions in favour of the knowledge of the therapist. Like diagnosis more generally, what counts instead, from a person-centred perspective, is the 'formulation' provided *by the client* of his experiences at any given moment. However, such a view conflicts with the more medicalised ways of working promoted by cognitive-behavioural and psychodynamic methods of working, and as such reiterates the challenge presented by those adopting a more person-centred perspective.

Whether the person-centred critique of disorder-specific diagnosis is right or wrong, its radical stance has certainly had an effect on the standing of the approach within the contemporary mental health field. Person-centred therapy is now commonly viewed as inadequate as a form of psychological therapy, particularly for those with significant difficulties who have complex needs, and whom are thus seen to require a more direct or theoretically sophisticated form of intervention. This view has led to many difficulties for practitioners, as Joseph and Worsley (2005: p.1) explain:

> The Person-Centred Approach does not adopt the medical model to understanding psychopathology and does not make the assumption than there are specific disorders requiring treatment. Insofar as practitioners in psychology and psychiatry do make this assumption... we can see why the Person-Centred Approach has become marginalised...Some person-centred practitioners have indeed revelled in living on the edges, taking great satisfaction in the radical nature of the paradigm.

While there is no doubt that any constructive criticism is worth considering, from a person-centred perspective, the many criticisms made of it from a medicalised perspective derive not only from a one-sided view of how best to attend to psychological distress, but also from an over-simplified and outdated view of person-centred therapy itself. Contemporary person-centred approaches have evolved a range of alternative understandings providing both theoretical and practical insights for those wishing to work with a range of complex client difficulties. These afford considerable dialogue with standpoints differentiating between disorders and requiring assessment, diagnosis and formulations processes to be undertaken. Indeed, much time has been spent developing uniquely person-centred understandings of what these processes may involve.

Person-centred alternatives

Person-centred assessment

For many (although not all: c.f. Bozarth, 1998) within the person-centred framework it is not so much the concept of assessment that is objectionable but its purpose within a medicalised context (Wilkins and Gill, 2003). If an assessment of a client is undertaken as a method of making a *diagnosis* of a client in terms of his 'illness' or 'disorder' then this is entirely discordant with the basis of the approach and hence resisted for the reasons stated previously. However, if an assessment is conducted with a view to establishing the extent to which a therapist believes he or she is able to build a potentially effective *person-centred relationship* with the client, then far fewer philosophical and practical issues arise. From such a view it is not the client who is being assessed and diagnosed but her potential involvement in a person-centred *relationship* (Wilkins, 2005a).

This *relationship*-based formulation of assessment follows directly from the 6 'necessary and sufficient' conditions (Rogers, 1957) which specify a range of requirements which *must* be met in order to facilitate change. If, during an initial assessment, it appears that one or more of these conditions seems unlikely to be met, then change cannot be assured and therapy is contra-indicated (i.e. indicated against). Such an outcome may occur when, for example, a client with severe disturbance (e.g. psychosis) seems unable to establish contact (contravening the requirement for contact to be established and thus requiring *pretherapy* to take place: Van Werde, 2005), in a circumstance whereby the client is not anxious or vulnerable (condition 2) and sees no need for therapy to take place, or when a therapist feels unable to offer a particular client empathy or unconditional positive regard for a particular reason (e.g. the client is suicidal and the therapist feels unable to work with someone in such a situation).

In order to provide a framework for a person-centred method of assessment, Wilkins and Gill (2003) have identified 6 questions to guide the practitioner in whether or not person-centred therapy is indicated or contra-indicated with a particular client. Each of these questions, based on the 6 conditions specified by Rogers (1957), must be answered affirmatively for person-centred therapy to be seen as of benefit. The questions are as follows (Wilkins and Gill, 2003: pp.184–185):

1. Are my potential client and I capable of establishing and maintaining psychological contact?
2. Is my potential client in need of, and able to make use of therapy?
3. Can I be congruent in the relationship with the potential client?
4. Can I experience unconditional positive regard for this potential client?
5. Can I experience an empathic understanding of the potential client's internal frame of reference?
6. Will the potential client perceive, at least to a minimal degree, my unconditional positive regard and my empathy?

Although these questions do not attempt to develop a diagnosis of the client's particular disorder, they do require a practitioner to evaluate the extent to which a relationship is possible between her and the client in question. This places a great deal of importance on the practitioner's assessment of the likelihood of a therapeutic relationship being established, a process which necessitates an implicit evaluation of the client's psychological state, albeit one that does not attempt the diagnosis of any particular disorder. In advocating an assessment process such as this, Wilkins and Gill (2003) acknowledge a possible role for diagnosis (i.e. of the *potential* for relationship) within the person-centred framework and thus call into question the anti-diagnostic stance traditionally advocated by many within the framework. This adds to those within the approach highlighting a pragmatic need for finding ways of engaging with medicalised methods of working, simply to prevent person-centred therapy becoming extinct within the healthcare domain, as Sanders (2005: p.38) suggests:

> There are those who take a pragmatic position, knowing that if we reject the medical model and diagnosis, person-centred therapists would effectively disenfranchise themselves ... in the majority of services which accept the medical model and require assessment and diagnosis as routine ... with disenfranchisement comes disempowerment.

A person-centred approach to classifying distress

Articulation

In response to criticisms as well as theoretical advances, two areas of work dedicated to the development of person-centred approaches to medicalised standpoint have emerged in recent years. The first of these has been to strengthen the 'articulation' (Mearns, 2003) between person-centred theory and existing diagnostic systems such as the DSM IV. This follows on from the pragmatic view mentioned previously and is represented by the work of Lambers (1994) who has explored a number of common mental health disorders, such as 'personality disorder' and 'psychosis' from a person-centred perspective. Lambers draws on the terms and concepts of person-centred personality theory to develop a uniquely person-centred understanding of such difficulties, which she argues arise as a consequence of (1994: p.106):

1. The *nature* of the predominant conditions of worth the person has experienced.
2. The person's particular way of *coping* with the conflict between these conditions and the 'self'.
3. The combination of 1 and 2 with other predisposing hereditary, cultural, social and situational factors.

So, for example, 'borderline personality disorder', a 'disorder' defined within the DSM IV as associated with symptoms including mood swings, intense anger, self-destructive acts, persistent identity disturbance and frantic attempts to avoid abandonment real or imagined (APA, 1994), is seen from a person-centred perspective as a product of

(Lambers, 1994: p.111) 'inconsistency in conditions of worth, lack of validation of experience, abuse and emotional neglect' that has led to the development of a 'vulnerable, unstable self-concept'. Lambers stresses that working with a client presenting in such terms can be a challenging experience for the person-centred therapist, mainly due to the threat presented to the client by a close, valuing relationship focusing on understanding his 'self'. Hence, she argues the role of congruence is paramount in enabling the therapist to maintain his own sense of 'self' as well as avoid becoming drawn into the client's internal conflicts and fears (1994: p.111).

The analysis undertaken by Lambers (1994) uses person-centred theory to provide a more detailed understanding of how a particular 'disorder' is seen to arise, as well as offering an analysis of some of the issues likely to emerge in its 'treatment'. Hence she goes some way to providing an alternative method of formulating particular forms of distress to those made by other psychological views (i.e. psychodynamic explanations) while at the same time working within a medicalised framework of diagnosis and classification. A similar approach has been undertaken by other person-centred practitioners, such as Speirer (1998) who has developed a model interpreting existing psychiatric classifications in terms of how they link to *incongruence*.

Diagnosing and working with 'process'

The second area of work in relation to supporting person-centred working in medicalised frameworks has been to develop an *alternative* system of understanding (and classifying) significant and severe psychological distress. Work in this area has been conducted almost exclusively within the experiential domain (e.g. Elliot et al., 2004; Purton, 2004c) and, as a result, has tended to focus on identifying particular client 'processes' (i.e. ways of relating to internal and external stimuli) which may be attended to in different ways. What makes this stance different to 'diagnostic-specific' (Schmid, 2003) approaches taken within a medicalised domain is that the client is still seen as an active participant in the act of therapy, with the *actualising tendency* seen as central to the enactment of change (Takens and Lietaer, 2004). Indeed, in focusing upon particular psychological processes, the emphasis remains upon the client, as a *constructive agent* and *holistic being,* rather than on the disorder or illness only. The role of the therapist, in such regard, is that of expert in offering ways of working with a particular psychological *process*, but not on the *content* of the client's experiences themselves (such as is implied by the process of making interpretations or identifying maladaptive cognitions – see Chapter 3 for further discussion on this). Clients are not diagnosed as having particular disorders, but instead seen as employing particular forms of process or 'patterns of difficulty' in their experiencing (Elliott et al., 2004). As a result, they are viewed as beings with choices and alternatives, and not pathologised (i.e. attended to and classified entirely in terms of the pathology or disorder diagnosed).

One of the most significant theorists developing a person-centred approach to psychological distress based on process is Margaret Warner (e.g. 2006). Warner has identified three styles of 'difficult' process – fragile, dissociated and psychotic (Warner, 2000, 2002) – describing their developmental basis as well as how best to work with them from a person-centred perspective. Her work provides a rebuttal of any remaining concerns that person-centred therapy has insufficient basis for working with those experiencing significant difficulties.

For example, in describing the developmental roots of 'fragile process' (ways of processing often discussed in terms of narcissistic or borderline 'personality disorder' within the DSM IV) Warner (e.g. 2000: p.147) draws upon theories of cognition and information-processing (e.g. Wexler, 1974) and suggests that a number of key experiential capacities are central to any person's ability to effectively process their experiences. These capacities are, a) to hold experience in attention at moderate levels of arousal, b) to modulate the intensity of experiential states and, c) to relate words to experience. As infants embark upon the journey of establishing a discrete and autonomous awareness of 'self', they are entirely dependent upon the empathic attunement and attention of caregivers to enable emotional experiences to be soothed (e.g. the anxiety associated with hunger) and for accurate symbols (e.g. words) to be related to feelings. If caregivers are unable, for whatever reason, to empathically relate to the infant, he is unlikely to develop these capacities. One possible outcome of this is that the infant becomes unable to encounter his feelings without being overwhelmed by them (i.e. unregulated) and feels of little, if any, inherent value in his transactions with others. Hence he becomes unable to interact in an intimate way without feeling threatened or misunderstood, while at the same time remaining unable to regulate the feelings that such experiences present to him.

For Warner (1996), like Lambers (1994) working with 'fragile' process in an adult client places great demands on a person-centred therapist. As well as therapist congruence, she highlights the role of empathy in ensuring the individual is able to gradually re-connect with emotional experiences in a context that is sufficient soothing and valuing to prevent this process becoming overwhelming. Such therapeutic work requires intensive *empathic attention* to be paid to the moment-by-moment experiences of the client in a context that is secure and supportive. Although often difficult, as Warner (2000: pp.152–153) suggests, it is of vital importance in facilitating change in the form of emotional processing enacted by the client;

> Ideally, therapy with adults who have a fragile style of processing creates the kind of empathic holding that was missing in the child's

early childhood experiences. If the therapist stays empathically connected to the significant client experiences, the clients are likely to feel the satisfaction that comes from staying with their experiences in an accepting way ... over time ... clients are likely to find that their reactions make more sense to them than they thought and that seemingly inexorable feelings go through various sorts of positive change and resolution.

The therapeutic approach advocated by Warner for fragile process is highly intensive and demanding. However, equally challenging, if not more so, is work with clients encountering impaired 'contact' with reality (Van Werde, 2005). While medicalised approaches to such difficulties (e.g. psychosis) rely heavily on pharmacological interventions (Breggin, 1993), the person-centred approach offers an alternative method based on therapeutic relating. Again this work serves to demonstrate the ongoing development of a highlight theorised, but person-centred, method of working with those experiencing severe disturbance.

Working with psychosis – the role of 'pre-therapy'

Although explored by a number of person-centred therapists (e.g. Warner, 2000), the application of person-centred therapy to psychotic experiencing has crystallised around the work of Gerry Prouty (e.g. 1990) who has developed a method of working with psychosis such as those who are developmentally impaired, experiencing dissociation or have Alzheimers (Prouty et al., 2002). Prouty (1990) starts with the condition of psychological contact, one of the 6 conditions Rogers (1957) proposed as 'necessary and sufficient' for change to occur, arguing that its place within the theory of therapy – that each person makes some *perceived difference* in the experiential field of the other (Rogers, 1957, cited in Kirschenbaum and Henderson, 1990b: p.96) – prevents person-centred therapists from working with those for whom contact may not be in place (Prouty, 1994).

For Prouty (1998), psychological contact encompasses three elements; contact with reality, contact with other people and contact with self. Each of these types of contact is significantly impaired in clients experiencing psychosis (or other contact impaired populations), preventing such individuals from meeting the required 'contact' condition for person-centred therapy to be indicated. To bridge this gap, Prouty has developed a form of 'pre-therapy' with the aim of assisting clients with 'contact difficulties' to re-connect their own experiencing (affective contact), other people (communicative contact) and reality (reality contact).

Pre-therapy, according to Prouty (1994) is essentially a theory of psychological contact. It contains a practice description (contact reflections), a description of internal client functioning (contact functions) and an assessment of consequent observable behaviour (contact behaviours). Its aim is to use contact reflections by a therapist to stimulate a greater level of psychological contact with self, others and reality (contact functions) which is then manifested in contact behaviours (i.e. relating to these domains in a manner that demonstrates contact is being achieved). Content reflections take five forms, each of which is designed to assist the client gain greater contact functioning or contact behaviour. They are very concrete in form, for example, simply providing an accurate reflection of what a client is doing or saying.

The five forms of contact reflections are:

1. Situation reflections – aspects of the client's situation or context are accurately pointed out (e.g. 'Susan is drawing a picture').
2. Facial reflections – highlighting the emotional content that is implicit in a facial expression (e.g. 'you look angry').
3. Body reflections – stating accurately the movement or posture of the client's body (e.g. 'your finger is pointing').
4. Word-for-word reflections – accurately and clearly repeating what a client is saying or socially comprehensible noises he or she is making (e.g. 'that's a car').
5. Reiterative reflections – repeating previous reflections that seemed successful in establishing contact in order to strengthen the contact made and facilitate the client's experiencing.

Each of these forms of contact reflection work in different ways to facilitate contact functions and contact behaviours. For example, a facial reflection such as 'you look sad' is designed to assist the client make contact with their own feelings of sadness, or in other words, establish affective (i.e. emotional) contact with themselves. Similarly, situational reflections work to facilitate contact with a concrete reality, by offering, as Prouty (1998, cited in Merry, 2000a: pp.69) states, 'a pointing towards the world'. Such reflections directly attend to the features of the contextual 'reality', thereby helping the client make connections to it.

Box 6.4   Example vignette of pre-therapy (from Prouty, 1998, cited in Merry 2000a: p. 73)

C: The voices (client puts hand on head)
T:BR Your hands are on your head
C: (moves hands to cover face)
T:FR Your hands cover your eyes
T:BR You are breathing deeply
C: (The client removes her hands from her eyes and looks at the floor)

(Continued)

(Continued)	
T:SR	You're looking at the floor
T:SR	There is a green carpet in this room
C:	(no response)
T:SR	We're standing here together
T:SR	You're breathing easier now
C:	(the client looks directly at the therapist)
T:SR	You looked directly at me
C:	The client puts her hands on the side of her head and over her ears) I hear voices
T:WWR	You hear voices
C:	The voice says 'you die, you should kill yourself'
T:WWR	The voice says 'you should die, you should kill yourself'
T:RR	You said earlier you heard voices
C:	(looking directly at the therapist, the client begins to tell her story about an actual experience of sexual abuse)
Key:	C (client), T (therapist), SR (situation reflection), BR (body reflection), FR (facial reflection) RR (reality reflection), WWR (word-for-word reflection).

Although the direct and concrete nature of the contact reflections advocated by pre-therapy can be uncomfortable for inexperienced therapists in the early stages of establishing contact with a client (Sommerbeck, 2005), they highlight the significant role of person-centred relating with even the most severely disturbed individuals. This is not to suggest that clients who are 'out of contact' do not need other forms of practical and social care to ensure their well-being is attended to. However, pre-therapy offers a person-centred alternative to methods of working predicated solely on medicalised grounds. Indeed, as 'contact' is increasingly established with an individual, it is seen as possible to integrate person-centred therapeutic work into the pre-therapy being undertaken, as occasional moments of contact allow the client to experience the empathy, unconditional positive regard and congruence of the therapist (Van Werde, 2005). This allows the incongruence causing the psychotic experiencing to be attended to via the client's actualising tendency, and as such offers a first step toward a fuller person-centred therapeutic relationship.

Summary

- The 'medical model' dominates contemporary mental health settings. Most psychological disturbance is understood in medicalised terms, and thus diagnosed and treated as specific 'disorders' or 'illnesses'.

- The person-centred approach takes an 'anti-diagnostic' stance, preferring to view individuals with psychological distress in terms of their potential and resourcefulness rather than in terms of specific mental 'illnesses'.
- Due to its resistance to medicalised ways of psychological working, the person-centred approach has become increasingly marginalised in many mental health settings. It is often seen as insufficiently sophisticated to deal with complex difficulties.
- In recent years person-centred practitioners have evolved a number of methods of engaging with medicalised ways of working. The two main ones are articulation and process-differentiation.
- Person-centred therapy now offers a growing framework for practitioners wishing a theoretical basis for working with severe difficulties. This includes the work of Prouty et al. (2002) which outlines how person-centred theory and practice may be applied to those clients with 'contact' impairments such as psychosis.

SEVEN   Research and the Person-centred Approach

Introduction

Counselling Psychology as an area of applied psychology highlights the vital importance of empirical research as a basis for therapeutic practice (Frankland, 2003). Indeed, one of the things that differentiates counselling psychology from other disciplines within the counselling field is the significance it accords to the need for practitioners to engage in, and/or understand, research as part of their professional activities.

In this chapter we shall explore the relationship between person-centred therapy and the research domain, focusing firstly on the beginnings of person-centred research in the early 1940s and then moving on to examine the key developments since then. Following this, we shall explore some of the main challenges faced by person-centred researchers in recent times, focusing particularly on the need to provide *evidence* demonstrating the effectiveness of person-centred therapy as a form of counselling psychology. This requirement has presented a number of very real difficulties to those in the approach, for it is a need arising from a medicalised perspective assuming different forms of distress (i.e. disorders) require different types of treatments. Research, in such terms, is viewed as a means of demonstrating 'what works for whom' (Roth and Fonegy, 1996), a motivation which conflicts with many conceptual principles of the person-centred perspective.

Following our consideration of issues arising from the need for an 'evidence-base' for person-centred practice, we shall examine what contemporary research tells us about person-centred therapy as a psychological approach, both in relation to the need to demonstrate effectiveness with different 'disorders' as well as in terms of its contribution to understanding how the approach works to enable change. This will also allow recent trends to be identified and possible future developments to be explored.

Box 7.1   What are the main types of research conducted into person-centred therapy?

Although research into person-centred therapy takes various forms, in reading this chapter you will come across two main types. The first of

(Continued)

these focuses on the *outcome* of therapy in terms of the change it yields within the client. This type of research is important for it establishes the extent to which the therapy does what it intends to, or in other words, whether it is effective or not. The focus is simply on whether or not the client's psychological wellbeing is better at the end of therapy than when he began.

The second type of research into person-centred therapy is called *process* research. This type of research examines what actually happens during therapeutic encounters, rather than simply whether or not therapy as a whole is effective. Research on process also often examines the effects of what happens during therapy, such as the impact of a therapist's use of empathy on a client's experiences. Hence it is often also known as *process-outcome* research, for it often looks at the 'outcomes' of the processes it is interested in.

The short history of person-centred research

Research into person-centred therapy began in the 1940s when Carl Rogers and like-minded associates began to seek ways of applying the principles of empirical analysis to the processes of therapeutic activity (Barrett-Lennard, 1998) to support the development of their new approach. Rogers was the first psychologist to do this and, as such, was a pioneer in using empirical research to examine the processes and outcomes of psychological therapy.

For Rogers (1961) the facts were 'always friendly' (p.25), a perspective derived from his long-standing interest in natural science. As a result he was determined to establish an empirical basis for his therapeutic ideas which would allow him to develop an *accurate* and *testable* theory (McLeod, 2002), something vital if his approach was to be what he wished it to be; a truly effective method based on a robust empirical grounding. However, research in the 1940s was no easy matter and Rogers had a number of challenges to overcome in order to realise his ambition. How, for example, could he gain a fully detailed and accurate account of what actually happened during a therapeutic interaction without the audio and video technologies that we use today? Sitting in the therapy room watching what was happening would clearly influence both client and counsellor, thus distorting their interaction. Relying on participants' memories would introduce a whole range of different difficulties. Hence Rogers decided to utilise up-to-the-minute developments in gramophone technology to record, and then transcribe, each therapeutic session word-for-word. This was no easy process at that time, as he explains (Rogers, 1942 - cited in Kirschenbaum and Henderson, 1990a: p.211):

'At Ohio State University it has been possible to install equipment which permits electrical recording of counselling interviews on phonograph records ... The equipment consists of a concealed nondirectional microphone in the clinic interviewing room, which is connected to a double turntable recording machine in another room. This permits continuous recording of the interview on blank phonograph discs ... we have devised a machine which enables the stenographer to type the material as she would from a Dictaphone, listening to the record through earphones. A foot pedal allows her to raise or lower the needle at will, so that she can listen to a sentence, type it, and then listen to the next...'.

In analysing and transcribing therapy sessions using such methods, vital questions regarding the nature and process of non-directive therapy, such as how its procedures differed – in practice – to those of other approaches, and in what ways clients and non-directive therapists interacted with one another (e.g. Snyder, 1945) could, for the first time, be subjected to empirical scrutiny. The initial focus on the *process* of therapy (i.e. what happened during therapeutic encounters) enabled specific theoretical hypotheses to be generated, such as that *non-directive* empathic responding assisted a client attend to her own inner feelings and experiences (Rogers, 1949). These provided the building blocks for later research and supported the development of a theoretical basis for the client-centred approach.

By 1949, a groundswell of studies had been completed and Rogers and his many associates presented them to the wider psychological community in a special issue of the *Journal of Consulting Psychology*. These studies became known as the 'parallel studies' because they were all based on data derived from 10 cases (i.e. work with 10 clients over a period of time) of therapy. They all analysed aspects of the non-directive approach from various angles, such as terms of the relationship between therapy interactions and the client's evaluations of 'self' (e.g. Stock, 1949). Also included in these studies was one of the first pieces of *outcome* research ever conducted in the field of psychological therapy, a study tentatively exploring the extent to which each case was successful or not (e.g. Raskin, 1949).

Although Rogers' initial focus had been on understanding the processes of therapy and their effects, his interest in outcome research developed substantially over the following few years. Indeed, the next collection of studies (Rogers and Dymond, 1954) took as its primary focus the acquisition of evidence indicating the effectiveness of what was now *client-centred* counselling interventions. These comprised 11 research reports and two case studies based on data derived from 54 therapeutic cases. Unlike previous research, the cases were organised into a research study in which clients received different levels of therapeutic input (i.e. number of sessions) in the context of a variety of experimental controls. Their outcomes were, on the whole, extremely positive for client-centred therapy, thus demonstrating its effectiveness in assisting clients reduce psychological distress (Dymond, 1954).

Box 7.2   The first steps in measuring outcomes to explore the effectiveness of therapy

Testing the outcomes of client-centred therapy required careful measurement and control of key variables, as well as a clear understanding of how psychological 'change' was to be defined and measured. This latter issue was a most contentious one, for any definition of change was wholly dependent on the personality theory being employed and its underlying assumptions. Hence the formulations employed by Rogers and associates (Rogers and Dymond, 1954) drew on familiar client-centred constructs such as the 'self-concept' and 'self-regard', and employed measures linked to these, such as assessing a client's level of self-acceptance by comparing the match between her stated actual and ideal 'self' (Dymond, 1954), and her level of her psychological defensiveness (as measured via a test of 'emotional maturity', Rogers, 1954). In using measures such as this, administered pre- and post-therapy (i.e. before a course of therapy had begun and then again following its conclusion), the researchers were able to compare scores in order to evaluate whether it had been successful or not. Furthermore, they were able to follow up this evaluation a number of months later to see if any change recorded was long-standing.

Allied to the comparison of pre- and post-therapy measures, the principles of experimental psychology required further testing to be sure that any change could really be attributed to the therapy itself (i.e. the independent variable) and not any other factors influencing the change process, such as the natural evolution of a person's experiencing over time. This required experimental control, which in the cases detailed in Rogers and Dymond (1954) took the form of a waiting list group, who started therapy two months later than the experimental group and thus received less therapeutic input, as well as an actual control group of individuals receiving no therapy at all (something which may raise ethical issues now!). In comparing scores between these three groups before and after therapy was completed, the experimenters could argue that any statistically significant differences were attributable to the therapy itself, and thus empirically-derived evidence of its effectiveness in facilitating change.

While the focus of the 1954 studies on outcome was an important one, process research was also continuing at this time with research mostly focusing on testing and refining client-centred theory, particularly in terms of understanding *how* the client-centred therapeutic relationship worked to facilitate change (e.g. Bown, 1954; Standal, 1954). This work provided the basis for Rogers' eventual papers (Rogers 1957, 1959) outlining the necessary and sufficient conditions for change, which in turn produced a mass of further studies investigating the effect of its central therapeutic variables, namely empathy, unconditional positive regard and congruence (Sachse and Ellliot, 2001). A particular pioneer in this regard was Barrett-Lennard (1962), whose relationship inventory provided an important quantitative framework for assessing the client's *experience* of the therapist conditions (such as unconditional positive regard and empathy). This inventory was hugely innovative, for previous rating work had tended to evaluate these conditions through external raters analysing transcripts of sessions, a process fraught with potential bias and inaccuracy.

By 1958, a bedrock of research into the client-centred approach had been established and Rogers, encouraged by the success of his research ventures thus far, developed an ambitious plan to examine the applicability and effectiveness of client-centred therapy within a more demanding clinical cohort, namely schizophrenic clients. To accompany his personal move to Wisconsin (where his role spanned both psychology and psychiatry departments), a large-scale study was agreed which would examine the processes and outcomes of individual client-centred therapy within a local psychiatric hospital. Although an intricately planned piece of research, this study, generally known as the 'Wisconsin project' proved hugely difficult, as McLeod (2002, pp.90–91) explains:

> The Wisconsin project was a lengthy, challenging and frustrating piece of work. Many of the schizophrenic patients were people who had received invasive and coercive treatments, and were mistrustful of professional helpers. They resisted completing assessment measures, did not turn up for therapy sessions, and frequently said little during sessions.

Allied to the practical problems of collecting data were some unfortunate tensions within the research team as well as a series of very inconclusive results regarding the effectiveness of client-centred therapy with such clients. This outcome was hugely disappointing for Rogers, and the final report of the project, published eventually in 1967 (Rogers et al., 1967) was both late and lengthy, documenting as it does, a relative lack of evidence for the effectiveness of a client-centred approach within a psychiatric setting. Although this lack of evidence was influenced by the many practical and political challenges of conducting rigorous research in such a complex environment, the project as a whole was generally seen as a failure (Kirschenbaum, 1979), and consequently became somewhat of a watershed for Rogers and his associates. The previously close-knit research group fragmented and Rogers himself effectively abandoned his interest in research to focus his attentions on the application of client-centred principles within community and group settings, a decision strongly influenced by his disillusionment with his job at the University of Wisconsin and subsequent move to California.

Box 7.3   Rogers' abandonment of research

As well as feeling frustrated over the outcomes of the Wisconsin project, a number of other reasons contributed to Rogers' decision to focus his attentions on other applications of person-centred attitudes and principles. Many of these linked to his questioning of the role of empirical research within the domain of therapeutic psychology. A particular issue here was his recognition (Rogers and Dymond, 1954), that a client's subjective perceptions of himself and the picture revealed by scientific measures often differed substantially. This 'problem of perceptual vantage points' (1954: pp.431–432) sowed a seed of doubt for Rogers as to the extent scientific measurement may be able to *objectively* measure an individual's experiences, and hence its relevance to psychological research.

By 1968 these doubts had deepened, and Rogers found himself grappling with some complex questions regarding the extent to which his role as a 'scientist' could be reconciled with his experiences as a therapist and person (Rogers, 1968). These were particularly challenging in the context of a psychological discipline at that time utterly dominated by empirical perspectives, and one which seemed, to Rogers, to be moving in entirely the wrong direction, toward a cold, detached, mechanistic and 'medicalised' view of people; neglectful of the subjective meanings and personal creativity so central to the experience of being a person. He wished for a new form of 'science', one which (Rogers, 1968, cited in Kirschenbaum and Henderson, 1990a: p.277) 'would put the stress on meaning, not simply on statistical significance at the .01 level...'. Hence, once again he was ahead of his time in highlighting a need for research of the kind found in recent developments such as qualitative methodologies.

The further evolution of person-centred research

After the Wisconsin project and the fragmentation of Rogers' research group in the late 1960s, the disparate interests of individual researchers evolved into a number of different strands of work, mainly focused on the therapeutic process. This was a difficult time for the approach, for the coherence and energy that had been part of person-centred research up until that point evaporated. Furthermore, the close link between theory and practice began to loosen as researchers pursued their individual interests and ideas. This work generally fell into two main categories, the first of which involved the further testing and refinement of the 'necessary and sufficient' conditions specified by Rogers (1957).

Research on the therapist 'conditions'

Of these conditions, it was empathy that attracted the greatest attention, with various studies since that time demonstrating a strong correlation between empathic understanding and therapy outcome (Zimring, 2000). Indeed, on the basis of a historical meta-analysis undertaken as part of a major review of 'Empirically Supported Therapy Relationships' (Norcross, 2002), Bohart et al. (2002) demonstrated not only that empathy is strongly correlated with outcome in therapy, but also that it 'accounts for as much, and probably more, outcome variance than does specific interventions' (Bohart et al., p.96). What this means is that therapist empathy would seem to be an even more important factor influencing therapeutic outcome than the therapeutic approach being employed. This is an issue we shall explore later in the chapter, for it points to the significance of what is called 'common factors' in the therapy process.

As well as demonstrating that empathy is strongly correlated to outcome, the review conducted by Bohart et al. (2002) also explored what research studies over the years have indicated why this may be the case. They propose that research into empathy has highlighted four factors to account for its strong relationship with a positive (i.e. statistically significant – indicating that the result is not a product of chance) outcome. These are, a) empathy as a relationship condition – it supports a close relationship between client and counsellor enabling trust and self-disclosure to occur, b) empathy as a corrective emotional experience – an empathic relationship offers a client a direct learning experience of being understood and valued by another person, c) empathy and cognitive processing – empathy promotes cognitive re-structuring by encouraging reflection and meaning creation, and d) empathy and the client as active self-healer – empathy encourages the client to become more actively involved in the healing process. As we saw in Chapter 3, many of these factors are stressed by person-centred therapy in its theoretical rationale and, as such, research would seem to provide an empirical grounding for the envisaged role of empathy in facilitating psychological change.

As well as empathy, much research has also been undertaken into the other conditions such as unconditional positive regard. Somewhat like empathy, research studies generally point toward an association between therapist 'positive regard' and therapy outcome; (the *conditionality* of the regard is not assessed for conceptual and methodolgical reasons). However, findings on this condition are less clear cut than with empathy, with just over half (51%) of the recent studies examined by Farber and Lane (2002) demonstrating a statistically significant positive association between positive regard and therapy outcome, and the rest demonstrating no such significant positive effect (although no negative effect). This even split between significant and non-significant findings reflects most research on positive regard since the 1970s, although when the therapist's positive regard and therapy outcome is rated by the client, rather than a neutral observer, the proportion of studies demonstrating a statistically significant positive effect increases substantially (Farber and Lane, 2002), indicating that, in generalised terms, clients who claim to have experienced positive regard from a therapist tend to perceive therapy as successful.

The third condition identified by Rogers (1957) is congruence. Like empathy and positive regard, this condition has been subject to considerable empirical scrutiny over the years. However, the range of studies included in the review conducted by Klein et al. (2002) for the Norcross (2002) investigation into empirically supported therapy relationships, highlighted far less evidence for a positive association between congruence and therapy outcome than for the other two conditions (34% of studies demonstrating statistically significant positive results). However, one possible reason for such inconclusive findings may be the conceptual and methodological difficulties in evaluating congruence as a *single condition* (Sachse and Elliott, 2001); as Klein et al. (2002: p.207) suggest:

> while the empirical evidence for congruence as an independent condition for therapy outcome is mixed, there remains both empirical and theoretical support for it to be considered as an important component of a more complex conception of the psychotherapy relationship.

Hence, when taken as part of a strong therapeutic bond between client and counsellor, therapist congruence (or percieved genuineness) may be seen to exert an indirect, but positive, influence on therapy outcome (Horvath and Bedi, 2002). Indeed, the difficulties of empirically examining congruence as an independent condition may be generalised to any of the other conditions due to the fact that the six specified as 'necessary and sufficient' (Rogers, 1957) are inextricably linked (Tudor, 2000), and as a result cannot be easily be operationalised as independent variables.

Research on client experiencing

The second main area of person-centred research following Rogers focused upon client experiencing, further examining some of his ideas, as well as their implications, from the 'process conception' of psychotherapy (Rogers, 1961). A particular interest emerged in finding ways of facilitating change itself (i.e. in terms of assisting clients move from one level of psychological process to another), an area of work motivating the 'experiential' tradition and first captured in a book by Wexler and Rice (1974), titled *Innovations in Client-Centred Therapy.*

As well as a chapter by Eugene Gendlin on his focusing approach (Gendlin, 1974), this book presented research by Rice (Rice, 1974) highlighting the role of what she termed 'evocative empathy' (i.e. evoking aspects of a client's experiencing) in facilitating the processing of specific emotional experiences. Rice's research was pivotal for it specified different types of empathic responses as techniques for different types of client difficulties, a proposition that opened up the possibility of other techniques and strategies being developed for specific types of difficulty. Hence, experiential researchers began to devise and evaluate techniques designed to facilitate client processing in specific ways, a focus that subsequently resulted, for example, in the model of 'emotion-focused' therapy proposed by Greenberg et al. (1993) and the application of process-experiential methods to specific 'disorders', such as PTSD (Elliott et al., 1995).

A coherent person-centred research progamme?

Despite the sophistication of research within the experiential field as well as ongoing investigations into the therapeutic conditions, following Rogers move to California person-centred therapy became increasingly detached from the rigorous research base that was its founding characteristic. This lack of a coherent research programme and the increased suspicion of empirical methods by many person-centred practitioners meant that 'classical' person-centred theory stagnated while 'experiential' theory and practice was insufficiently advanced to become a predominant dimension of the approach, recognisable to others.

As time passed, person-centred therapy fell behind other psychological therapies (e.g. cognitive-behavioural approaches) in providing an up-to-date empirical link between theory and practice (Elliott, 1998), a differential highlighted by the huge lack of any systematic research examining its *effectiveness,* as an approach to psychological therapy, in treating specific 'disorders'. Since the 1970s, such research had become increasingly important due to the medicalised nature of mental health provision and its need to determine effective treatments for different diagnosed problems, person-centred therapy became further marginalised as a form of mainstream psychological working, viewed not only as theoretically insubstantial but also lacking in empirical validation.

As we saw in Chapter 7, a medicalised approach to mental health raises some specific difficulties for person-centred practitioners. Certainly the *type* of 'clinical trial' research that is now required to justify the use of a particular psychological approach within a medicalised setting makes some very specific demands which do not easily accord with person-centred principles and procedures. Hence, in recent years, person-centred researchers have been faced with a dilemma; either accord with medicalised methods of researching or challenge them with the consequence of further alienating the approach from the mainstream. Each of these standpoints has been adopted in particular ways. We will explore the latter first, exploring both the need for an evidence-base for practice as well as person-centred objections to the types of evidence commonly required.

Evidence-based practice and the person-centred approach

A move toward an evidence-based framework

Over the last few decades there has been a significant increase in the level of interest in determining which psychological therapies provide the greatest tangible benefit to clients with different problems and difficulties (Roth and Fonegy, 1996). This interest stems from a move toward greater accountability in public services, and is often translated into a desire to maximise effectiveness and quality of medical provision (Mace and Moorey, 2001). As psychological therapies have increasingly become part of such provision, a pivotal role has been ascribed to research evidence in demonstrating that a particular type of therapy treats particular client difficulties both safely and more effectively than others. Such evidence is then used to develop guidelines for practitioners (and clients) regarding the best type of psychological therapy for common 'disorders' such as depression and anxiety (Rustin, 2001). They thus provide the link between diagnosis (and psychololgical formulation) and treatment planning.

This process of translating research evidence into guidelines for treating specific psychological difficulties (such as depression) is now entrenched within both the UK and elsewhere (Elliott, 1998). In the USA, for example, Division 12 (Clinical Psychology) established a *Task Force on Promotion and Dissemination of Psychological Procedures* (c.f. Chambless and Hollon, 1998) to identify which forms of therapy are empirically validated for particular disorders. In the UK, a similar process has been undertaken by the Department of Health, and published in a document entitled *Treatment Choice in the Psychological*

Therapies (DoH, 2001). This attempts to 'address who is likely to benefit from psychological treatment, and which of the main therapies currently available in the NHS is most appropriate for which patients' (Parry 2001: p. 3), work that is now carried forward in various ways, such as by The National Institute for Clinical Excellence (NICE), whose recommendations on treating psychological difficulties such as anxiety (NICE, 2004) inform the flow of funding in the NHS. These generally advocate cognitive-behavioural methods on the basis of many studies demonstrating their effectiveness in treating a range of client difficulties.

Although research can take a multitude of forms, the type of evidence given strongest weight by those developing guidelines for treatment choice is derived from clinical studies and organised into a hierarchy linked to its perceived robustness or grade. Most commonly, this hierarchy accords greatest weight to data acquired in experimental studies akin to medical trials (such as those used to evaluate pharmacological treatments), with randomised controlled studies (i.e. when the therapeutic outcomes of two groups of people, randomly allocated to a no-treatment control group and a treatment group are compared) providing what is often called the 'gold standard' (Wessley, 2001) of research evidence. This is often followed by data elicited using a range of other experimental methods, for example 'cohort' studies (where a *non-randomised* sample of patients receiving treatment is tracked over time and compared to a similar group of patients not receiving the same treatment) as well as a number of other experimentally derived material. Non-experimental data, such as that elicited from qualitative research studies, is seen as of low quality from such a perspective.

In weighting experimental evidence (and in particular, the methods of the 'clinical trial') above all else, researchers wishing to demonstrate the effectiveness of any type of psychological therapy are required to adhere to many of the terms and assumptions of the medical model, as applied to the psychological domain. These include identifying particular psychological disorders (i.e. the dependent variable), defining the treatment being offered (i.e. the independent variable) in the form of standardising procedures and techniques (this is called 'manualisation' for it involves writing a manual for practitioners in which the specific therapeutic procedures or protocols to be used are outlined) and determining what experimental controls are required to minimise interference from extraneous variables. Hence, embedded within this type of research are some very clear assumptions that derive strongly from a medicalised viewpoint. It is assumptions such as these that are at the heart of what is often termed the *Empirically Supported Treatments Controversy* (Elliott, 1998), and to which many person-centred practitioners have taken great exception.

Person-centred responses

Although the principle of developing a research base to evaluate psychological practice was central to the evolution of the person-centred approach (e.g. Rogers and Dymond, 1954), the clinical trial type of research required to provide robust empirical support for person-centred therapy as a form of psychological 'treatment' is problematic from a person-centred point of view.

Unlike much research in the person-centred tradition, to provide robust evidence in a medicalised context requires studies in which disorders are identified (i.e. diagnosed) and then treated in a 'manualised' manner (Bohart et al., 1998). Both of these processes are problematic because, a) the requirement to focus on diagnosed 'disorders' runs contrary to a person-centred anti-diagnostic standpoint (see Chapter 6) and, b) the need to work in a manualised manner assumes a therapeutic intervention that is amenable to 'manualisation' (Henry, 1998). Although this assumption may suit those psychological therapies which rely primarily on specific treatment techniques (such as those used within cognitive-behaviour therapy to identify and challenge 'maladaptive' thinking), it does not accord with the person-centred emphasis on client autonomy, nor its presumption that the relationship itself has a primary role in facilitating change (i.e. a problem because the nature of the relationship between two people cannot be standardised sufficiently to be 'manualised' as a set of procedures). Hence, requirements for medicalised evidence derive from a different set of assumptions to those of person-centred therapy and as a result are challenged by person-centred researchers, who suggest (Bozarth, 1998: pp.163–164):

> Our entire mental health education and treatment system is virtually founded on a sham and the pretense of scientific support for the effectiveness of treatment by techniques and methods of expertise (which I label the 'specificity myth') … The fundamental fictional foundation of the system is that there are specific treatments for specific disorders.

Arguments such as these highlight the vigour which many person-centred practitioners resist the medicalised terms and assumptions of the research commonly used as 'evidence' to guide practice (e.g. Brodley, 2005). However, they also call into question application of medicalised research practices (i.e. clinical trials) within the psychological domain, highlighting a number of methodological and practical flaws that undermine their capacity to establish a reliable battery of evidence demonstrating what therapies are effective for which disorders. A key issue raised in such terms is that of researcher allegiance.

The allegiance of a researcher to a particular type of therapy has been shown to be strongly related to a positive outcome for that therapy when compared to any others in many research studies (c.f. Wampold, 2001). As most researchers employing a medicalised, 'clinical trial' model tend to favour a cognitive-behavioural standpoint, this has been shown to influence the extent to which the approach is so often found to have the highest level of effectiveness in a range of studies (Elliott et al., 2004).

Linked to this is the issue of external validity, or the extent to which findings of a clinical trial of psychological therapy may be generalised to real-life therapeutic settings. Seligman (1995), for example, questions the generalisability of clinical trial studies conducted in experimental settings and offering consistent, measured 'doses' of a particular type of therapy which is 'manualised'. He goes on to argue that, unlike clinical trials, psychological work, in the field, often involves variable length of 'treatments' (i.e. different patients often being seen for different lengths of time), different therapeutic strategies being tried out (i.e. when one approach does not seem to work another is often employed) and a more general interest in working toward an improvement of overall functioning rather than simply the alleviation of specific symptoms associated with a specific disorder, such as anxiety. Hence, from such a perspective, clinical trials of psychological therapies offer very little indication of what works in real-life settings.

Box 7.4 Evidence-based practice or practice-based evidence?

As a consequence of the move toward establishing an 'evidence base' for practice, much 'clinical trial' research has been undertaken into a whole range of health (e.g. occupational therapy) and counselling psychology approaches. Yet, the results of much of this have been found by many practitioners to bear little relevance to what actually happens in real-life settings (Margison, 2001). As a consequence, there has been a move to develop a method of generating 'evidence' via evaluating the outcomes and processes of actual clinical services (Barkham and Barker, 2003). This kind of research is not experimental but based on real therapeutic practice, such as in therapists and clients monitoring their progress using questionnaires and other measures completed regularly. To reflect the emphasis on deriving evidence from actual practice rather than experimental trials, data from of this kind of research is often called 'practice-based evidence'.

To address these problems of ecological validity, Seligman (1995) proposes that researchers wishing to validate particular types of therapeutic intervention should turn their attention away from 'clinical trial' research models and focus instead on evaluating the effectiveness of psychological interventions in real life. One method for doing so is evaluating actual clinical services (see Box 7.4). Another, he suggests, is large-scale consumer surveys.

In citing an example of one such survey involving 7000 readers (who had experienced therapy of one kind or another) of an American consumer magazine, Seligman (1995) argues that the results demonstrated both that treatment by a mental health professional usually worked and, most importantly, that 'no modality of psychotherapy did any better that any other for any problem' (1995: p. 968). This finding would seem to run contrary to the principle of establishing different treatments for different client problems or disorders, suggesting instead that all forms of therapy do as well as each other. One reason for this may be that it is what they have *in common* that is more important than where they differ. This idea is known a the 'common factors' hypothesis (c.f. Lambert and Barley, 2002), and constitutes a hugely significant aspect of the person-centred critique of medicalised approaches to 'evidence-based' practice.

Box 7.5   What has a 'dodo-bird' got to do with person-centred therapy?

In 1975, Lester Luborsky (Luborsky et al., 1975) suggested that research into counselling and psychotherapy seemed to be doing the same thing as the 'dodo-bird' in Lewis Carroll's *Alice in Wonderland*. While the 'dodo-bird' first suggests a running race takes place, after half an hour of running he stops it to announce that 'everyone has won and everyone must have prizes'! In other words, the 'dodo-bird' decides that all runners are equal and thus each should be equally rewarded. This conclusion seemed, to Luborsky et al. (1975) to parallel much research in counselling psychology which found that no one form of therapy did better or any worse than any other, a finding arrived at by statistically aggregating the results of a range of studies into what is called a 'meta-analysis'. This finding is still regularly replicated (Wampold, 2001), and points to the importance of the aspects shared by all approaches, such as the therapeutic relationship, rather than their differences. These are called *common factors*.

Neglect of common factors

One of the strongest challenges to the clinical trial model, and indeed the very project of establishing an evidence-base for differentiated psychological therapy from a person-centred perspective is that it simply *ignores* the conclusions of decades of research which suggest that what works is dependent not on the type of treatment used in therapy, but instead the strength of the client-counsellor relationship coupled with the self-resources of the client (Bozarth, 1998). There is certainly much evidence also showing that the quality of therapeutic relationship between client and counsellor is a key factor in the success or failure of the therapeutic work, irrespective of the 'disorder' being attended to or the therapeutic approach employed.

Crits-Cristoph and Mintz (1991), for example, have demonstrated that different therapists vary in their degree of therapeutic efficacy, even when using a 'manualised' form of psychological therapy such as CBT. This points to the possibility that it is less the technical nature or philosophical basis of the intervention that influences outcome, but instead an individual therapist's skill in establishing and maintaining an effective therapeutic relationship with an individual client. Similarly, a meta-analysis by Martin et al. (2000) showed that a strong therapeutic 'alliance' between therapist and client was consistently related to positive therapy outcomes in 79 major studies.

Client self-resources (i.e. personal characteristics, psychological capabilities and support systems) are also of great importance and, indeed, generally shown to account for the greatest degree of variance in therapeutic outcomes or, in other words, make the greatest contribution (estimated to be around 40%: Lambert and Barley, 2002) to the change process, even more than the therapeutic relationship and the techniques of the therapist herself (Lambert and Barley, 2002). For example, Clarkin and Levy (2004) summarise a range of personal and social variables that have been strongly related to successful therapeutic outcomes. These include issues such as attribution style (the extent to which a client attributes responsibility for his experiences to internal and external factors), socio-demographic characteristics, and a number of personality variables such as client expectations of therapy outcome, readiness to change and 'psychological mindedness' (i.e. capacity to conceptualise things in psychological terms). Many of these resonate strongly with Rogers' (1957) conditions suggesting that a client must be both willing and able to undertake therapy for it to be a success. However other 'extratherapeutic' variables are also relevant, such as self-help, friends and family, as well as association with others with similar difficulties.

On the basis of findings such as these, Henry (1998) argues that the only reason for neglecting the primary role of common-factors is that of politics, in that it suits those promoting medicalised approaches to psychological therapy to maintain a search for evidence demonstrating one 'treatment' is more effective than another for particular disorders, as he suggests, (Henry, 1998: p.128):

I believe that to a neutral scientific panel from outside the field the answer would be obvious, and empirically validated. As a general trend across studies, the largest chunk of outcome variance not attributable to pre-existing patient characteristics involves individual therapist differences and the emergent interpersonal relationship between patient and therapist, regardless of technique or school of therapy. This is the main thrust of three decades of empirical psychotherapy research. Nonetheless, the implications of these findings are being systematically ignored, while an incompatible research paradigm continues to further entrench itself, most appallingly, *in the name of science.*

Arguments such as these make clear the extent to which many within the person-centred approach challenge the *assumption* that particular therapies may be found to have more of an evidence-base than others, ignoring, as it does, the strong evidence suggesting a pivotal role for 'common factors', such as the therapeutic relationship, which support many of the propositions of person-centred theory and practice (Bozarth and Matomasa, 2005). For some, issues such as these highlight a need for the approach to challenge medicalised assumptions and maintain a stance of 'principled opposition' to its demands (e.g. Sanders, 2005). Such a stance would continue to identify the significant problems associated with the application of 'clinical trial' methodologies within the psychological domain, as well as potentially stressing once again the concerns about empirical methods first made by Rogers in the 1960s (see Box 7.3).

For others within the approach, (e.g. Elliott, 2001a), there is more to be gained by finding ways of developing relevant evidence of person-centred therapy as an effective means of working with psychological distress. Hence it is argued the person-centred researchers must strive to provide robust evidence of its effectiveness in treating a range of disorders. Like those adhering to the need to engage with diagnosis, many within the approach have accepted the pragmatic case for the development of a relevant evidence-base and an increasing number of studies are being conducted in order to *empirically validate* the person-centred approach as a legitimate form of psychological treatment. It is to work in this area that we now turn.

Recent research: person-centred therapy as an 'evidence-based' approach

In evaluating recent evidence for person-centred therapy via a painstaking and comprehensive meta-analysis, Elliott et al. (2004) argue that there is now much 'solid evidence for the efficacy and effectiveness' of the person-centred approach (which they term 'experiential' psychotherapy) for a wide range of psychological disorders.

A study by Greenberg and Watson (1998), for example, used an experimental methodology in a piece of outcome research to examine the effectiveness of both process-experiential and classical (which they term 'client-centred') person-centred approaches in treating 34 people diagnosed with depression (17 in each group) over 16–20 sessions. In both instances, the clients showed considerable improvement, both at the termination of therapy and following an intervening six-month period. In examining why the therapy was successful, the authors report that the working alliance and the relevance of the therapeutic 'task' to the client were the predominant factors in enabling success. However, as they suggest (Greenberg and Watson, 1998: p.220):

> these results cannot be seen as demonstrating the equivalence of the two treatments. The addition of the active experiential interventions to purely client-centred treatment appears to facilitate greater change at termination in interpersonal problems, self-esteem and general distress.

Hence they go on to argue that the process-experiential model was slightly more beneficial to clients because of its use of particular tasks over and above the relationship to facilitate experiencing. This is a finding often replicated, although the differences are often extremely slight and also strongly mediated by factors such as research allegiance which calls into question their generalisability (Bozarth et al, 2001). Greenberg and Watson are 'process-experiential' therapists.

As well a multitude of studies demonstrating the effectiveness of the person-centred approach as a method of treatment for various disorders, there is increasing evidence to suggest that it is equally effective as other therapeutic approaches, such as Cognitive-Behaviour Therapy (CBT), which is at present the approach with the greatest evidence-base for effectively treating a wide range of client problems. For example, a recent Randomised Controlled Trial (RCT) in the UK (King et al., 2000) found that 'classical' person-centred therapy (termed 'non-directive' counselling in this study) and CBT had equivalent outcomes in the management of depression and mixed anxiety and depression in primary care. As the authors state (King et al., 2000: p.37):

> when the two psychological therapies were compared directly (in an analysis that included patients randomised by either allocation method, to provide twice the effective sample size) there were no significant differences in clinical outcome between the therapies at either the 4- or 12-month follow up...The current trial does not support the view that CBT in primary care offers clinical effectiveness superior to NDC [person-centred therapy].

As a result, this study would seem to suggest that the person-centred approach is an equally effective therapeutic method to CBT, a finding that is increasingly emerging in studies looking at a wide range of different client problems, ranging from depression and mixed anxiety and depression (as above) to trauma (e.g. Clarke, 1993) and severe personality disorder (e.g. Eckert and Wuchner, 1996). Although this is not yet represented in guidelines produced by NICE or associated bodies, such a state of affairs is a product of the *quantity* of studies demonstrating the effectiveness of CBT being far greater than those examining person-centred therapy. A lack of research on, and thus evidence for, person-centred therapy cannot be taken to indicate that it doesn't work! One future trend in person-centred research is thus to continue to further expand the evidence for the approach when applied to a widening number of client problems (Timulak, 2003).

Recent process research

Although the development of research aiming to strengthen the evidence-base for person-centred therapy as an effective psychological intervention has been a priority for many person-centred researchers, there also remains considerable interest in the *processes* of person-centred therapy. A number of researchers within the approach are thus further elaborating how person-centred therapeutic interactions work to facilitate change in a client, building on the research into conditions such as empathy we explored previously. At the forefront of this has been David Rennie (e.g. 1996, 2001), whose focus upon the client's experiences of the therapeutic process highlights many important dimensions that can help or hinder the processes of change. What makes Rennie's approach so important is that it focuses in significant depth, on the moment-by-moment meanings for the client and how particular factors (such as a therapist disturbing a client's train of thinking/feeling by an unhelpful comment or suggestion) affect the processing of experience (Rennie, 2001).

Similarly important understandings of what Elliot et al. (2004) term 'micro-processes' of therapy have been provided by Sachse (e.g. 1998), whose work has explored how clients with different types of problem relate to their experience during a therapeutic interaction. This is linked to a more general recognition that clients have different 'processing styles', or in other words, ways of relating to internal and external events, which influence the way they may be helped by a therapeutic encounter (Sasche, 1998). This work reflects the emphasis on client process highlighted within the experiential tradition.

In further exploring therapeutic processes, another trend among a number of person-centred researchers has been the application of innovative research methodologies, and in particular those employing a qualitative, rather than quantitative approach, to many issues of interest. Qualitative methods, in emphasising *meanings*, mesh strongly with the phenomenological standpoint of the person-centred approach (McLeod, 2003a) and have been drawn upon widely by researchers in exploring a number of therapeutic concerns.

Box 7.6 Being a person-centred researcher?

As well as being an approach to psychological therapy, the person-centred perspective encompasses a range of philosophical principles that can be applied to the conduct of any research in any area of psychology. Mearns and McLeod (1984) have translated these into five principles in which the researcher; a) maintains an interest in empathically understanding the participant's subjective experiences, b) sees research as a process and not an activity simply focused on an outcome, c) maintains a congruent stance in relation to her participants, d) accepts participants and their experiences in a non-judgemental manner and, finally e) treats individuals who take part in research projects as equals, *as participants* rather than *subjects* (the latter being a term that denotes the authority of the researcher).

Being a participant in a research project offers the individual a share in the research, such as in terms of guiding the research questions being asked and playing an active role in determining findings. This is in contrast to objective empirical approach of many psychologists who attempt to maintain tight control of all variables measured to minimise any subjective bias. Involving participants in research would thus seem to run contrary to empirical quantitative approaches in psychology, and perhaps be more in tune with the focus on the particpant's subjective views and experiences commonly associated with many qualitative research methods (McLeod, 2000).

The use of qualitative methods in psychological research is still unfamilar to many students of the person-centred approach. However, some common qualitative methods that may be employed are:

- Phenomenological research – interviewing participants to develop a deep appreciation of the subjective meanings attached to a particular 'lived experience' (e.g. being counselled). An increasingly popular phenomenological approach is Interpretive Phenomenological Analysis (IPA) which examines phenomenological accounts and interprets them using existing theoretical concepts to generate findings.
- Grounded Theory – a research method that generates theory entirely on the basis of data collected (i.e grounded in the data) rather than through testing pre-conceived ideas or hypotheses. A common grounded theory approach is interviewing different participants and then analysing their responses for themes and patterns.
- Discourse Analysis – a qualitative research method that focuses on the relationship between language and power by examining how participants talk in particular contexts (e.g. in a counselling encounter).

(Continued)

- Narrative Analysis – an approach, like Discourse Analysis, which focuses on talk but highlights the types of accounts (or stories) people tell about themselves and their experiences.
- Action Research – an approach which marries the research process with the desire to perform a particular 'action', such as using research on counselling to develop and test new ways of supporting those in need of help.

Worsley (2003), for example, has examined the role of 'small-scale phenomenological research' in supporting therapist self-development. Such research involved a deep, rigorous and systematic interrogation of personal meanings linked to a particular topic (in this case, anorexia) as a means of widening self-awareness. A different, but also qualitative, approach was that of Moerman and McLeod (2006), whose exploration of the client's experiences of 'self' during person-centred therapy for alcohol problems used a method termed Interpersonal Recall Analysis which they describe as 'an interview procedure in which a taped counselling session is replayed for the client so that the individual can recall and describe experiences related to particular moments in the session' (p.232). This study found that the difficulties experienced by clients in maintaining a 'rational self ' had very significant implications for their capacity to manage change relating to alcohol. It also suggested, again, that clients seemed to use the therapy in different ways due to differences in 'processing style' being influenced by the severity of their problem.

Although use of qualitative research is most commonly associated with a focus on therapy process, the requirement to demonstrate 'evidence' over therapy outcomes has led Elliott (2001b) to argue that a case-study method may allow the integration of these concerns. Using both qualitative and quantitative methodologies he has developed what he terms a Hermeneutic Single Case Efficacy Design (HSCED) (e.g. Elliot, 2001b). This draws on a comprehensive array of data (called a Rich Case Record) including both outcome measures and qualitative interviews to both assess effectiveness as well as understand process, in one integrated method. Work such as this is undoubtedly at the cutting edge of person-centred research and offers an interesting and important avenue for future developments.

A research policy?

Although it is clear that research into person-centred therapy is again reestablishing a strong evidence-base for the approach, linking theory to practice in the context of a wide range of methodological innovations, it is important to ensure that this momentum is maintained rather than diminished as has happened previously. For McLeod (2002), the priority is therefore a central person-centred research 'policy', designed to guide and integrate research practice and to promote the central role of research among person-centred practitioners. Such an idea may seem somewhat alien to those more familiar with the practice of person-centred therapy, yet it suggests a return to the kind of coherent research programme of the kind perhaps first associated with Rogers and his associates. In many ways such a move may represent a return to the past, but at the same time do so with a view to the future.

Summary

- Research into the person-centred approach began in the 1940s when Carl Rogers and his associates began applying empirical methods to the process and outcome of therapeutic cases.
- In the 1950s and 1960s researchers underook many studies to help test and refine the theory and practice of person-centred therapy, demonstrating its effectiveness as a psychologcal approach.
- Following a relatively unsuccessful research project examining the application of person-centred therapy within a psychiatric setting, Carl Rogers abandoned his interest in further empirical research to focus instead on working with groups and communities.
- In the 1970s and 1980s person-centred research diminished in visibility and coherence, leading to accusations that the approach was insufficiently 'evidence-based'.
- The requirement to demonstrate an 'evidence-base' for therapeutic practice in relation to different 'disorders' has grown in recent years, but is challenged by person-centred researchers due to the 'medicalised' assumptions underpinning it. These include stressing the 'clinical trial' as the best way of ascertaining therapeutic effectiveness.
- While some within the person-centred community have resisted the demands to provide 'evidence' in the form required by medicalised perspectives, others have preferred to undertake research designed to 'empirically validate' person-centred therapy as an effective way of working with a variety of 'disorders'.
- Contemporary person-centred research utilises a range of methods to further explore key issues linked to the process of person-centred therapy. These are both quantitative and qualitative in approach, although qualitative methods are seen by some as more in keeping with the underpinning philosophy of a person-centred standpoint.

EIGHT   Social Constructionism and the Person-centred Approach

Introduction

In the previous three chapters we have examined how the person-centred approach may be considered to relate to key aspects of counselling psychology theory, practice and research. In this chapter we will broaden our focus to consider how contemporary critiques of psychological practice impact upon person-centred theory and practice. These critiques are often described as 'critical', 'postmodernist' or 'post-structuralist' (c.f. Burr, 1995), although in this chapter we shall use the general title 'social constructionist' to refer to the bundle of ideas that have called into question some of the most fundamental assumptions and practices of modern psychology. Many of these are highlighted within the arena of counselling psychology and hence represent an important consideration for person-centred practitioners.

Social constructionist ideas are not straight-forward, and are grounded in a very different philosophical perspective to that under-pinning much contemporary psychology (Parker et al., 1995; Gergen 1999). Hence, they cannot be easily discussed in relation to the person-centred approach without some prior (simplified!) exploration. Our first task, then, is to explore some important social constructionist propositions and the questions they ask of psychology generally. Following this, we shall turn our attention to the person-centred approach and examine these questions in relation to it. In doing so we shall organise our investigation around the three broad themes of knowledge, power and selfhood. These themes encompass a number of crucial aspects of social constructionist thinking and offer a useful bridge to an examination of their implications for person-centred theory and practice.

A brief introduction to social constructionism

As a philosophical standpoint, social constructionism has many different dimensions and purposes. Social construction offers a *critique* of our existing forms of psychological theory and practice, as well as an alternative *viewpoint* on how instead we can understand, and act in, the world around us as psychological practitioners. Although it is possible to elaborate these critical ideas in a number of ways, Neimeyer (1998) provides a useful framework identifying 3 core themes in its critique. These are as follows.

a) Knowledge – Social constructionism rejects the core assumptions of the empirical form of psychology that has dominated the discipline over the last century. It particularly challenges the search for objective, generalisable, scientific facts or 'truths' about psychological phenomena, arguing that the search for such truths is problematic because all knowledge is a human product and therefore invariably subject to cultural, historical and political factors. Hence, psychology can never be wholly objective in its search for facts, for this would require no prior assumptions to be made about how things are, which is impossible. Social constructionism thus argues that empirical psychology presents *constructions* of reality based on its own assumptions and resulting methods of examination, rather than truths elicited via empirical examination. Indeed it argues that all psychological knowledge is socially constructed and thus *relative*.

b) Power – The second theme highlighted by social constructionism is that of power, and reflects a sensitivity to the ways in which the theories and practices of psychologists work to support particular types of power relationships over others. Central to this process is language, and the 'discourses' (particular collections of culturally specific concepts and ideas) that, it argues, define or 'carve up' (Neimeyer, 1998) the world in particular ways. For instance, a common discourse informing Western psychology is the medical discourse (Foucault, 1974) which provides us with certain assumptions about how we should understand psychological distress (i.e. as an individual 'illness'). These differ to alternative discourses, such as those of spirituality which define such difficulties as a consequence of misdemeanour or even 'possession'. There is no fundamental way of *proving* which of the explanations proposed by these discourses is right, for each understands 'evidence' and knowledge in different ways; psychology involving the ideas of empirical testability; spiritually assuming the centrality of 'god's will'. Therefore, the issue is one of power, and the extent to which each discourse is able to make the ideas of the other seem illegitimate and its own 'common sense' (Parker, 1989). In most therapeutic contexts within the Western world, medicalised explanations are dominant, and hence claim the authority to define how best to attend to psychological difficulties; diagnosing what is wrong in terms of identifying particular 'disorders' and then offering appropriate treatment for these. Alternative explanations for an individual's psychological suffering (e.g. sociological factors such as poverty, or 'possession' by the devil), are rendered illegitimate, even if these accord more strongly with the client's own value system than those of the practitioner. It is power imbalances produced through discourse that social constructionism challenges.

c) Selfhood – Rather than seeing people as having a single fixed 'self' (i.e. series of personal qualities or personality traits) which they carry round with them, social constructionism sees the 'self' as contextual, like an elastic band that adopts different shapes and patterns in accordance with the circumstances and relationships that surround it. Our identity (i.e. who we see our self to be) is thus enmeshed in the contexts and relationships within which we participate and hence we evolve a range of different, contextual versions of who we are which over time become 'sedimented' (Wetherell and Potter, 1992) to provide us with a consistent sense of 'self'. Although this may seem a somewhat strange idea, it is not uncommon for people to talk about different 'parts' of themselves (Mearns, 1994). Social constructionism sees such parts as an inevitable consequence of our identity being negotiated on an ongoing basis, and extends this idea to argue that our identity is thus *distributed* among the different relationships and contexts within which we participate (Bruner, 2004), rather than being fixed and contained within us. In assuming the latter, social constructionism argues that much psychology is wrong in focusing on individuals as separate from others (i.e. in terms of assuming personal traits and consistent views of who we are that we carry around with us), seeing this as a product of Western values prioritising individualism over the importance of context and interpersonal relationships.

Box 8.1   A rejection of modernism

Many social constructionist arguments are based on a critique of 'Modernism', which was the dominant philosophical standpoint within the Western world between the end of the 18th century to around the middle of the 20th century. Modernism emphasised human progress, utilising industrial technologies and science to move away from medieval, mystical preoccupations (Neimeyer, 1998). It strove toward 'absolute truths' (things proved beyond doubt by scientific examination) to enable progress through understanding, a view that is reflected in empirical psychology and its belief in a psychological reality that is both knowable and measurable. It is this belief, and its associated practices, that are being called into question by social constructionist, and *post-modern*, standpoints.

Social constructionism and the person-centred approach

From our brief run-through of social constructionist ideas, it is clear that these ask a number of questions of contemporary psychology. As an approach embedded within a contemporary psychological context, person-centred theory and practice may be examined in relation to these. This is not a straightforward task, for the person-centred approach maintains a somewhat uneasy relationship with many other approaches within the psychological domain while at the same time sharing a number of core assumptions and procedures. Our exploration will therefore attempt to chart a somewhat unique dialogue, focusing once again upon the broad themes of knowledge, power and selfhood.

Knowledge

One of the primary concerns of social constructionism is to challenge what it sees as *truth claims* made by psychological theories (Gergen, 1991). These claims are generally based on the *scientific principles* (i.e. testing hypotheses to generate facts) of empirical psychology and used to present one theory as offering the truth over all others, a proposition social constructionism argues misrepresents the nature of knowledge, as well as masking the impossibility of objective, assumption-free data. Such truth claims are also often embedded within what Lyotard (1984) terms a 'meta-narrative' (i.e. an all encompassing, universal theory), which social constructionism argues ignores the many differences between peoples, cultures and historical periods. What may be applicable to us living in the 21st century Western world at the present time may not explain the psychological realities of all people in different parts of the globe or during a different time in history. Psychological theories which ignore this by generalising their conclusions to all people, often on the basis of empirical research conducted solely on a Western population in recent times, are seen as diminishing the legitimacy of alternative cultural standpoints and philosophies. Thus they may be seen to constitute a form of cultural imperialism.

In looking at person-centred theory it is clear that many of its dimensions, like many psychological theories based on empirical methods, make a number of truth claims derived from empirical examination (Jones, 1996). Furthermore, its conclusions are presented in the form of 'meta-narrative' that suggests its propositions are generalisable to all people, irrespective of context of circumstance.

A particular example of this is the theory of therapy, personality and interpersonal relationships, presented by Rogers in 1959. Rogers (1959, cited in Kirschenbaum and Henderson, 1990a: p.239), describes this theory, based on empirical testing and refinement, as 'of an if-then variety. If certain conditions exist (independent variables), then a process (dependent variable) will occur which includes certain characteristic elements. If this process (now the independent variable) occurs, then certain personality and behavioural changes (dependent variables) will occur'. In using concepts such as independent and dependent variables, he clearly defines the approach in terms assumed by empirical psychology and claims for it *factual* status by suggesting that personality and behavioural changes *will* occur if particular conditions (i.e. independent variables) are met. These claims suggest the theory holds true for *all* people, and gives no scope whatsoever for alternative possibilities or different ways of understanding. Similar claims are made for a number of the concepts inherent within person-centred theory, such as that *all* individuals possess an actualising tendency which promotes constructive growth (Rogers, 1951).

On the basis of such propositions, it would seem clear that person-centred theory is enmeshed within a Western empirical psychology adopting a modernist approach to knowledge which, as we have seen, is strongly criticised by social-constructionist ideas (Jones,1996). Yet, this is not all there is to person-centred therapy, for the approach is also informed by a second kind of knowledge, one which emphasises *subjective meanings* and *perceptions* and thus one which challenges any notion of objective, scientific truth over and above what is relevant to an individual at any given moment. As we saw in Chapter 5, this *phenomenological* standpoint is highlighted in its therapeutic philosophy and procedures (i.e. focusing primarily on the client's frame of reference) and resonates with social constructionist propositions regarding the relative, personal and contextual nature of truths and thus the equal value of subjective meanings to those provided by empirical science.

One way of understanding the presence of these different types of knowledge is to view person-centred theory as a combination of Rogers' enthusiasm for empirical methods allied with his recognition of the importance of subjective experiencing (derived from his personal experience as a therapist and his awareness of alternative philosophical standpoints such as existential philosophy: Sartre, 1956). Hence, his approach encompassed a tension between its underpinning theory and its therapeutic practice (as we saw in Chapter 5), with the latter, promoting the value of personal meaning and, hence, subjective understandings. For Jones (1996), this highlights a parallel between Rogers' focus on the client's perspective and the type of non-directive, 'interested enquiry' now proposed by social constructionist psychologists such as Gergen (1991) and Shotter (1993). Hence, as O Hara (1995) argues, as well as being a modernist, Rogers was a post-modern pioneer, grappling with the difficulties of applying scientific principles to human beings in the context of multiple, personal truths. Indeed, as we saw in Chapter 7, Rogers himself came to question the role of empirical methods in psychology. Was there room, he asked, for an alternative method of psychological understanding (Rogers, 1959, cited in Kirschenbaum and Henderson 1990a: p.251):

there is a rather widespread feeling in our group that the logical positivism in which we were professionally reared is not necessarily the final philosophical word in an area in which the phenomenon of subjectivity plays such a vital and central part... Is there some view, possibly developing out of an existential orientation, which might find more room for the existing subjective person...? This is a highly speculative dream of an intangible goal.

Power

The second theme of a social constructionist critique as applied to the person-centred approach is that of power. Social constructionism argues that psychology, as a discipline, has taken very little interest in its own power (Parker et al., 1995) with the effect of masking the ways in which its theories and practices work to legitimise particular types of power relationships over others (Foucault, 1974). One example of such relationships is the way in which medicalised approaches place significant power in the hands of the practitioner to 'diagnose' psychological disorders and treat these using specific methods and skills (see Chapter 6). Another is the *individualised* focus of much psychological work, a focus that has attracted criticism from a social constructionist viewpoint for detracting from the potential societal basis of psychological difficulties, such as the link between poverty and depression (e.g. Russell, 1999). This critique is directly relevant to the focus of person-centred therapy.

In common with much Western psychology, person-centred therapy may be seen to offer particular psychological concepts (e.g. the actualising tendency) and explanations (i.e. incongruence as a basis for psychological difficulties) that situate the source of psychological difficulty *within* the individual. One outcome of such a 'psychologised' (Pilgrim, 2000) perspective on mental health is to dismiss explanations of distress which highlight structural and economic dimensions as causal factors. Hence, it may be argued that person-centred therapy, in theorising psychological difficulties as caused by incongruence, upholds unequal relationships of power within society by not acknowledging the significance of socio-political oppression (e.g. racism, poverty, homophobia etc.) on individual wellbeing (Smail, 2001). As Diamond (2004: p.244) suggests:

A psychology that attends primarily to the individual is only partially informed and is reactive to the predominantly psychiatric concepts of pathology and illness. It is seduced by the zeitgeist that the individual is both omnipotent and culpable. A serious corollary for psychotherapy is that with the attention focused upon the individual, the person feels culpable for distresses they had little if any, influence over and may well have little, if any, control and power in changing.

What is being suggested here is that situating the individual as at the centre of her distress maintains a therapeutic focus upon inner experiencing rather than the socially oppressive factors involved in creating and maintaining it (Sanders and Tudor, 2001). For Waterhouse (1993), this can lead to an undue weight being attributed to an individual's capacity to change (i.e. become congruent) when what is actually at the root of her problem is, for example, unemployment and a consequent lack of social power. Indeed, it may even be argued that a person-centred therapeutic approach working in such terms may be compounding the problem by giving inadequate recognition of the structural factors contributing to her distress and constraining the choices she is able make (Diamond, 2004), a critique that reflects existential-phenomenological arguments (c.f. Cooper, 2004) over the lack or attention paid to the constraints of existence within a person-centred framework. In this vein, Cromby (2004) points to the visible 'contrast between opulence and poverty' (p.184), asking how these legitimise the powerlessness and hopelessness experienced by those with depression.

While it is certainly true that person-centred therapy may be seen to take an individualised stance in its theory and practices, a number of person-centred practitioners have argued that it is a misnomer to suggest that issues of power are neglected by the approach (Wilkins, 2003).

Natiello (1990), for example, has argued that person-centred therapy actually places awareness of power at the very heart of its practice, in its active resistance of medicalised psychological explanations and practices (such as identifying and diagnosing particular psychological disorders) and working toward a sharing of power between therapist and client. Hence the approach may share a focus upon the individual with other psychological approaches, but does this in a way far more sensitive to the potential power inequalities inherent in the process of psychological therapy (Proctor, 2002) than most.

It is also possible to view person-centred theory as adopting a socially aware standpoint, rather than a psychological perspective fully grounded in an individualistic stance (Cameron, 1997). Rogers (1977), for example, draws attention to the fact that oppressive external realities can often become *internalised* as conditions of worth. Hence, rather than ignoring the social context, the approach views it as enmeshed within personal experiencing, seeing 'the personal as political and the political as personal' (Tudor, 1996). Such an idea of internalised oppression parallels, to a degree, social constructionist arguments that social power inequalities are often enacted through individual identities (Sampson, 1989). Hence the approach may be seen to advocate social change through personal change (Perrett, 2006), for example in a client overcoming oppressive conditions of worth and thus influencing the world around him as a result.

In addition to the social effects of its personal therapeutic work, the approach continues to develop many strands that address power and politics at a social level (e.g. Proctor et al., 2006). Toward the end of his working life, for example, Rogers became increasingly interested in the possibility of person-centred relating (i.e. in terms of the 6 conditions of therapy previously defined) in wider contexts, such as those involving community struggle or political conflict. Indeed, he wrote widely on issues relating to global peace and conducted a number of workshops designed to facilitate communication in conflict situations. In relation to one such workshop (The 'Rust' workshop), he describes the intention as being to create 'a climate in which persons could meet as persons, not in their official capacities ... to facilitate free expression ... in such a way as to increase mutual understanding, reduce tensions and foster good communication' (Rogers, 1986, cited in Kirshenbaum and Henderson, 1990a. p.460). Hence his interest was in social change through dialogue, mutual respect and empathic understanding, themes that clearly resonate with the therapeutic climate he advocates. This aim is continued by many contemporary practitioners of the approach, such as Tudor and Worrall (2006) who link the political concept of 'alienation' introduced by Karl Marx to the lack of 'authenticity' associated with incongruent personal experiencing.

Despite the critical, socially engaged nature of such work, there undoubtedly remains a number of questions over how many person-centred therapists actually work with issues of power, and in particular, the material circumstances (and constraints) of their clients' lives (Sanders, 2006). One particular factor in this is that of training. Kearney (1997), for example, makes references to the lack of attention paid within person-centred training courses to issues of power and social inequalities. She argues that practitioners *should* be trained to be more aware of these issues to enable them to work pragmatically, as well as empathically, with clients actual experiences, such as in recognising the impact of social oppression in limiting her choices. As things presently stand, however, the primary focus in training is upon the 'individual' level, which can make it difficult, in practice, for person-centred practitioners to view their work in a more socially aware manner (Sanders and Tudor, 2001).

Box 8.2   Working with power: a person-centred agenda

On the basis of a recognition that power is central to the theory and practices of any form of psychology, including the person-centred approach, Proctor (2002) has proposed four criteria for practitioners to meet in order to work effectively with it. These are (Proctor, 2002: p.87);

- We do not forget the structures of power involved in the roles of therapist and client.

(Continued)

- We do not obscure inequalities in the relationship with respect to states of (in)congruence and the effect of personal histories.
- We aim to understand the socially positioned individual.
- We look at our own positions as therapists regarding power and our potential for oppression.

How easy do you think it would be for a practitioner to meet each of these criteria in working with every client? What are the main challenges you think a person-centred therapist would face in doing so?

Selfhood

The third theme of a social constructionist critique is that of selfhood. Although a range of issues is relevant in examining the person-centred approach from such a standpoint, we shall concentrate on just three concerns. These are the 'self' as independent, authentic and unitary.

An independent self

As we explored earlier, social-constructionism questions the possibility of an individual whose identity is in any way separate from the varied contexts and interpersonal relationships within which she participates (Wetherell and Maybin, 1996). Yet this is the dominant assumption made within much contemporary psychology (particularly in the West), through its 'individualised' focus upon the independent bundle of traits, attributes and cognitions that each one of us is seen as carrying from one context to another (Shotter, 1993).

As we have seen, one consequence of this view is that relatedness is neglected as a central feature of selfhood (i.e., being a 'self'), a perspective that is reflected in person-centred 'self' theory in a number of ways. A particular example of this is the concept of the 'actualising tendency', a concept which presents individual motivations such as independence and personal autonomy at the core of personal fulfilment (Jones, 1996), as Rogers (1951: p.488) states:

> The organism actualises itself in the direction of greater differentiation or organs and of function ... It moves in the direction of greater independence or self responsibility, ... in the direction of increasing self-government, self-regulation and autonomy, and away from heteronymous control, or control by external forces.

From such a perspective, the person-centred approach may be seen to take an individualistic stance, stressing an independent, autonymous 'self' over views of identity emphasising the importance of relatedness and *interdependence* (c.f. Wilkins, 2003). This has a number of problems from the social constructionist perspective, for it neglects the relational, contextual basis of identity (Wetherell and Potter, 1992). Furthermore it promotes individual autonomy and growth over collective wellbeing, a view which has been challenged in a number of ways.

Laungani (1999), for example, argues that the independent, individualised 'self' promoted within the person-centred approach renders the therapeutic method inappropriate for those living within Asian cultures, particularly those from the Indian sub-continent, where the boundary between culture, family, and individual identity is more blurred. A person-centred therapy giving primacy to individual autonomy and personal fulfilment is likely, he argues, to be ineffective within such a context, ignoring as it does the greater extent to which such communities (unlike those in the West) acknowledge the related basis of their experiences and wellbeing (1999: p.343). Similar arguments have also been made suggesting the individual focus of the approach on autonomy and independence encourages selfish living and egocentrism (c.f. McMillan, 2004), rather than collective responsibility and relationship.

To address some of the concerns raised about the over-emphasis on Western notions of individuality and separateness in person-centred views, Holdstock (1993) has argued for a significant 'revisioning' of the person-centred concept of 'self'. Rather than assuming separateness and independence in terms of an individualised view of 'self' and actualising tendency prompting greater autonomy, he proposes that a more *inter*dependent understanding of 'self' would actually be more in keeping with the relational basis of the therapy itself, where a primary role is accorded to the therapeutic relationship in overcoming incongruence. Indeed, such a view has much in common with more general shifts within the field of counselling and psychotherapy, as McLeod (2004: p.353) suggests;

> The discourse of therapy, as an enterprise concerned with the structure of the individual self, has gradually been supplanted by a discourse of relatedness ... a relatedness that is about what happens between actual people on an everyday basis.

Following on from such propositions, a number of person-centred practitioners have attempted to develop person-centred theory to account for a more inter-related view (Cooper et al., 2004). This has taken two main forms. Firstly, the work of researchers such as Mearns and Cooper (2005) and Schmid (2001) has provided a dialogical, relational understanding of the therapeutic encounter (see Chapter 4) in which the individual is viewed inherently *interdependent* with others, rather than as a fixed, independent 'self' (Bruner, 2004). This understanding, as Mearns and Cooper (2005: p.5) state, assumes that:

> We are fundamentally and inextricably intertwined with others ... our being is first and foremost a 'being-in-relation' ... we do not exist as individuals first and then come together with others to form relationships. Rather ... we exist with others first, and only after that come to develop some notion of individual or separateness.

Although such a view of 'self' is very different to that proposed by Rogers, it accords with developing intersubjective perspectives within the approach (e.g. Barrett-Lennard, 2005) and thus may be considered to demonstrate an increasing accommodation of social constructionist concerns within the person-centred framework.

The second area of person-centred theory highlighted in arguing that the approach does assume an overly independent 'self' lies in its view of the actualising tendency. Brodley (1999), for example, has argued that an often neglected aspect of the actualising tendency is its *pro-social* basis, in that it promotes a constructive form of human functioning which views human beings as essentially interdependent, and consequently motivates personal growth through relationship with others rather than away from them. This social dimension has been developed by Mearns and Thorne (2000), who have proposed that, within the 'self', the promptings of the actualising tendency are subject to a process of 'social mediation', or in other words, an internal appraisal of the likely effects of its promptings upon a client's existing circumstances. When its promptings are too threatening or challenging for the individual's existing 'life-space', various forms of resistance emerge, such as worries about what will happen if a particular form of change is enacted or, indeed, more intuitive experiences of doubt that lead to a general 'holding back'. These kinds of resistance take a variety of forms and constitute a reactive force which is an essential part of moderating the actualising tendency with regards to the demands of existing relationships and contexts. Hence, Mearns and Thorne (2000) argue that the concept of an 'actualising tendency' should be instead formulated as an *actualising process*, which takes greater account of the contextual, relational basis of identity and thus the process of change. As they suggest (Mearns and Thorne, 2000: p.186):

> Our theoretical offerings seek to restore a balance where both the actualising tendency within the individual and also the forces of social mediation are respected, with neither being given dominance over the other and with therapy, as well as a fruitful adolescence and other facilitative human events, encouraging us not only to strike a balance but to be fluid in that balance.

Authenticity

The second aspect of a social constructionist critique linked to selfhood challenges the person-centred notion of authentic relating due to the fact that this implies a real or core dimension to human experiencing. Russell (1999), for example, highlights the person-centred idea of the organismic valuing, and suggests that (Russell, 1999: p.5):

> Within the humanistic therapies, the notion of the *real* 'self' is paramount. The Rogerian attitude and philosophy characterises the beliefs about the 'self' intrinsic to mainstream humanistic counselling, which is that when entrusted to pure phenomenological experience, the person may discover a 'self' thats/he truly is, which will, given the right conditions, be a harmonious self.

As we have seen in previous chapters, one of the cornerstones of person-centred therapy is the potential integration of organismic experiencing into the 'self-concept' to resolve incongruence. It is only when a state of congruence is reached, and organismic experiences are no longer denied or distorted, that the individual is able to encounter his 'true' experiential being, so as Rogers (1961: pp.108–109) surmises 'When a person comes to me … he begins to drop the false fronts, or the masks, or the roles with which he has faced life. He appears to be trying to discover something more basic, something more truly himself'.

Words such as these are often seen to highlight the possibility (and desirability) of an authentic form of selfhood that may ultimately be discovered when the false 'self' created by conditions of worth are disgarded in favour of congruent awareness of the 'true' experiencing of the organism. From a social constructionist standpoint such a possibility is an illusion, Although there will always be biological or other mechanisms influencing experiencing (Edwards, 1997) at any given time, the *meanings* (and identities) attributed to their promptings or sensory products (e.g. an urge to sleep) are inevitably interpretations and thus socially constructed. Hence, from a social constructionist perspective, no experience of 'self' can be any more authentic than any other. Of course such an argument undermines a hugely important aspect of person-centred theory (the idea of *authentic* organismic experiencing) and has been strongly challenged by a number of person-centred practitioners. Moore (2004), for example, draws together Eastern and Western perspectives to argue for the possibility of a pre-verbal, unconditioned, 'self' which is seen as a bodily, rather than psychological, process; a 'not-me', of pure bodily sensation and experiencing. Eugene Gendlin also argues for a bodily basis of an authentic 'felt sense' (1964). Indeed, he provides a strong rebuttal of social constructionist arguments prioritising the social context and interpersonal relationships above this 'felt sense', as he suggests (Gendlin, 2003: p.110) 'the current fascination with social construction is a mistake. It is a mistake to tell people that they are only the products of culture, interaction, or their family. A human being is the person inside'. In such terms, social constructionist critiques are thus rejected in favour of the presumption that there is, in actual fact, an authentic dimension to human experiencing.

A unitary 'self'

The final aspect of the social constructionist critique linked to identity relates to the many assumptions of a single (often termed 'unitary') 'self'. Such a version of 'self' may be seen as reflected in Rogers' (1951) description of the 'self-concept', which he defines as the 'portion of the total private world that becomes recognised as "me", "I", "myself"'. Hence the 'self-concept', as initially conceived within person-centred theory, implies one, consistent version of personal identity irrespective of context and seen to be maintained (to a greater or lesser extent) by processes of denial or distortion. Indeed, it is inconsistencies or contradictions in this view (i.e. incongruence) that are seen as giving rise to all psychological difficulties.

From a social constructionist perspective, the formulation of a single 'self-concept' fails to account for the *multiplicity* of 'selves' that we construct in the different situations we encounter (Bruner, 1990) and the plurality of identities we thus occupy. As these identities may each be considered to offer a different experience of selfhood, social constructionism proposes a 'plural' rather than single 'self-concept'. As Gergen (1991) suggests, we now live in a state of what he terms 'multiphrenia', where 'each truth about ourselves is a construction of the moment, true only for a given time and within certain relationships' (1991: p.16).

On the basis of social constructionist arguments regarding self-plurality, there has been a growing recognition of the 'self-concept' as multiple rather than singular entity within the person-centred framework (Lyddon, 1998). Much work has been done to examine person-centred 'self' theory from a pluralistic view. Cooper (1999), for example, has argued that the notion of a plural 'self' is not a new one, and that Rogers himself was grappling how to explain his experiences of clients' 'violent fluctuations in the concept of self' (Rogers, 1959: p.201). Indeed, Cooper (1999) goes on to propose that the idea of multiple self-concepts is not, in fact, dissonant with person-centred self-theory at all.

In exploring the possibilities open to an individual whose self-concept is significantly at odds with his/her organismic experiences, Cooper (1999) argues that one of two things may occur. Firstly, as Rogers (1951) suggested, the individual may deny and distort those organismic experiences to ensure that they are not seen as part of the 'self'. Secondly, however, Cooper (1999) goes on to suggest that it may equally be possible for that individual to radically re-structure his self-concept in order to fit with the organismic experiences being encountered in the particular circumstances at hand, so as to resolve the tension arising from incongruence. This latter possibility would account for the way in which people may change from one view of themselves to another, as he suggests (1999: p.63):

> As an entity which can only be defined in relation to what it is not, the 'self-concept' is not a thing but an outline between figure and ground: a configuration which as the gestalt psychologists recognised, is always open to reversal ... in this figure/ground reversal, a remarkable degree of consistency is actually preserved. The boundary between self and not-self remains fixed. The only difference is now that the individual is viewing it from the other side of the fence.

Although this extension may potentially account for fluctuations between oppositional 'self-concepts' within the individual when moving through different contexts, it may also be extended to explain the multiplicity of different 'selves' highlighted within social constructionist understandings. Keil (1996) for example, argues that it is possible to view the 'self' as a 'systematic process of interactions of inner persons', each of which has a different concept of 'self' to the others. She locates the basis of this in the fact that to maximise positive regard (and positive self-regard), any individual is required to play a range of different 'roles' in the multiple contexts within which they participate. As a result, a number of qualitatively different 'selves' evolve over time, each of which has congruent and incongruent aspects, and, accordingly differs in its capacity to fully experience the totality of organismic experiencing in any given moment. This view has been further developed by Mearns (e.g. Mearns, 2002; Mearns and Cooper, 2005) through the notion of self-configurations which, he suggests (2002: p.21), have a pragmatic function;

> Essentially, what is being described is a system for the development of the self that generates enormous latitude for adaptability. The self may develop a range of aspects, or configurations, which allows a wide range repertoire of ways of meeting different social challenges. The person is not just a single 'self', but a multiple cast of players, each firmly attached and coherent to allow a congruence of expression...What we are witnessing in the multiplicity of configurations within the self is creativity and expressiveness as well as an incredibly sophisticated adaptive system that can even allow the person to present quite opposite aspects of self congruently and in different contexts.

Box 8.3 Working with different 'configurations of self'

A view of people as having a number of different self 'configurations' has significant practical implications for person-centred practitioners in their therapeutic activities. For Mearns and Thorne (2000) these include some basic requirements for the therapist to:

1. Stay close to the client's symbolisation – some configurations will be more dominant than others in the client's reflective understanding. Although dominant configurations may be aware of one another, there are others which may not be accurately symbolised or acknowledged within the client's reflective view of 'self'. They urge therapists to exercise caution in listening to how a client talks about his or her different configurations, and not to name (or re-name) those that are not presently part of the client's reflective experiencing.

2. Avoid 'zero-sum' responding – Different configurations can cancel each other out. For example, a client's experience of 'stuckness' may be created by the conflict between a 'for growth' and a 'not for growth' configuration. Rather than work simply with the product of this conflict (stuckness), it is important to offer empathy, congruence and unconditional positive regard to the configurations themselves.

3. Adopt a stance of multi-directional partiality – This stance, derived from 'family therapy', presupposes a 'family' of configurations, each of which requires attention, understanding, valuing and respect. The therapist must not value or 'prize' one configuration over all others.

4. Be congruently aware of his own configurational dynamics – The therapist should explore his own configurations and be aware of how these 'selves' interact with one another and the client's own configurations. Such awareness is of great significance if the congruent offering of empathy and unconditional positive regard is to be maintained.

Another aspect of person-centred theory that engages with social constructionist arguments regarding self 'plurality' is that stressing the *process* of experiencing. Van Kalmathout (1998), for example, has drawn attention to the importance attached by Rogers to phenomenological basis of experiencing and the way the 'self-concept' only became a construct within person-centred theory as a result of clients repeatedly referring to themselves as having a 'self' with particular features and attributes (Rogers, 1959). Certainly, the therapeutic focus of the approach on the moment by moment experiencing (i.e. her frame of reference at any given time) of the client is one that affords a considerable fluidity in 'self', allowing for a multiplicity of identities or 'selves' to emerge (Vahrenkamp and Behr, 2004). Indeed, for Wilkins (2003) person-centred self-theory never formulated the 'self-concept' as a single, fixed entity, but as one entirely dependent upon the individual's perceptions at any given moment. Hence it is a mistake to view the 'self-concept' in fixed or singular terms, as often assumed. Instead, he suggests (2003: p.32), 'the nature of the "self" people describe changes from moment to moment and year to year.... a person's 'self' is whatever he or she believes it to be'. Hence the 'self-concept' is always a work in progress; a perspective that resonates strongly with social constructionist propositions and one that challenges any notion of 'self' as anything other than fluid, multiple and inherently related to context. Indeed, for Warner (Warner, in Cooper et al., 2004), the term 'selfing' is preferable to 'self' to denote the ongoing process of experiencing and thus of identity negotiation. However, in accordance with person-centred theory, the greater 'openness' (or congruent) an individual is to her organismic experiencing, the more possibilities are available to her in terms of the potential self 'identities' she is able to acknowledge and thus negotiate.

Summary

- Social constructionism takes a critical stance in relation to many aspects of Western psychology. In particular it questions the possibility of objective 'truths' being acquired via empirical means. Issues linked to power and the presumption of a individual, single 'self' are also raised.
- Person-centred therapy is challenged by social constructionism for its claims to offer the 'truth' about psychological change. However, the value it places on subjective meanings accords with social constructionist propositions regarding the impossibility of objective knowledge.
- Social constructionism highlights the individualised basis of psychological distress as proposed within person-centred theory. This, it argues, neglects the socially oppressive dimensions of a client's life circumstances that may influence her psychological wellbeing and constrain change.
- The person-centred theory of 'self' is problematised by social constructionist critiques calling into question its overly independent nature, its presumption of authentic experiencing and relating, and its initial formulation implying a single (or unitary) 'self-concept'.

NINE   Training as a Person-centred Practitioner

Introduction

In this chapter we will consider some important issues relevant to anyone with a psychological background wishing to train as a practitioner in the person-centred approach. Although we could spend much time exploring a range of concerns related to training in counselling, psychotherapy or counselling psychology, this general information is available from a variety of sources (e.g. Bor and Watts, 2006). Hence our focus here is simply on training in person-centred therapy.

  Firstly we will explore what is involved in training to become a person-centred practitioner, looking briefly at the different levels of programmes on offer and considering the range of professional 'identities' available. We will then examine how person-centred training courses operate, exploring their key features and methods of working. In doing this we shall focus on the 'realities' of person-centred working in therapeutic settings, such as training placements in the NHS. Such placements can present some very significant difficulties for practitioners wishing to work from a person-centred perspective. These shall be explored, and some possible ways of managing them discussed. Finally, the chapter will conclude with an investigation of what is involved in applying and preparing for a person-centred training programme.

What is a person-centred training?

Unlike many psychological models, the place of training in the person-centred approach is far from clear-cut. Generally speaking, a 'training' process is considered to result in development of particular competencies and theoretical understandings relevant to a specified outcome (Gillon, 2002). However, such a competency-based model does not acknowledge that person-centred therapy involves a philosophical stance rather than simply a series of techniques. Thus, as Rogers (1951: p.432) himself argued, 'no student can or should be *trained* to become a client-centred therapist'.

In making this assertion, Rogers was proposing that the therapeutic *attitudes* required of a person-centred practitioner are not competencies that can be simply acquired, like, say, learning a particular way of communicating or by mastering a specific therapeutic technique (although this form of learning is necessary to learn various experiential methods and techniques). Instead, they are personal qualities, attitudes unique in both their acquisition and manifestation. Hence, there is no right and wrong way to learn what to do as a practitioner. Taken to its logical conclusion, such a view implies that any attempt to impose a uniform, predetermined curriculum for training person-centred practitioners is problematic, for such a proscriptive stance diminishes the unique capabilities and learning needs of any particular individual while at the same-time placing the power to determine necessary outcomes in the hands of external 'experts' (Natiello 1998), an act that fundamentally contravenes the philosophical basis of person-centred relating.

In order to recognise the need to foster individual capabilities, many training programmes in person-centred therapy attempt to marry their processes of development and examination to the principles of individual self-determination and self-assessment (Mearns, 1997). This is no easy task, particularly in the context of the ever growing regulatory demands of administrating organisations (e.g. universities) and quality assurance regimes within which they operate. As a result, programmes differ in the balance that they strike, with some clinging as ferverently as they can to the self-directed principles upon which the approach rests, while others take a more structured standpoint, formally assessing work and providing students with significant degrees of guidance over what competent 'practice' often looks like. However, whichever end of the spectrum is preferred, person-centred training still offers one of the most radical perspectives on practitioner development in the counselling and counselling psychology fields.

Training as person-centred practitioner

Counselling, psychotherapy and counselling psychology have increased in popularity over the last decade. As a result, a myriad of different types of training programmes have developed adhering to a wide range of professional standards and quality frameworks, such as those linked to vocational education and training (i.e. NVQs), distance learning, subdegree, undergraduate, graduate and postgraduate levels. Although many of the programmes now on offer draw strongly on person-centred ideas, many do not constitute a formal training in person-centred therapy. This can lead to a great deal of confusion or disappointment to trainees on such courses, particularly if person-centred work covered is only part of a more 'integrative' or 'eclectic' focus (see Box 9.1). To avoid any misunderstandings, it is vitally important to check exactly what any proposed course covers and how it links to the various qualification frameworks presently in place. The British Association of Counselling and Psychotherapy (www.bacp.co.uk) produces a range of publications that offer further information on appropriate courses and training pathways.

Box 9.1   Are person-centred counselling training courses ever the same as general, integrative or eclectic counselling training programmes?

No they are not. The person-centred approach has a very particular philosophy that is reflected in the focus and nature of training offered. This is the same as training courses in other therapeutic approaches, such as psychodynamic counselling or cognitive-behavioural therapy. There are many programmes which are heavily influenced by person-centred therapy, but present themselves as integrative or eclectic in nature. To undertake a person-centred training, it is advisable to seek a course which is structured in accordance with the underpinning theory and practice of the approach. The British Association for the Person-Centred Approach (www.bapca.org.uk) or Person-Centred Therapy Scotland (www.pctscotland.co.uk) is able to supply lists of courses which these practitioner bodies regard as offering fully person-centred trainings.

Despite the array of courses available, a general rule of thumb may be to consider person-centred training courses in terms of the following layers, each of which offers different things to the prospective practitioner:

- Programmes focusing on developing *counselling skills* – There are many short courses (e.g. evening classes) designed to develop person-centred *counselling skills*. These courses are intended to be introductory and provide a basic awareness of the 'core conditions' as applied within a caring setting (such as nursing). They *do not* encompass many elements of programmes training individuals to become practitioners of person-centred therapy and often have little academic content. However, they are often a vital first step in learning more about a counselling role, and in experiencing what person-centred practice might be like.
- Programmes offering a *certificate* in person-centred counselling – A certificate level course in person-centred therapy is the well-trod preparation for *practitioner* training programmes. Certificate courses often last about one-year, part time, and include many aspects of a

practitioner training programme at a less advanced level. Certificate courses are a useful 'taster' and are a good method of gaining the skills and experience required for admission to a training course. They involve a certain amount of personal development work, but do not allow participants to practice counselling work with real clients.

- Programmes offering *a Diploma/HND/PG Diploma/M.Sc* in person-centred counselling – A Diploma or M.Sc. is generally understood to be a practitioner training in person-centred counselling. Following the successful completion of this qualification, the individual is deemed sufficiently competent to practise as a person-centred counsellor. Although there are no hard and fast rules, a Diploma programme involves around 400–450 hours of training, and takes about one year of full-time study, or two- to three-years of part-time work. It is now fairly common for students to augment the practical element of such a course with a research project leading to the award of an M.Sc. This is a path to be recommended if at all possible. Having both a counselling and research qualification adds much value in an employment market searching for practitioners able to evaluate research 'evidence' effectively. It is important to note here that not all Diploma level trainings are at the graduate or postgraduate level – an issue that will present difficulties if a career in *counselling psychology* is desired.

- *Advanced Diploma/M.Sc/Doctorate in Counselling* – A small number of courses now exist offering person-centred practitioners the opportunity to extend their knowledge and training to more advanced levels. These are only accessible to those with significant experience in practice and/or research in the approach.

Accrediting bodies and training pathways

Becoming a person-centred practitioner is seen by many as a method of securing a career in the counselling or counselling psychology field. Although an increasing number of therapeutic jobs are available, it is important to bear in mind that competition for these is intense, and that employers tend to prefer people whose training and experience has enabled them to become 'Accredited', 'Registered' or 'Chartered' by a relevant professional body (e.g. The British Psychological Society). Although a psychological background may also be advantageous in the employment market, being formally recognised by a professional body is seen to demonstrate that the individual has not only undertaken a specified amount of formal therapeutic training, but also that she has a significant amount of experience and is able to operate effectively and independently as a professional practitioner. Although many experienced therapists have not, as yet, chosen to engage in these processes of evaluation, it is becoming increasingly necessary for all recently qualified practitioners to become formally recognised in one way or another. The statutory regulation of counselling, counselling psychology and psychotherapy is now in the final planning stage, and all practitioners will soon be legally *required* to register with a professional body in the same way that doctors, dentists and other health professionals do at present.

Although there are different professional bodies overseeing the accreditation of practitioners employing the person-centred approach, each specialises in different aspects of the counselling, counselling psychology and psychotherapy arenas. Any student wishing to train in person-centred therapy (or, indeed, counselling or counselling psychology in general) is strongly advised to consider firstly the kind of career she desires in order to identify the most appropriate professional identity to aim for. Once this is determined, appropriate training pathways become much clearer.

For students from a psychological background wishing to become a person-centred practitioner, three main professional identities are available. These are:

- Person-centred *counsellor*
- Person-centred *psychotherapist*
- *Counselling psychologist*.

We shall consider each of these in turn.

Person-centred counsellor

Many psychologists who are also practitioners of the person-centred approach like to identify themselves as professional *counsellors*. For these individuals, by far the most popular professional body is the British Association for Counselling and Psychotherapy (BACP),[1] who now operate a popular accreditation scheme for training courses which meet its criteria as well as for individual practitioners. As there is much debate on the differences between psychotherapy and counselling – the person-centred approach does not see them as different from one another, (Wilkins, 2003) – the organisation recently changed its name from the British Association for Counselling, adding the term *psychotherapy* to allow for the practitioners in its membership wishing to describe themselves as psychotherapists.

Becoming 'Accredited' by the BACP involves the completion of a 'core training' course (normally a Diploma or equivalent) of at least 450 hours training, and a minimum of 450 hours of supervised clinical work. This clinical work must take place over a minimum period of three years, and a maximum of five years, following the first session conducted with a 'real' client during the training process. At least 150 of these clinical hours must be undertaken after the training course has been completed. For those wishing to become Accredited as a person-centred counsellor, the most advisable route is a Diploma-level training in person-centred counselling followed by further clinical placements. Although those with psychological backgrounds may benefit from such knowledge in the employment market, the identity of 'counsellor' is not one that requires prior psychological work and may, to an extent, limit the degree to which this additional psychological expertise is valued. Also, it is important to bear in mind that counselling remains a substantially non-graduate profession, a fact which has certain implications for future career prospects as well as pay.

Person-centred psychotherapist

Although far from common, there are now a small number of training courses in person-centred (or what is often termed *client-centred*) psychotherapy that satisfy the demands of the United Kingdom Council for Psychotherapy (UKCP) for registration (with them) as a psychotherapist. The UKCP defines psychotherapy in more stringent terms than the BACP and its registration process is thus more demanding, requiring longer periods of training, more hours of supervised clinical practice as well as a psychiatric placement. It is highly unusual for a person-centred practitioner individual to embark on such a programme without significant amount of previous clinical work and training.

Counselling psychologist

Perhaps the most inviting training route for graduate psychologists (with a degree conferring the British Psychological Society (BPS) graduate basis for registration (GBR)) is that leading to Chartership as a counselling psychologist. There are a huge number of advantages to this pathway, not least the fact that the number of employment opportunities for counselling psychologists is greater than those for counsellors or psychotherapists. Chartered counselling psychologists are increasingly considered for jobs traditionally associated with clinical psychology (e.g. in the NHS) and many employers of counsellors or psychotherapists view the extensive psychological training involved in becoming a chartered counselling psychologist as offering added value. This gives counselling psychologists a competitive edge in many employment contexts (Frankland, 2003).

Training to become a chartered counselling psychologist takes three years, full time or the equivalent on a part-time basis. There are two training pathways, the 'taught' route and the 'independent' route. The 'taught' route is a formal programme conducted within a university setting leading to a Practitioner Doctorate (or equivalent) in counselling psychology. There are around 10 such programmes in the UK at present, mostly concentrated within the South East of England, although this is changing. The 'independent' route requires the trainee to put together, agree and complete a comprehensive 'plan of training' (involving one 'core model' training at postgraduate level plus other specialist courses). This must provide the competences required to fulfil the 'Qualification' in counselling psychology, a BPS award which comprises various assessed components, including clinical case studies, academic essays, supervised clinical practice and a research dissertation (of at least Masters level). Award of the Qualification confers eligibility for Full Membership of the Division of Counselling Psychology and thus Chartership as a counselling psychologist.

As things stand, the 'independent' route to becoming Chartered as a counselling psychologist is the *only* method available for individuals wishing the person-centred approach to be their *core therapeutic model* during the training process. Although a number of existing taught programmes in counselling psychology cover the person-centred approach in considerable depth, none offer the content required to adhere fully to its philosophical underpinning and relational demands. Individuals strongly committed to the person-centred approach may therefore prefer to undertake a Diploma or M.Sc in person-centred counselling followed by further specialist work to complete the BPS Qualification. It is vital that this programme meets the standards required by the BPS (such as being at *postgraduate* level) and any reader considering this route is strongly advised to contact the Registrar for the Division of Counselling Psychology via the British Psychological Society (www.bps.org.uk) at the earliest possible stage.

Although those wishing a 'core' person-centred training will do best to follow the route described above, another option for those with a more general interest in humanistic/existential approaches may be to consider one of the taught courses in counselling psychology emphasising these standpoints. As we explored in Chapter 5, they have much in common with person-centred therapy and thus emphasise similar concerns in the conduct of psychological therapy. Details on these programmes can again be obtained via the BPS.

A final point to be made here is that working toward qualification as a chartered counselling psychologist does not exclude any individual from also becoming registered with the BACP or UKCP as a counsellor or psychotherapist. Indeed, it is quite common for practitioners to be members of more than one of these professional bodies. Again however, it is important to note that counselling psychology is, by definition, an integrative (Clarkson, 1996) professional identity which presents certain dilemmas for individuals viewing themselves as solely person-centred therapists.

Basic elements of person-centred training

As we have already touched upon, person-centred training programmes at Certificate and Diploma level or above have a number of key features linked to the philosophy of the approach, highlighting the importance placed on therapist attitudes in facilitating change within a client. There is thus a great deal of emphasis on personal development and experiential learning to enable each trainee to develop her own approach to therapeutic working. Much of this work is conducted in group contexts, for the course membership is seen to represent a 'microcosm' of society and is thus viewed as the vehicle through which different types of people and personalities may be encountered. Hence, group working is seen as a key mechanism through which trainees can understand more about themselves and how they relate to a range of other people, a vital component of the capacity to practice as a professional person-centred therapist. As a result, person-centred training courses are often viewed as 'therapeutic communities' (Mearns, 1997), where the ethos of the programme is underpinned by a desire to facilitate and support the personal growth of the individual in the context of learning how to practise as a person-centred counsellor. These dimensions are seen as intertwined with one another.

Course structure

Person-centred training programmes have a number of different mechanisms for facilitating trainee learning. Some of the most common of these are discussed below.

The large group

The large group is made up of the whole course 'community', with the term 'community' being used here to describe all those involved in the course, trainees and staff alike. This group is the place where all course members (including staff) come together to discuss issues arising on the course. Large group meetings provide an open forum for individuals to say what they wish about the course itself, their experiences of others on it, or indeed, anything else that matters to them. A survey by Hill (2002) suggests that the large group is seen by counselling tutors as having the following functions: enhancing connectiveness between course members, experiential learning in translating counselling theory into practice, enhancing selfhood by enabling positive personality change, creating a social microcosm where social issues (e.g. prejudice) are explored, as an arena for interpersonal learning through developing listening and communication skills and, finally, as a means for maintaining the health of the course by allowing organisational issues to be addressed.

Due to its size (potentially up to 40 members) and open, often unstructured, nature, the large group tends to invoke strong feelings in its members. For some, the most common experience is one of boredom, for others, exhilaration and/or fear (Hughes and Buchanan, 2000). In actual fact, most people go through a range of emotions during meetings (which may last for between 1–2 hours). Although it is possible just to turn up and sit quietly in the circle of chairs (as they are usually arranged), it is extremely difficult not to become absorbed in what is happening in some way or other. It is certainly unlikely that any member of the large group will not be involved directly in its process at some stage during the course.

For many, the opportunity to explore personal issues in a large group context is too good an opportunity to miss. However, as Brodley and Merry (1995) point out, large groups do not always offer gentle or positive experiences, and the group itself can be experienced as a very dangerous place when conflicts are exposed (as they often are) between members. The learning in such experiences is often around how best to offer constructive feedback, cope with criticism in a non-defensive way or to maintain a congruent (genuine) stance in relation to a disagreement with others.

Personal development group

Although the large group offers many opportunities for personal growth, smaller personal development groups also often meet on a regular basis. These groups are normally a formal part of the curriculum and are facilitated by a course tutor or other person-centred practitioner. They operate with the sole aim of supporting trainees in their personal development and are places where personal issues may be explored in more intimacy and depth than in the large group. They are very much 'therapy' groups and their content is confidential.

Personal therapy

With personal growth central to *all aspects* of the curriculum, further individual personal therapy (i.e. individually seeing a person-centred counsellor) is not generally compulsory within person-centred trainings. Indeed, for some it would be incongruent for an approach stressing self-direction and a sharing of power to *require* someone to undertake personal work unless he or she personally felt it necessary (Mearns, 1997). Needless to say, many trainees do chose to enter personal therapy at some point during their training programme and for most (e.g. Williams et al., 1999) it is seen to be beneficial. It should be stated at this point that all individuals wishing to qualify as chartered counselling psychologists will be *required* to undertake a minimum of 40 hours personal therapy at some point during their training, although not necessarily during the person-centred component.

Skills training

A significant proportion of a person-centred training programme is dedicated to skills development, focusing on the capacity of the trainee to experience and maintain the relational conditions of empathy, unconditional positive regard and congruence and, in some programmes, developing methods and techniques associated with experiential working (e.g. focusing). Training takes place in a very 'hands-on' manner, with tutor-led discussion and presentation minimised to ensure the trainee spends the maximum amount of time developing her personal competencies. Although there are different ways of supporting this, two common techniques are role plays and in-vivo counselling with a fellow course member.

Role plays use fictional scenarios and clients to provide the individual in the counselling role a chance to experience what it is like to undertake the counselling task. Similarly, in-vivo practice, where a course member counsels another course member on real issues of concern, is an effective method of working with 'real-life' difficulties and personalities. Both methods are often undertaken in groups of three (triads) where the roles of counsellor, observer and client are rotated. Following practical exercises, it is common for the group to reflect on particular issues or dilemmas, and share experiences as a means of enhancing learning. This process is commonly enhanced by the use of video and audio recordings, where a particular role play or in-vivo session is used as a basis for individual, or even group-based, discussion and exploration.

Theory and professional issues

The degree of emphasis placed on theoretical and practical considerations associated with professional practice varies considerably between different person-centred training programmes. Some trainings offer comprehensive and demanding explorations of the underpinning theory and professional issues associated with person-centred working, while others are more concerned with maintaining the experiential basis of the approach and assume a somewhat 'lighter touch'. The kinds of theoretical and practical issues generally explored reflect, in many ways, the content of this book – such as person-centred personality and therapy, the approach's relationship to other therapeutic paradigms and methods of working, its research tradition as well as a range of issues associated with the dominant 'medicalised' context of psychological working.

Therapeutic practice

As well as the elements discussed previously, a core aspect of any training process in person-centred therapy is work with real clients in clinical placements. This starts as soon as possible (on Diploma-level trainings or above) in accordance with the person-centred philosophy of training being an experiential, rather than theoretical, endeavour. Although the commencement of work with real clients can seem a hugely daunting prospect, this aspect of the course can often turn out to be one of the most rewarding experiences of all. However, it can also present a number of challenges, particularly for students undertaking placements within healthcare contexts dominated by 'medicalised' perspectives. Such placements are particularly common, and of great importance, for those training to be counselling psychologists, who by virtue of their 'psychologist' identity, may face additional challenges when choosing to work in a person-centred manner.

As we have seen throughout this book, the person-centred approach presents a challenge to the more 'medicalised' viewpoints predominant within the contemporary psychology and mental health fields. Working as a person-centred practitioner (counselling psychologist or otherwise) in a training placement or otherwise, is an embodiment of this challenge, and it is inevitable that difficulties will arise in how best to employ the approach in the context of competing understandings and practices. Some of the key challenges likely to be encountered are discussed as follows. (Readers who have not already done so are advised to consult Chapter 6, where the 'medicalised' terms of contemporary therapeutic contexts are discussed, prior to reading on.)

A pre-dominant philosophy of 'deficiency'

Much contemporary counselling and applied psychology work is underpinned by an 'illness' rather than 'potentiality' model (Sanders, 2005), so person-centred practitioners must become accustomed to a language of pathology and psychiatric diagnosis (e.g. 'personality disorder', 'schizophrenia') rather than one highlighting personal resources and agency. For Mearns (2004), the frequent neglect of the 'human curriculum' reflects the ongoing desire of society for a manualised, symptom orientated 'quick fix'. This, he argues, is part of a process increasingly enmeshed with tabloid journalism and its trivialised and judgemental narratives on the demonic consequences of distress. Hence, a need to control and manage rather than to *understand* emerges, with many consequences for person-centred practice.

To work in a person-centred manner in many placement settings is highly demanding, requiring a constant balancing of person-centred principles with contextual requirements to understand and talk about 'patients' in diagnostic terms. Although each practitioner has to find a way of managing these demands in the circumstances around them, one possible mechanism is to view the context itself from a person-centred framework. Hence the practitioner may wish to *empathise* with the assumptions and language employed by others, respecting this in its own terms, while at the same time maintaining a recognition of his or her *congruent* experiencing, which at times may be expressed (e.g. 'I understand you use the term *patient*, but I personally prefer using the term client'). Such an approach will certainly require ethical compromises to be made, but also potentially create the possibility for dialogue and mutual respect (Sommerbeck, 2005).

A 'diagnostic' framework for practice

With a language of deficiency and psychiatric classification dominant in many settings, it is common for person-centred practitioners to be expected to undertake therapeutic practices associated with such a philosophy. A particular example of this is an 'assessment' session, where a therapeutic interview is conducted to establish a client's primary difficulties, develop a psychological formulation (and diagnosis), and to establish how this may be addressed or managed (treatment planning). As we explored in Chapter 6, the concepts of 'assessment' and 'diagnosis' are extremely contentious from a person-centred perspective (Wilkins, 2005a). Although there are now a number of mechanisms that have been proposed to enhance the dialogue between person-centred approaches and more medicalised standpoints, many healthcare contexts still require specific 'diagnoses' to be identified (often in terms of psychiatric classifications), reports written and treatments planned, processes which for some may compromise personal philosophies and person-centred ways of working.

Related to this is a common requirement to make use of various quantitative measures to assess client functioning at different stages of the therapeutic process. CORE (Clinical Outcome for Routine Evaluation) is a typical example of such measures and involves an initial (therapist completed) assessment questionnaire being compared with an outcome measure filled in at the end of the therapy by the client (Barkham et al., 1998). Any therapist-driven assessment and evaluation activity does not easily accord with a person-centred stance emphasising the clients' subjective meanings and experiences, and many practitioners thus experience a dilemma in determining how best to undertake it (Watkins, 1993).

One possible method of managing contextual demands for 'assessment', diagnostic and evaluation activities may be to view such requirements, from a person-centred perspective, as *collaborative exercises* (Proctor, 2005b), sharing their purpose with each client and working jointly toward a negotiated understanding over how best to undertake them. This may involve, for example, discussing with a client the kinds of 'diagnosis' that may be relevant to their distress (e.g. 'depression), asking for feedback on letters and reports written about them, jointly determining goals and treatment plans, and working as closely as possible in the completion of outcome measures and ratings. For the client, such an approach may be deeply empowering. Unlike in many 'medicalised', methods, such a way of working actively involves *her* in determining her own difficulties and needs, as well as in determining how best to progress in attending to them within the realities of contemporary clinical contexts.

The use of time limits

Most therapeutic services, particularly within healthcare settings, are in great demand and therefore limit the number of sessions available to any individual client, often to around 8–12 (Purves, 2003). Working in a time-limited way presents a number of challenges to person-centred practice (Thorne, 1999). For example, the 'external' imposition of limits may be seen to undermine the client's capacity to determine his own needs or to provide the time to enable him to 'process' his distress in order to become more congruent. Furthermore, the development of a deep person-centred therapeutic relationship, particularly one affording relational depth (Mearns and Cooper, 2005) often takes longer than brief therapy allows, potentially undermining the efficacy of the approach.

Box 9.2   Brief companionship

For Brian Thorne (1994), time-limited, short-term work is possible in person-centred terms, but only with clients who *actively choose* to work in such a manner. He cites an example of an experiment at the University of East Anglia where student clients were offered what he termed *focused counselling* from a list of therapeutic options. Such counselling involved a process of three individual sessions followed by the option of further work in a group setting. Thorne (1994) argues that such 'brief companionship' can be of great help, but only for individuals who are, a) self-exploring people recognising their own needs as suitable for brief counselling work and, b) requiring therapy to complete an already well-advanced process (p. 63).

Despite their potential, there are a number of creative options open to person-centred practitioners required (or desiring) to work in such a way. First and foremost, it may be possible to view the constraints of short-term working as an opportunity rather than a challenge, and again work constructively *with* a client to determine how best to use what is available as helpfully as possible for them. In such terms, the principles of person-centred working may be applied to empower *the client* to determine his greatest need, and thus to choose the content and focus of therapy in the context of time-limited working (Proctor, 2005b). This process is not something that necessarily takes place simply as part of a 'contracting' dialogue at the commencement of therapy, but may also be an ongoing concern raised, wherever necessary, by the therapist in terms of the choices the client is making in focusing (or not) upon particular aspects of her experiencing as the sessions progress. Certainly, in acknowledging the role of the context and the choices the client is making in relation to it on an ongoing basis, the therapist potentially highlights the client's *autonomy*, a process that may support his development of a more internalised locus of evaluation.

A second possibility arising from person-centred working within a time-limited setting relates to supporting the client's use of 'extratherapeutic' resources, such as her existing support networks, contacts, skills and methods of managing. Research evidence generally shows that such resources are, in actual fact, the most important variable in accounting for the variance in therapy outcome (Ahn and Wampold, 2001). Hence, practitioners may be able to adopt an empathic stance that attends to these directly as part of the therapeutic encounter, as a means of facilitating a client's change process during (and following) therapy. Such a stance may involve, for example, relating to 'configurations' which are 'for change' (Mearns and Thorne, 2000), to acknowledge these within the client and to examine what they may provide for her once therapy has been completed.

As well as strategies such as these, it is also important to acknowledge the person-centred view of the person as trustworthy, resourceful, and possessing an actualising tendency promoting growth wherever possible. Hence, while it may not be ideal that therapy is constrained by time, clients should still be seen as able to make use of the resources available to them in a constructive manner, and thus be capable of exerting maximum benefit from a person-centred therapeutic relationship, even on a time-limited basis. Added to this is the possibility of working at 'relational depth' a human-to-human experience that may have profound implications for future experiencing and relating, even on the basis of a single encounter (Mearns and Cooper, 2005).

Misunderstanding and misrepresentation of the person-centred approach

One of the hardest problems faced by practitioners within the person-centred framework is the extent to which the approach may be distrusted or maligned by those working from other therapeutic or professional perspectives. Although there are many professionals with a very positive view of what person-centred therapy can offer, there are others who view the approach in a less favourable light, often due to philosophical disagreements or, more frankly, a lack of understanding of its psychological basis and complexity. Humanistic psychology has been marginalised over the last 30 years, mainly due to its philosophy and practices not according with the need to appear 'efficient' and 'diagnostic-specific' as a form of psychological intervention (Seeman, 2001). Medicalised, diagnostic viewpoints now dominate most clinical settings (Joseph and Worsley, 2005). Hence, person-centred philosophy and practice is widely rejected, leading to some common criticisms and objections. These criticisms and objections, as well as how to answer them, are considered in Box 9.3.

Box 9.3 Common criticisms and objections to the person-centred approach

Person-centred therapy is just about being 'nice' to clients, not about challenging them to deal with their issues.

The idea that person-centred therapy is about being 'nice' derives from the philosophy of trusting the client in the context of an empathic, unconditionally valuing relationship. Such a relationship offers the client, often for the first time, a chance to allow difficult feelings to be consciously acknowledged and explored in a non-defensive manner. What could be a greater challenge to someone than a relationship that allows them to let down defences and really acknowledge their difficult, painful feelings about things?

Unconditional positive regard (UPR) is impossible. It requires a therapist to accept things that are morally or personally repugnant.

Positive regard for a client is offered in various degrees at different times, with the notion unconditionally referring to the *ideal* of as few therapist requirements and judgements being placed on the client as possible. Highly self-regarding therapists have little need to judge others and find the offering of *unconditional* positive regard as far easier than those therapists still grappling with many personal conditions of worth. Such individuals are also able to differentiate between actions and persons (Purton, 1998). Thus, while someone's

(Continued)

(Continued)

personality and behaviour may be objectionable, it is possible, at the same time, to recognise that he too is a person worthy of respect and compassion. Unconditional positive regard does not suggest that all actions are acceptable or to be valued.

The person-centred approach is too passive. Clients need more expert support and guidance to assist them to deal with their problems.

There is little doubt that certain clients are used to being guided on what to do, particularly those accustomed to medical intervention or psychological 'treatments'. However, the person-centred approach requires an extremely active, dynamic relationship between client and practitioner that is focused entirely upon facilitating the client's capacity to function as an independent, self-regarding being. It is true that person-centred therapists prefer not to take 'expert' stances over their clients by making interpretations (e.g. psychodynamic practitioners) or by acting as teachers of particular personal management skills (e.g. Cognitive-Behavioural Therapy). Instead they trust the client to know what she needs, which is the exact opposite of fostering an approach dependent on the expertise of others. Certainly, person-centred therapy makes no apologies for trusting in the constructive potential of all human beings.

Person-centred therapy is not an 'evidenced-based' approach.

As we explored in Chapter 7, the nature of 'evidence' often used to justify the use of a particular psychological therapy derives from a clinical trial model which is unsuitable for evaluating therapeutic approaches emphasising the relationship between client and counsellor and avoiding manualised, diagnostic-specific, methods of working. Hence, there is far less 'evidence' demonstrating person-centred therapy as an effective method of working than there is for other common approaches, such as CBT. This does not, however, indicate that the person-centred approach is *not effective,* merely that there have been fewer 'clinical' trial research studies on it. This is gradually changing and there have been a number of recent studies which have evaluated the effectiveness of person-centred therapy in a range of settings. These generally conclude that the approach is equivalent in effectiveness to CBT in treating a range of disorders (e.g. King et al. 2000). Hence claims that it is not 'evidence-based' and thus not effective are both misleading and out of date.

Person-centred therapy is not appropriate for those with complex psychological difficulties.

It is true to say that person-centred therapy does not embrace the processes of psychiatric diagnosis, and thus may be seen as unsuited

(Continued)

to work with individuals given such labels. However, the difficulty here lies not in the person-centred approach, but in the psychiatric categorisation of people and their distress. There has been a considerable amount of work undertaken in applying person-centred ideas to those with severe psychological distress (e.g. pre-therapy: Prouty et al., 2002). This provides a strong framework for any suitably trained and experienced person-centred practitioner wishing to work with such individuals. Yet, in common with all psychological therapies, the person-centred approach cannot undo the many challenges to individual well-being presented by the social and cultural context (Hawtin and Moore, 1998). Hence, for those with very severe disturbances, the depth of person-centred work required cannot easily be provided within the social care pathways presently in place. This is a social and political problem, not one resulting from any inadequacies of the person-centred way of working.

Person-centred therapists are insufficiently aware of psychological theory to function effectively as psychological practitioners.

It is true that some person-centred trainings do not dwell to any great extent on theoretical debates in psychology. This is a deliberate stance linked to its emphasis on personal relationship over abstract theorising. However, the approach is inherently psychological in its reasoning, having a consistent logic tracing the roots, causes and consequences of psychological disturbance and offering a clear, tested, method for its effective treatment. In learning about person-centred therapy, the individual gains a practical knowledge of its psychological basis which can be articulated where necessary.

Supervision

When working with clients in training placements, all trainees receive regular supervision to ensure they are practicing effectively (Dryden et al., 1995). Indeed, the supervisory process takes on added significance during a training programme where key competencies are being developed and refined. The primary focus of supervision, from a person-centred perspective, is the counsellor's own resources (e.g. capacity to maintain empathy and congruence) in working with a client rather than the technical (or theoretical) exploration of a client's 'disorder' and how best to work with it (Patterson, 1983). In accordance with the self-directed philosophy of the approach, this exploration often takes the form of a 'collaborative inquiry' (Merry, 1999), where the supervisor offers empathy, unconditional positive regard and congruence to the supervisee, which assists engagement with those difficult, personally threatening issues that may be impeding her ability to experience say, unconditional positive regard toward a client. Supervisors are also charged with ensuring competent and ethical practice (Tudor and Worrall, 2004), and hence it is normal for any concerns of this nature to be raised with the supervisee as soon as they arise (Mearns, 1994). During the training process, supervision often takes place at a ratio of around 1 hour of supervision to every 6 hours of client work.

In addition to individual supervision, it is common for peer group supervision to be offered during a person-centred training programme. Peer groups are generally made up of a small number of trainees (e.g. 6–10, plus a facilitator), and provide an opportunity for members to discuss their client work and to receive feedback upon it. Again, the focus of such groups is upon the experiences of the trainees in the context of their individual work with clients, and deep personal issues can occasionally arise (which will be dealt with within the group or elsewhere). Peer supervision takes place on a regular basis, and many groups decide to schedule additional meetings outside the formal curriculum to enable members to support one another in meeting the demands of client work.

Although most person-centred training courses offer person-centred supervision, some placements may require a trainee to engage in additional, service-specific, supervision processes. These may not assume a person-centred stance (i.e. being, instead, psychodynamic or cognititive-behavioural in emphasis) and, as such, may present some difficulties for those more accustomed to person-centred methods. Common challenges that arise in such circumstances are that the supervisor is experienced as cold and unsupportive, overly concerned with the client's 'pathology' and life history, primarily interested in the unconscious processes of the relationship (i.e. transference), disinterested in the supervisee's personal experiencing (unless directly connected to a particular client), directive, and mainly interested in a client's thinking patterns above all else.

Coping with supervision from a different therapeutic orientation can be particularly difficult for trainee person-centred practitioners. It can be very confusing, and de-skilling, to be supervised by someone who does not necessarily share your therapeutic philosophy and way of doing things. Yet, there are a number of things that can be done to help in such circumstances. These may include:

• Making contact with more experienced person-centred practitioners (if there are any) within the placement setting itself.

- Using peer support within the course.
- Recognising that your placement-based supervisor/peers may feel uncertain about what person-centred therapy offers and thus need some guidance as to your working philosophy and methods.
- Acknowledging that comments or criticisms made about your work may reflect difference between you and your supervisor's approach, rather than your competence.
- Finally, being open to alternative possibilities and ideas provided by your supervisor rather than rejecting these out of hand. Remember, the theory of therapy specified by Rogers (1957) was intended to integrate different perspectives, not exclude them.

Student assessment

How best to assess trainees is a thorny issue for many person-centred trainers (Mearns, 1994). For some, the philosophical principles of the approach do not fit well with externally derived assessment regimes, such as tutor marked work or external observation of clinical role-play. However, the reality of funding, quality assurance, institutional requirements and, indeed, the philosophy of different course programmes, means that, in practice, trainees are invariably required to subject themselves to varying degrees of scrutiny from peers and tutors. Such scrutiny often takes the form of the submission of pieces of course-work, such as client studies (where work with a particular client is critically evaluated), process reports (where a single counselling session is recorded and critically evaluated) and essays pertaining to different aspects of the approach. Another common mechanism in the assessment of a trainee is a 'self-assessment' process (Natiello, 1998) in which he evaluates his own learning about the approach and proposes, to the course, whether or not he believes he has met the requirements to pass and why. This process is undertaken in dialogue with peers, tutors and clients and informs, to varying degrees, the basis of the final decision made by examiners.

Preparing for a person-centred training programme

It is vital that any prospective trainee from a psychological background or otherwise prepares as fully as possible prior to applying, and/or accepting, a place on a person-centred training programme at Diploma level or above. There are a number of important reasons for this, not least the costs, financial and otherwise, of pulling out once training has commenced. Therefore, it is vitally important to be absolutely clear on what purpose any training course will serve in meeting your career aspirations, how this proposed training assists your move toward acquiring a particular professional 'identity' (such as chartered counselling psychologist), why a particular course has been selected over and above all others and, finally, what to expect on any chosen course once it has commenced. Good people to ask in determining answers to the these questions are university or college lecturers familiar with person-centred framework, graduates, current trainees and tutors on any proposed course being considered, all those associated with the training pathway being contemplated (such as the Registrar for the Division of Counselling Psychology) and, finally, any friends and family who will be affected by your decision to go ahead. Reading the many advisory guides to training in counselling, psychotherapy and counselling psychology is also vital. Doing this in conjunction with the above should, hopefully, prevent the unfortunate circumstance of a wrong choice being made.

Box 9.4   Some common questions asked by prospective trainees

How can I prepare for the practical, experiential focus of person-centred training?

Academic psychology courses are often more theoretical and research orientated compared to the practical, experiential nature of a person-centred training. Work experience in a caring role or other counselling skills training may be a useful way of bridging the two, as well as a good way of testing your suitability for counselling or counselling psychology as a career. It might also be worth undertaking some personal therapy with a person-centred practitioner to explore your motivations for training and see how it works, in action. It is very likely that you will be required to have some previous experience of personal development work, as well as practical experience, before being accepted onto a Diploma or M.Sc course.

Am I personally ready for a person-centred counselling training?

Training as a person-centred practitioner is a personally demanding process which requires maturity, sensitivity and personal strength. Perhaps the main source of personal difficulty is the impact of previous trauma (e.g. bullying) or psychological distress (e.g. depression) indirectly or directly raised via deep relating with peers and/or clients. Such personal 'baggage' is common and, indeed, often of importance in assisting therapeutic awareness. However, it is important to ensure that any personally difficult experiences have been explored in therapeutic activities prior to commencing a training programme if they are

(Continued)

likely to present you with significant challenges to your well-being in working with other trainees or clients.

Is a person-centred training the right training for me?

There is a wide range of different models in counselling, counselling psychology and psychotherapy. Although the person-centred approach is one of the best known of these, it is important to ensure that other possible approaches are not too readily excluded. Different therapeutic approaches suit different people. It is important to be fully aware of the other possibilities prior to deciding person-centred work is best suited to you.

I know what training course I want to do, but how do I make a successful application?

Most person-centred training courses, at Diploma level or above, operate a two-stage application process, an application form followed by an interview. Usually the course team will be looking to ensure a wide spread of participants from differing backgrounds. Hence it is very difficult to predict what attributes a successful applicant will possess. However, it is likely that the following criteria will be influential in determining a successful outcome:

- A demonstrable interest in counselling, such as a successfully completed counselling skills programme or counselling psychology module.
- Experience in a caring role, such as voluntary work or personal caring responsibilies.
- Maturity in outlook, although not necessarily age.
- Awareness of the format of person-centred counselling training, and an appreciation of the likely demands placed, by this, on yourself and your relationships.
- A capacity to talk about yourself (and be asked about) your motivations and personal difficulties without becoming overly defensive.
- A demonstrable preparedness to critically reflect on yourself and an openness to learning.
- Demonstrable experience of relating to other people in groups.
- A clear desire to enter counselling or counselling psychology professionally, rather than to use the training programme as a means of personal development.
- A demonstrable capacity to fund the programme.
- A capacity to meet the academic requirements of the programme, particularly if it is at M.Sc level.

(Continued)

(Continued)

What shall I do if I am rejected by a course?

It is not uncommon to be turned down for a place on a person-centred training programme. Often this is due to the course being oversubscribed. However, on occasion, it may be the case that the course team do not feel you are ready to undertake such a training at the present time. If you are not accepted onto a course, either on the basis of an application form or after an interview, it is always worth asking for some feedback as to why this was so. Finding out the reasons for your rejection will help you understand what you may have to do to get a place in the future, or indeed things you may wish to consider doing instead.

Once accepted, how can I prepare for the course?

Once accepted onto a training course it is important to prepare as much as possible for the demands it will place on you. Ensuring that you are in physical and mental good health is vital, as is making sure all practical aspects such as finance, accommodation and family responsibilities are sorted out prior to starting. It is also useful to set up any required placements or supervision arrangements as early as possible.

Next steps

In this chapter we have explored some of the many key issues related to training as a practitioner of the person-centred approach. Needless to say, we have only been able to touch upon the surface of these, so the reader is strongly advised to do some further 'homework' should a training programme still appeal. Furthermore, contact should be made as early as possible with various professional bodies in the area to ensure the rapidly evolving statutory framework has not changed since this chapter was written.

Although the chapter has sounded many cautionary notes for any prospective trainee of the person-centred approach, it is important to also remember that it constitutes one of the most profound, rewarding methods of psychological working. Not to be entered into lightly, for it is both personally demanding and professionally challenging, a person-centred training will, without a doubt, change your life.

Summary

- Person-centred therapy has a unique philosophy that is reflected in its training programmes. Personal development is emphasised as a basis of developing empathy, unconditional positive regard and congruence.

- There are various courses available, with a Diploma or M.Sc offering a professional training course in person-centred therapy. Lower level courses, such as certificates, do not train an individual to practise as a person-centred therapist.
- Individuals should work toward becoming a person-centred counsellor, person-centred psychotherapist or chartered counselling psychologist. Each of these 'identities' has a different training pathway.
- Person-centred training courses are 'therapeutic communities', in which course members are constantly engaged in personal development activities. Group working is central to this process.
- Placements assuming a more 'medicalised' stance can present a range of challenges for any individual wishing to work in a person-centred way. A common way of managing these is to work as collaboratively with a client as the context allows.
- Preparing for the realities of person-centred working is an important task for any trainee or prospective trainee.

Note

1 Counsellors living in Scotland have the alternative of joining Counselling and Psychotherapy in Scotland (COSCA).

References

Ahn, H., & Wampold, B. (2001). Where oh Where are the Specific Ingredients: A meta-analysis of component studies in counselling and psychotherapy. *Journal of Counselling Psychology, 48*, 251–257.

Assagioli, R. (1965). *Psychosynthesis: A manual of principles and techniques.* New York: Hobbs, Doorman and Company.

APA (American Psychiatric Association), (1951). *Diagnostic and Statistical Manual.* Washington DC: American Psychiatric Asociation.

APA (American Psychiatric Association), (1994). *Diagnostic and Statistical Manual of Mental Disorders (4th Ed.).* Washington DC: American Psychiatric Association.

APA (American Psychiatric Association), (1995). *Template for Developing Guidelines: Interventions for mental disorders and psychosocial aspects of physical disorders.* Washington DC: American Psychological Association.

APA (American Psychiatric Association), (2000). *Diagnostic and Statistical Manual of Mental Disorders – text revision (4th ed).* Washington DC: American Psychiatric Association.

Baker, N. (2004). Experiential Person-Centred Therapy. In P. Sanders (Ed.), *The Tribes of the Person-Centred Nation.* Ross-on-Wye: PCCS Books.

Barkham, M., & Barker, C. (2003). Establishing Practice-Based Evidence for Counselling Psychology. In R. Woolfe, W. Dryden & S. Strawbridge (Eds.), *Handbook of Counselling Psychology.* London: Sage.

Barkham, M., Margison, F., Evans, C., McGrath, G., Mellor-Clark, J., Milne, D., Connel, J. (1998). The Rationale for Developing and Implementing Core Outcome Batteries for Routine Use in Service Settings and Psychotherapy Outcome Research. *Journal of Mental Health, 7*(1), 35–47.

Barrett-Lennard, G. T. (1962). Dimensions of Therapist Response as Causal Factors in Therapeutic Change. *Psychological Monographs, 76*(43, whole no. 562).

Barrett-Lennard, G. T. (1981). The Empathy Cycle: Refinement of a nuclear concept. *Journal of Counselling Psychology, 28*, 91–100.

Barrett-Lennard, G. T. (1984). Understanding the Person-Centred Approach to Therapy: A reply to questions and misconceptions. In D. McDuff & D. Coghlan (Eds.), *The Person-Centred Approach and Cross Cultural Communication: An international review volume II.* Dublin: Centre for Cross-Cultural Communication.

Barrett-Lennard, G. T. (1998). *Carl Rogers' Helping System: Journey and Substance.* London: Sage.

Barrett-Lennard, G. T. (2005). *Relationship at the Centre: Healing in a Troubled World.* London: Whurr.

Beck, A. (1967). *Depression: Clinical, experimental and theoretical aspects.* New York: Hoeber.

Beck, J. S. (1995). Cognitive Therapy: Basic and Beyond. New York: Guilford.

Bentall, R. P. (2004). *Madness Explained: Psychosis and human nature.* Harmondsworth: Penguin.

Berne, E. (1968). *Games People Play.* Harmondsworth: Penguin.

Biermann-Ratjen, E. M. (1996). On the Way to a Person-Centred Psychopathology. In R. Hutterer, G. Pawlowsky, P. F. Schmid & R. Stipsis (Eds.), *Client-Centred and Experiential Psychotherapy: A paradigm in motion* (pp. 11–24). Frankfurt: Peter Lang.

Biermann-Ratjen, E. M. (1998). On the Development of Persons in Relationships. In B. Thorne & E. Lambers (Eds.), *Person-Centred Therapy: A European perspective*. London: Sage.

Blackburn, I. M., & Davidson, K. (1995). *Cognitive Therapy for Anxiety and Depression*. Oxford: Blackwell.

Bohart, A. C. (1982) Similarities Between Cognitive and Humanistic Approaches to Psychotherapy. *Cognitive Therapy and Research, 6*(3), 245–249.

Bohart, A. C., Elliot, R., Greenberg, L. S., & Watson, J. C. (2002). Empathy. In J. C. Norcross (Ed.), *Psychotherapy Relationships that Work* (pp. 89–108). Oxford: Oxford University Press.

Bohart, A. C., & Greenberg, L. S. (1997). *Empathy Reconsidered: New directions in psychotherapy*. Washington DC: American Psychological Association.

Bohart, A. C., O Hara, M., & Leitner, L. M. (1998). Empirically Violated Treatments: Disenfranchisement of humanistic and other therapies. *Psychotherapy Research, 8*(2), 141–157.

Bor, R., & Watts, M. (2006). *The Trainee Handbook: A guide for trainee counsellors and psychotherapists (2nd Ed)*. London: Sage.

Boss, M. (1979). *Existential Foundations of Medicine and Psychology*. New York: Jason Aronson.

Bowlby, J. (1969). *Attachment*. New York: Basic Books.

Bown, O. H. (1954). *An Investigation of Therapeutic Relationship in Client-Centred Psychotherapy*. Unpublished PhD, University of Chicago, Chicago.

Boy, A., Seeman, J., Schlien, J. M., Fischer, C., & Cain, D. (1989/2002). Symposium of Psychodiagnosis. *Person-Centred Review, 4*, 132–182.

Bozarth, J. D. (1984). Beyond Reflection: Emergent modes of empathy. In R. F. Levant & J. M. Schlien (Eds.), *Client-Centred Therapy and the Person-Centred Approach: New directions in theory, research and practice* (pp. 59–75). London: Praeger.

Bozarth, J. D. (1993). Not Necessarily Necessary but Always Sufficient. In D. Brazier (Ed.), *Beyond Carl Rogers*. London: Constable.

Bozarth, J. D. (1996a). Client-Centered Therapy and Techniques. In R. Hutterer, G. Pawlowsky, P. F. Schmid & R. Stipsis (Eds.), *Client-Centered and Experiential Therapy: A Paradigm in Motion*. Frankfurt am Main: Peter Lan.

Bozarth, J. D. (1998). *Person-centred Therapy: A revolutionary paradigm*. Ross-on-Wye: PCCS Books.

Bozarth, J. D. (2001). An Addendum to Beyond Reflection: Emergent Modes of Empathy. In S. Haugh & T. Merry (Eds.), *Rogers' Therapeutic Conditions, Evolution, Theory and Practice: Empathy*. Ross-on-Wye: PCCS Books.

Bozarth, J. D., (2002). Empirically Supported Treatment: Epitome of the specificity myth. In J. C. Watson, R. Goldman & M. S. Warner (Eds.), *Client-Centred and Experiential Psychotherapy in the 21st Century: Advances in theory, research and practice*. Ross-on-Wye: PCCS Books.

Bozarth, J. D., & Brodley, B. T. (1991). Actualisation: A functional concept in client-centred psychotherapy. *Journal of Social Behaviour and Personality, 6*(5), 45–59.

Bozarth, J. D., Zimring, F., & Tausch, R. (2001). Client-Centred Therapy: The evolution of a revolution. In D. Cain & J. Seeman (Eds.), *Humanistic Psychotherapies*. Washington DC: American Psychological Association.

Bozarth, J. D., & Motomasa, N. (2005). Searching for the Core: The interface of client-centred principles with other therapies. In S. Joseph & R. Worsley (Eds.), *Person Centred Psychopathology: A positive psychology of mental health*. Ross-on-Wye: PCCS Books.

Brandt, D. (1981). *Becoming a writer*. New York: Jeremy P. Tarcher.

Brazier, D. (1993). The Necessary Condition is Love: Going beyond self in the person-centred approach. In D. Brazier (Ed.), *Beyond Carl Rogers*. London: Constable.

Breggin, P. (1993). *Toxic Psychiatry*. London: Harper Collins.

Brodley, B. T. (1990). Client-Centred and Experiential: Two different therapies. In G. Lietaer, J. Rombouts & R. Van Balen (Eds.), *Client-Centred and Experiential Therapy in the Nineties*. Leuven: Leuven University Press.

Brodley, B. T. (1996). Empathic Understanding and Feelings in Client-Centred Therapy. *The Person-Centred Journal, 3*(1), 22–30.

Brodley, B. T. (1997a). The Non-Directive Attitude in Client-Centred Therapy. *Person-Centred Review, 4*, 18–30.

Brodley, B. T. (1997b). Concerning 'Transference', Counter-Transference and Other Psychoanalytically-Developed Concepts from a Client-Centred Perspective. *Renaissance, 9*(2).

Brodley, B. T. (1998). Congruence and its Relation to Communication in Client-Centred Therapy. *The Person-Centred Journal, 5*(2), 83–106.

Brodley, B. T. (1999). About the Non-Directive Attitude. *Person-Centred Practice, 7*(2), 79–82.

Brodley, B. T. (2001). Observations of Empathic Understanding in a Client-Centred Practice. In S. Haugh & T. Merry (Eds.), *Rogers' Therapeutic Conditions, Evolution, Theory and Practice: Empathy*. Ross-on-Wye: PCCS Books.

Brodley, B. T. (2005). Client-Centred Values Limit the Application of Research Findings–An issue for discussion. In S. Joseph & R. Worsley (Eds.), *Person-Centred Psychopathology: A positive psychology of mental health*. Ross-on-Wye: PCCS Books.

Brodley, B. T. (2006). Non-directivity in Client-Centred Therapy. *Person-Centred and Experiential Psychotherapies, 5*(1), 36–52.

Brodley, B. T., & Merry, T. (1995). Guidelines for Student Participants in Person-Centred Peer Groups. *Person-Centred Practice, 3*(2), 17–22.

Brodley, B. T., & Schneider, K. J. (2001). Unconditional Positive Regard as Communicated Through Verbal Behaviour in Client-Centred Therapy. In J. Bozarth & P. Wilkins (Eds.), *Unconditional Positive Regard: Evolution, theory and practice*. Ross-on-Wye: PCCS Books.

Bruner, J. (1990). *Acts of Meaning*. Cambridge, MA: Harvard University Press.

Bruner, J. (2004). The Narrative Creation of Self. In L. Angus & J. McLeod (Eds.), *Handbook of Narrative and Psychotherapy*. London: Sage.

Bryant-Jeffries, R. (2005). *Counselling for Eating Disorders in Men: Person-centred dialogues*. Oxford: Radcliffe.

Buber, M. (1958). *I and Thou*. Edinburgh: T&T Clarke.

Bugenthal, J. F. T. (1964). The Third Force in Psychology. *Journal of Humanistic Psychology, 4*(1), 19–25.

Burr, V. (1995). *An Invitation to Social Construction*. London: Routledge.

Burton, M., & Davey, T. (2003). The Psychodynamic Paradigm. In R. Woolfe, W. Dryden & S. Strawbridge (Eds.), *Handbook of Counselling Psychology*. London: Sage.

Cain, D. (1993). The Uncertain Future of Client-Centred Counselling. *Journal of Humanistic Consulting and Development, 31*, 133–139.

Cain, D. (2001). Defining Characteristics, History and Evolution of Humanistic Psychotherapies. In D. Cain & J. Seeman (Eds.), *Humanistic Psychotherapies*. Washington DC: Americal Psychological Association.

Cameron, R. (1997). The Personal is Political: Re-reading Rogers. *Person-Centred Practice, 5*(2), 16–20.

Chambless, D. L. (1996). In Defence of Empirically Supported Psychological Interventions. *Clinical Psychology: Science and Practice, 3*, 230–235.

Chambless, D. L. & Hollon, S. D. (1998). Defining Empirically Supported Therapies. *Journal of Consulting and Clinical Psychology, 66,* 7–18.

Clarke, K. M. (1993). Creation of Meaning in Incest Survivors. *Psychotherapy, 28,* 139–148.

Clarkin, J. F., & Levy, K. N. (2004). The Influence of Client Variables on Psychotherapy. In M. J. Lambert (Ed.), *Handbook of Psychotherapy and Behaviour Change.* Wiley: New York.

Clarkson, P. (1996). The Eclectic and Integretive Paradigm. In R. Woolfe & W. Dryden (Eds.), *Handbook of Counselling Psychology.* London: Sage.

Cooper, M. (1999). If You Can't be Jekyll be Hyde: An existential-phenomenological exploration of lived plurality. In J. Rowan & M. Cooper (Eds.), *The Plural Self* (pp. 51–70). London: Sage.

Cooper, M. (2001). Embodied Empathy. In S. Haugh & T. Merry (Eds.), *Empathy* (pp. 218–229). Ross-on-Wye: PCCS Books.

Cooper, M. (2002). *Existential Therapies.* London: Sage.

Cooper, M. (2003). Between Freedom and Despair: Existential challenges and contributions to person-centred and experiential therapy. *Person-Centred and Experiential Psychotherapies, 2*(2), 43–56.

Cooper, M. (2004). Existential Appproaches to Therapy. In P. Sanders (Ed.), *The Tribes of the Person-Centred Nation.* Ross-on-Wye: PCCS Books.

Cooper, M., Mearns, D., Stiles, W. B., Warner, M. S., & Elliot, R. (2004). Developing Self-Pluralistic Perspectives within Person-Centred and Experiential Psychotherapies: A round table dialogue. *Person-Centred and Experiential Psychotherapies, 4*(1), 176–191.

Coulson, A. (1995). The Person-Centred Approach and the Reinstatement of the Unconscious. *Person-Centred Practice, 3*(2), 7–16.

Crits-Christoph, P., & Mintz, J. (1991). Implications of Therapist Effects for the Design and Analysis of Comparative Studies of Psychotherapies. *Journal of Clinical and Consulting Psychology, 59,* 20–26.

Cromby, J. (2004). Depression: embodying social inequality. *Journal of Critical Psychology, Counselling and Psychotherapy, 4*(3), 176–186.

Davy, J., & Cross, M. (2004). *Barriers, Defences and Resistance.* Milton Keynes: Open University Press.

Diamond, B. (2004). Expert-tease: The rise and rise of psychology. *Journal of Critical Psychology, Counselling and Psychotherapy, 4*(4), 242–246.

DoH (2001). *Treatment Choice in Psychological Therapies and Counselling: Evidence Based Clinical Practice Guidelines.* London: Department of Health.

Dryden, W. (2002). Rational-Emotional Behaviour Therapy. In W. Dryden (Ed.), *Handbook of Individual Therapy.* London: Sage.

Dryden, W., Horton, I., & Mearns, D. (1995). *Issues in Professional Counsellor Training.* London: Cassell.

Dymond, R. F. (1954). Adjustment Changes Over Therapy from Self-sorts. In C. R. Rogers & R. F. Dymond (Eds.), *Psychotherapy and Personality Change.* Chicago, IL: University of Chicago Press.

Eckert, J., & Wuchner, M. (1996). Long-Term Development of Borderline Personality Disorder. In R. Hutterer, G. Pawlowsky, P. F. Schmid & R. Stipsis (Eds.), *Client-Centred and Experiential Psychotherapy : A paradigm in motion.* Frankfurt am Main: Peter Lang.

Edwards, D. (1997). *Discourse and Cognition.* Sage: London.

Egan, G. (1998). *The Skilled Helper.* New York: Brooks Cole.

Ellingham, I. (1999). Carl Rogers' 'Congruence' as an Organismic, not a Freudian, Concept. *The Person-Centred Journal, 6*(2), 121–140.

Ellingham, I. (2002). Foundation for a Person-Centred Humanistic Psychology and Beyond: The nature and logic of Carl Rogers' 'formative tendency'. In J. C. Watson, R. Goldman & M. S. Warner (Eds.), *Client-Centred and Experiential Psychotherapy in the 21st Century*. Ross-on-Wye: PCCS Books.

Elliott, R. (1998). Editor's Introduction: A guide to the empirically supported treatments controversy. *Psychotherapy Research, 8*(2), 115–125.

Elliott, R. (2001a). The Effectiveness of Humanistic Therapies: A meta-analysis. In D. Cain & J. Seeman (Eds.), *Humanistic Psychotherapies*. Washington DC: American Psychological Association.

Elliott, R. (2001b). Hermeneutic Single-Case Efficacy Design: An overview. In K. J. Schneider, J. F. T. Bugenthal & J. F. Pierson (Eds.), *The Handbook of Humanistic Therapies*. Thousand Oaks, CA: Sage.

Elliott, R. (2002). Render unto Caesar: Quantitative and qualitative knowing in research on humanistic therapies. *Person-Centred and Experiential Psychotherapies, 1*(1 & 2), 102–117.

Elliott, R., & Greenberg, L. S. (2001). Process-Experiential Psychotherapy. In D. Cain & J. Seeman (Eds.), *Humanistic Psychotherapy*. Washington, DC: American Psychological Association.

Elliott, R., Greenberg, L. S., & Lietaer, G. (2004). Research on Experiential Psychotherapies. In M. J. Lambert (Ed.), *Bergin and Garfield's Handbook of Psychotherapy and Behaviour Change, (5th Ed)*. New York: Wiley.

Elliott, R., Suter, P., Manford, J., Radpour-Markert, L., Siegel-Honson, R., Layman, C., & Davis, K. (1995). A Process-Experiential Approach to Post-Traumatic Stress Disorder. In R. Hutterer, G. Pawlowsky, P. F. Schmid & R. Stipsis (Eds.), *Client-Centred and Experiential Psychotherapy*. Frankfurt am Main: Peter Lang.

Ellis, A. (1994). *Reason and Emotion in Psychotherapy: Revised edition*. New York: Carol Publishing.

Ellis, A. (2004). *The Road to Tolerance: The philosophy of rational-emotive behaviour therapy*. Amherst, NY: Prometheus Books.

Embleton-Tudor, L., Keemar, K., Tudor, K., Valentine, J., & Worrall, M. (2004). *The Person-Centred Approach: A contemporary introduction*. Basingstoke: Palgrave Macmillian.

Evans, R. I. (1975). *Carl Rogers: The man and his ideas*. New York: Dutton.

Farber, B. A., & Lane, J. S. (2002). Positive Regard. In J. C. Norcross (Ed.), *Psychotherapy Relationships That Work* (pp. 175–194). Oxford: Oxford University Press.

Ford, J. G. (1991). Rogerian Self-Actualisation: A clarification of meaning. *Journal of Humanistic Psychology, 31*(3), 101–111.

Foucault, M. (1974). *The Archaeology of Knowledge*. London: Tavistock.

Frankl, V. E. (1984). *Man's Search for Meaning*. New York: Washington Square Press.

Frankland, A. (2003). Counselling Psychology: The next ten years. In R. Woolfe, W. Dryden & S. Strawbridge (Eds.), *Handbook of Counselling Psychology*. London: Sage.

Frankland, A., & Walsh, Y. (2005). Talking Point: Division of counselling psychology 10th anniversary. *Counselling Psychology Review, 20*(4), 45–47.

Freeman, R. (1999). A Psychodynamic Understanding of the Dentist-Patient Interaction. *British Dental Journal, 186*(10), 503–507.

Freeth, R. (2004). A Psychiatrist's Experience of Person-Centred Supervision. In K. Tudor & M. Worrall (Eds.), *Freedom to Practise: Person-centred approaches to supervision*. Ross-on-Wye: PCCS Books.

Freier, E. (2001). Unconditional Positive Regard: The distinctive feature of client-centred therapy. In J. Bozarth & P. Wilkins (Eds.), *Unconditional Positive Regard: Evolution, theory and practice*. Ross-on-Wye: PCCS Books.

Freud, S. (1938). *An Outline of Psychoanalysis Vol. 16.* London: Penguin.

Geller, J. D., & Gould, E. (1996). A Contemporary Psychoanalytic Perspective: Rogers' brief psychotherapy with Mary Jane Tilden. In B. A. Farber, D. C. Brink & P. M. Raskin (Eds.), *The Psychotherapy of Carl Rogers: Cases and commentary*. New York: Guilford Press.

Gendlin, E. T. (1964). A Theory of Personality Change. In P. Worchel & D. Byrne (Eds.), *Personality Change*. New York: John Wiley.

Gendlin, E. T. (1974). *Client-centred and Experiential Psychotherapy*. In D. Wexler & L. N. Rice (Eds.), *Innovations in Client-Centred Therapy*. New York: Wiley.

Gendlin, E. T. (1978). *Focusing*. New York: Everest House.

Gendlin, E. T. (1996). *Focusing-orientated Psychotherapy: A manual of the experiential method*. New York: Guilford Press.

Gergen, K. (1991). *The Saturated Self: Dilemmas of identity in contemporary life*. New York: Basic Books.

Gergen, K. (1999). *An Invitation to Social Construction*. London: Sage.

Gilbert, P. (1992). *Counselling for Depression*. London: Sage.

Gillon, E. (2002). Do We Need to do More? Counselling Training and the Processes of Social Exclusion. *Counselling and Psychotherapy Journal, 13*(3).

Giovalolias, T. (2004). The Therapeutic Relationship in Cognitive Behavioural Therapy. *Counselling Psychology Review, 19*(2), 14–20.

Golsworthy, R. (2004). Counselling Psychology and Psychiatric Classification. *Counselling Psycholohgy Review, 19*(3). 23–29.

Goss, S., & Mearns, D. (1997). A Call for a Pluralistic Epistemological Understanding in the Assessment and Evaluation of Counseling. *British Journal of Guidance and Counselling, 25*(2), 189–198.

Grafanaki, S. (2001). What Counselling Research has Taught us About the Concept of Congruence: Main discoveries and unresolved issues. In G. Wyatt (Ed.), *Congruence*. Ross-on-Wye: PCCS Books.

Grant, B. (1990). Principled and Instrumental Non-Directiveness in Person-Centred and Client-Centred Therapy. *Person-Centred Review, 5*(1), 77–88.

Grant, B. (2004). The Imperative of Ethical Justification in Psychotherapy: The special case of client-centred therapy. *Person-Centred and Experiential Psychotherapies, 3*(3), 152–165.

Greenberg, L. S., & Geller, S. M. (2001). Congruence and Therapeutic Presence. In G. Wyatt (Ed.), *Congruence*. Ross-on-Wye: PCCS Books.

Greenberg, L. S., Rice, L. N., & Elliot, R. (1993). *Facilitating Emotional Change: The moment by moment process*. New York: Guilford Press.

Greenberg, L. S., & Watson, J. C. (1998). Experiential Therapy of Depression: Differential effects of client-centred relationship conditions and process experiential interventions. *Psychotherapy Research, 8*(2), 210–224.

Greenberg, L. S., Watson, J. C., & Goldman, R. (1996). Change Processes in Experiential Therapy. In R. Hutterer, G. Pawlowsky, P. F. Schmid & R. Stipsis (Eds.), *Client-Centred and Experiential Psychotherapy: A paradigm in motion* (pp. 35–45). Frankfurt am Main: Peter Lang.

Guthrie Ford, J. (1991). Rogerian Self-Actualisation: A Clarification of Meaning. *Journal of Humanistic Psychology, 31*, 101–111.

Haugh, S. (2001). The Difficulties in the Conceptualisation of Congruence: a way forward with complexity theory. In G. Wyatt (Ed.), *Rogers' Therapeutic Conditions, Evolution, Theory and Practice. Volume 1: Congruence* (pp. 62–67). Ross-on-Wye: PCCS Books.

Hawtin, S., & Moore, J. (1998). Empowerment or Collusion? The social context of person-centred therapy. In B. Thorne & E. Lambers (Eds.), *Person-Centred Therapy: A European perspective* London: Sage.

Henry, W. P. (1998). Science, Politics and the Politics of Science. *Psychotherapy Research, 8*(2), 126–140.

Hill, A. (2002). Lets Stay and Hate: The role of community meetings on counsellor training courses. *Counselling and Psychotherapy Research, 2*(4), 215–221.

Holdstock, L. (1993). Can we Afford not to Revise the Person-Centred Concept of Self. In D. Brazier (Ed.), *Beyond Carl Rogers*. London: Constable.

Hollanders, H. E. (2000). Eclecticism/Integration: Some key issues and research. In S. Palmer & R. Woolfe (Eds.), *Integretive and Eclectic Counselling and Psychotherapy*. London: Sage.

Horvath, A. O. & Bedi, R. P. (2002). The Alliance. In J. C. Norcross (Ed.), *Psychotherapy Relationships that Work: Therapist Contributions and Responsiveness to Patients*. New York: Oxford University Press.

Hughes, R., & Buchanan, L. (2000). *Experiences of Person-Centred Counselling Training*. Ross-on-Wye: PCCS Books.

Husserl, E. (1977). *Phenomenological Psychology*. The Hague: Nijhoff.

Jacobs, M. (2005). *The Presenting Past*. Milton Keynes: Open University Press.

Johnson, L. (2000). *Users and Abusers of Psychiatry: A critical look at psychiatric practice*. London: Routledge.

Johnson, S. M. (1994). *Character Styles*. New York: Norton.

Jones, M. (1996). Person-Centred Theory and the Post-Modern Turn. *Person-Centred Practice, 4*(2), 19–26.

Joseph, S. (2004). Client-centred Therapy, Post-traumatic Stress Disorder and Post-traumatic Growth: Theory and Practice. *Psychology and Psychotherapy: Theory, Research, and Practice, 77*, 101–120.

Joseph, S., & Worsley, R. (2005). Psychopathology and the Person-Centred Approach: Building bridges between disciplines. In *Person-Centred Psychopathology: A positive psychology of mental health*. Ross-on-Wye: PCCS Books.

Jung, C. G. (1963). *Memories, Dreams, Reflections*. London: Routledge and Kegan Paul.

Kahn, E. (1999). A Critique of Non-Directivity in the Person-Centred Approach. *Journal of Humanistic Psychology, 39*(4), 94–110.

Kang, S., Kok, P. G., & Bateman, A. (2005). Case Formulation in Psychotherapy: Revitalizing Its Usefulness as a Clinical Tool. *Academic Psychiatry, 29:* 289–292.

Keil, S. (1996). The Self as a Systematic Process of 'Inner Persons'. In R. Hutterer, G. Pawlowsky, P. F. Schmid & R. Stipsis (Eds.), *Client-Centred and Experiential Psychotherapy: A paradigm in motion* (pp. 53–66). Frankfurt am Main: Peter Lang.

King, M., Sibbbald, B., Ward, E., Bower, P., Lloyd, M., & Gabbay, M. (2000). Randomised Controlled Trial of Non-Directive Counselling, Cognitive Behaviour Therapy and Usual General Practitioner Care in the Management of Depression as well as Mixed Anxiety and Depression in Primary Care. *British Medical Journal* (321), 1383–1388.

Kirschenbaum, H. (1979). *On Becoming Carl Rogers*. New York: Dell.

Kirschenbaum, H., & Henderson, V. L. (Eds.). (1990a). *The Carl Rogers Reader*. London: Constable.

Kirschenbaum, H., & Henderson, V. L. (Eds.). (1990b). *Carl Rogers Dialogues*. London: Constable.

Klein, M. (1957). *Envy and Gratitude*. New York: Basic Books.

Klein, M. H., Kolden, G. G., Michels, J. L., & Chisholm-Stockard, S. (2002). Congruence. In J. C. Norcross (Ed.), *Psychotherapy Relationships That Work* (pp. 195–215). Oxford: Oxford University Press.

Kramer, R. (1995). The Birth of Client-Centred Therapy: Carl Rogers, Otto Rank and 'the beyond'. *Journal of Humanistic Psychology, 35*(4), 54–110.

Lambers, E. (1994). Person-Centred Psychopathology. In D. Mearns (Ed.), *Developing Person-Centred Counselling*. Sage: London.

Lambert, M. J., & Barley, D. E. (2002). Research Summary on the Therapeutic Relationship and Psychotherapy. In J. C. Norcross (Ed.), *Psychotherapy Relationships That Work* (pp. 17–32). Oxford: Oxford University Press.

Laungani, P. (1999). Client-Centred or Culture Centred Counselling. In P. Laungani & S. Palmer (Eds.), *Counselling in a Multicultural Society* (pp. 133–152). London: Sage.

Lazarus, A. A., & Colman, A. M. (1995). Introduction. In A. A. Lazarus & Colman, A. M. (Eds.), *Abnormal Psychology*. London: Longman.

Leahey, T. H. (1991). *A History of Modern Psychology*. Englewood Cliffs, NJ: Prentice Hall.

Lemma, A. (1997). *Invitation to Psychodynamic Psychology*. London: Whurr.

Levitt, B. E. (2005). Non-directivity: The foundational attitude. In B. E. Levitt (Ed.), *Embracing Non-directivity*. Ross-on-Wye: PCCS Books.

Lietaer, G. (1984). Unconditional Positive Regard: a controversial basic attitude in client-centred therapy. In R. F. Levant & J. M. Schlien (Eds.), *Client-Centred Therapy and the Person-Centred Approach: new directions in theory, research and practice* (pp. 41–58). New York: Praeger.

Lietaer, G. (1993). Authenticity, Congruence and Transparency. In D. Brazier (Ed.), *Beyond Carl Rogers* (pp. 41–58). London: Constable.

Lietaer, G. (2001). Unconditional Acceptance and Positive Regard. In J. Bozarth & P. Wilkins (Eds.), *Unconditional Positive Regard: Evolution, theory and practice*. Ross-on-Wye: PCCS Books.

Lietaer, G. (2002). The United Colours of Person-Centred and Experiential Psychotherapies. *Person-Centred and Experiential Psychotherapies, 1*(1&2), 4–13.

Luborsky, L., Singer, B., & Luborsky, L. (1975). Comparative Studies of Psychotherapy. *Archives of General Psychiatry, 32*, 995–1008.

Lyddon, W. J. (1998). Social Constructionism in Counselling Psychology: A commentary and critique. *Counselling Psychology Quarterly, 11*(2), 215–222.

Lyotard, J. F. (1984). *The Postmodern Condition: A Report on Knowledge*. Manchester: Manchester University Press.

Mace, C., & Moorey, S. (2001). Evidence in Psychotherapy: A delicate balance. In C. Mace, S. Moorey & B. Roberts (Eds.), *Evidence in the Psychological Therapies: A critical guide for practitioners*. Hove: Brunner-Routledge.

Margison, F. (2001). Practice-Based Evidence in Psychotherapy. In C. Mace, S. Moorey & B. Roberts (Eds.), *Evidence in the Psychological Therapies: A critical guide for practitioners*. Hove: Brunner-Routledge.

Martin, D. J., Garske, J. P., & Davis, M. K. (2000). Relation of the Therapeutic Alliance with Outcome and Other Variables. A meta-analytic review. *Journal of Clinical and Consulting Psychology, 68*, 438–450.

Maslow, A. H. (1954). *Motivation and Personality*. New York: Harper and Brothers.

Masson, J. (1992). *Against Therapy*. London: Collins.

May, R. (1982). The Problem of Evil: An open letter to Carl Rogers. *Journal of Humanistic Psychology, 22*(3), 10–21.

McCleary, R. A., & Lazarus, R. S. (1949). Autonomic Discrimination. *Journal of Personality, 18*, 171–179.

McLeod, J. (2000). Qualitative Research in Counselling and Psychotherapy. London: Sage.

McLeod, J. (2002). Research Policy and Practice in Person-Centred and Experiential Therapy: Restoring coherence. *Person-Centred and Experiential Psychotherapies, 1*(1 & 2), 87–101.

McLeod, J. (2003a). The Humanistic Paradigm. In R. Woolfe, W. Dryden & S. Strawbridge (Eds.), *Handbook of Counselling Psychology*. London: Sage.

McLeod, J. (2003b). Qualitative Methods in Counselling Psychology. In R. Woolfe, W. Dryden & S. Strawbridge (Eds.), *Handbook of Counselling Psychology*. London: Sage.

McLeod, J. (2004). Social Construction, Narrative and Psychotherapy. In L. Angus & J. McLeod (Eds.), *Handbook of Narrative and Psychotherapy*. London: Sage.

McMahon, G. (2000). Assessment and Case Formulation. In C. Feltham & I. Horton (Eds.), *Handbook of Counselling and Psychotherapy*. London: Sage.

McMillan, M. (1997). The Experiencing of Empathy: What is involved in achieving the 'as if' condition. *Counselling, 3*(3), 205–209.

McMillan, M. (2004). *The Person-Centred Approach to Therapeutic Change*. London: Sage.

Mearns, D. (1994). *Developing Person-Centred Counselling*. Sage: London.

Mearns, D. (1996). Working at Relational Depth with Clients in Person-Centred Therapy. *Counselling, 7*(4), 306–311.

Mearns, D. (1997). *Person-Centred Counselling Training*. London: Sage.

Mearns, D. (1999). Person-Centred Therapy with Configurations of Self. *Counselling, 8*(2), 125–130.

Mearns, D. (2002). Further Theoretical Propositions in Regard to Self Theory within Person-Centred Therapy. *Person-Centred and Experiential Psychotherapies, 1*(1&2), 14–27.

Mearns, D. (2003). The Humanistic Agenda: Articulation. *Journal of Humanistic Psychology, 43*, 53–65.

Mearns, D. (2004). Problem-Centred is not Person-Centred. *Person-Centred and Experiential Psychotherapies, 3*(2), 88–101.

Mearns, D., & Cooper, M. (2005). *Working at Relational Depth in Counselling and Psychotherapy*. London: Sage.

Mearns, D., & Jacobs, M. (Writer) (2003). Person-Centred and Psychodynamic Therapy: Colleagues or opponents? [Video]: CSCT, Birmingham.

Mearns, D., & McLeod, J. (1984). A Person-Centred Approach to Research. In R. F. Levant & J. M. Schlien (Eds.), *Client-Centred Therapy and the Person-Centred Approach*. New York: Praegar.

Mearns, D., & Thorne, B. (1999). *Person-Centred Counselling in Action (2nd Ed.)*. London: Sage.

Mearns, D., & Thorne, B. (2000). *Person-Centred Therapy Today: New frontiers in theory and practice*. London: Sage.

Merry, T. (1995). *Invitation to Person-Centred Psychology*. London: Whurr.

Merry, T. (1998). Client-Centred Therapy: Origins and Influences. *Counselling, 1*(1), 17–18.

Merry, T. (1999). *Learning and Being in Person-Centred Counselling: A text book for discovering theory and developing practice*. Ross-on-Wye: PCCS Books.

Merry, T. (Ed.). (2000a). *The BAPCA Reader*. Ross-on-Wye: PCCS Books.

Merry, T. (2000b). Person-Centred Counselling and Therapy. In C. Feltham & I. Horton (Eds.), *Handbook of Counselling and Psychotherapy*. Whurr: London.

Merry, T. (2004). Classical Client-Centred Therapy. In P. Sanders (Ed.), *The Tribes of the Person-Centred Nation*. Ross-on-Wye: PCCS Books.

Merry, T., & Brodley, B. T. (2002). The Non-Directive Attitude in Client-Centred Therapy: A response to Kahn. *Journal of Humanistic Psychology, 42*(2), 66–77.

Messer, S. B., & Wampold, B. (2002). Let's Face Facts: Common factors are more potent that specific therapy ingredients. *Clinical Psychology: Science and Practice, 9*, 21–28.

Mitchell, S. A. (2000). *Relationality: From attachment to intersubjectivity*. Hillsdale, NJ: The Analytic Press.

Moerman, M., & McLeod, J. (2006). Person-Centred Counselling for Alcohol-Related Problems: The Client's Experience of Self in a Therapeutic Relationship. *Person-Centred and Experiential Psychotherapies, 5*(1), 21–35.

Moore, J. (2004). Letting Go of Who I Think I Am: Listening to the unconditioned self. *Person-Centred and Experiential Psychotherapies, 3*(2), 117–128.

Moorey, S. (2002). Cognitive Therapy. In W. Dryden (Ed.), *Handbook of Individual Therapy*. London: Sage.

Natiello, P. (1990). The Person-Centred Approach, Collaborative Power and Cultural Transformation. *Person-Centred Review, 5*(3), 268–286.

Natiello, P. (1998). Person-Centred Training: A response to Dave Mearns. *The Person-Centred Journal, 5*(1), 39–47.

Natiello, P. (2001). *The Person-Centred Approach: A passionate presence*. Ross-on-Wye: PCCS Books.

Neimeyer, R. A. (1998). Social Constructionism and the Counselling Context. *Counselling Psychology Quarterly, 11*(2), 135–149.

Neisser. (1967). *Cognitive Psychology*. Englewood Cliffs, NJ: Prentice Hall.

Nelson-Jones, R. (2005). *The Theory and Practice of Counselling and Therapy*. London: Sage.

(NICE), (National Institute for Clinical Excellence). (2004). *Anxiety: Clinical guideline 22*.

Norcross, J. C. (2002). Empirically Supported Therapy Relationships. In J. C. Norcross (Ed.), *Psychotherapy Relationships That Work* (pp. 3–16). Oxford: Oxford University Press.

Norcross, J. C., & Newman, C. F. (1992). Psychotherapy Integration. In J. C. Norcross & M. R. Goldfried (Eds.), *Handbook of Psychotherapy Integration*. New York: Basic Books.

O'Hara, M. (1995). Carl Rogers: Scientist and mystic. *Journal of Humanistic Psychology, 35*(4), 40–53.

O'Hara, M. (1999). Moments of Eternity: Carl Rogers and the contemporary demand for brief therapy. In I. Fairhurst (Ed.), *Women Writing in the Person-Centred Approach*. Ross-on-Wye: PCCS Books.

O'Leary, E. (1997). Toward Integrating Person-Centred and Gestalt Therapies. *The Person-Centred Journal, 4*(2), 14–22.

Owen, I. R. (1999). Exploring the Similarities and Differences between Person-Centred and Psychodynamic Counselling. *British Journal of Guidance and Counselling, 27*(2), 165–178.

Padesky, C. A., & Greenberger, D. (1995). *Clinicians Guide to Mind Over Mood*. New York: Guilford Press.

Palmer, S., & Dryden, W. (1995). *Counselling for Stress Problems*. London: Sage.

Parker, I. (1989). Discourse and Power. In J. Shotter & K. Gergen (Eds.), *Texts of Identity*. London: Sage.

Parker, I., Georgaca, E., Harper, D., McLaughlin, T., & Stowell-Smith, M. (1995). *Deconstructing Psychopathology*. London: Sage.

Parlett, M., & Hemming, J. (2002). Gestalt Therapy. In W. Dryden (Ed.), *Handbook of Individual Therapy*. London: Sage.

Parry, G. (2001). Preface. In Department of Health (Ed.), *Treatment Choice in Psychological Therapies and Counselling: Evidence-based clinical practice guideline*. London: Department of Health.

Patterson, C. H. (1983). A Client-Centred Approach to Supervision. *The Counselling Psychologist, 11*(1), 21–25.

Patterson, C. H. (2000). *Understandng Psychotherapy: Fifty years of Client-Centred Theory and Practice*. Ross-on-Wye: PCCS Books.

Perls, F., Hefferline, R., & Goodman, P. (1951). *Gestalt Therapy*. New York: Dell.

Perrett, C. (2006). First Change the World, or First Change Yourself? In G. Proctor, M. Cooper, P. Sanders & B. Malcolm (Eds.), *Politicising the Person-Centred Approach: An agenda for social change*. Ross-on-Wye: PCCS Books.

Perry, J. C. (1993). Defences and their effects. In N. E. Miller, L. Luborsky, J. Barber & J. P. Docherty (Eds.), *Psychodynamic Treatment Research*. New York: Basic Books.

Persons, J. B. (1989). *Cognitive Therapy in Practice: A case formulation approach*. New York: Norton.

Persons, J. B. (2006). Case Formulation-Driven Psychotherapy. *Clinical Psychology: Science and Practice, 13*(2), 167–170.

Proctor, G. (2002). *The Dynamics of Power in Counselling and Psychotherapy: Ethics, politics and practice*. Ross-on-Wye: PCCS Books.

Proctor, G. (2005a). Clinical Psychology and the Person-Centred Approach: An uncomfortable fit? In S. Joseph & R. Worsley (Eds.), *Person-Centred Psychopathology: A positive psychology of mental health*. Ross-on-Wye: PCCS Books.

Proctor, G. (2005b). Working in Forensic Services in a Person-Centred Way. *Person-Centred and Experiential Psychotherapies, 4*(1), 20–30.

Proctor, G., Cooper, M., Sanders, P., & Malcolm, B. (Eds.). (2006). *Politicising the Person-Centred Approach: An agenda for social change*. Ross-on-Wye: PCCS Books.

Prouty, G. (1990). Pre-Therapy: A theoretical evolution in the person-centred/experiential psychotherapy of schizophrenia and retardation. In J. Rombouts & R. Van Balen (Eds.), *Client-Centred and Experiential Psychotherapy in the Nineties*. Leuven: University of Leuven Press.

Prouty, G. (1994). *Theoretical Evolutions in Person-Centred/Experiential Psychotherapy: Applications to schizophrenic and retarded psychoses*. Westport, CT.: Praeger.

Prouty, G. (1998). Pre-Therapy and the Pre-Expressive Self. *Person-Centred Practice, 6*(2), 28–32.

Prouty, G., Van Werde, D., & Portner, M. (2002). *Pre-Therapy: Reaching contact impaired clients*. Ross-on-Wye: PCCS Books.

Purton, C. (1998). Unconditional Positive Regard and its Spiritual Implications. In B. Thorne & E. Lambers (Eds.), *Person-Centred Therapy: A European perspective* (pp. 23–37). London: Sage.

Purton, C. (2002). Person-Centred Therapy Without the Core Conditions. *Counselling and Psychotherapy Journal (formerly Counselling), 13*(2), 6–9.

Purton, C. (2004a). Focusing-Orientated Therapy. In P. Sanders (Ed.), *The Tribes of the Person-Centred Nation*. Ross-on-Wye: PCCS Books.

Purton, C. (2004b). *Person-Centred Therapy: A focusing-orientated approach*. Basingstoke: Palgrave Macmillan.

Purton, C. (2004c). Differential Response: Diagnosis and the philosophy of the implicit. *Person-Centred and Experiential Psychotherapies, 3*(4), 245–255.

Purves, D. (2003). Time-Limited Practice. In R. Woolfe, W. Dryden & S. Strawbridge (Eds.), *Handbook of Counselling Psychology*. London: Sage.

Rank, O. (1936). *Will Therapy*. New York: Knopf.

Raskin, N. J. (1948). The Development of Non-Directive Therapy. *The Journal of Consulting Psychology, 12*(92), 92–110.

Raskin, N. J. (1949). An Analysis of the Six Parallel Studies of the Therapeutic Process. *Journal of Consulting Psychology, 13*(206–219).

Rennie, D. L. (1996). Fifteen Years of Doing Qualitative Psychotherapy Research. *British Journal of Guidance and Counselling* (24), 317–327.

Rennie, D. L. (1998). *Person-Centred Counselling: An experiential approach*. London: Sage.

Rennie, D. L. (2001). Experiencing Psychotherapy: Grounded theory studies. In D. Cain & J. Seeman (Eds.), *Humanistic Psychotherapies*. Washington DC: American Psychological Association.

Rice, L. N. (1974). The Evocative Function of the Therapist. In D. A. Wexler & L. N. Rice (Eds.), *Innovations in Client-Centred Therapy* (pp. 289–311). New York: John Wiley and Sons.

Rogers, C. R. (1939). *The Clinical Treatment of the Problem Child*. New York: Houghton Mifflin.

Rogers, C. R. (1942). *Counselling and Psychotherapy: Newer concepts in practice*. Boston: Houghton Mifflin.

Rogers, C. R. (1949). The Attitude and Orientation of the Counsellor in Client-Centred Therapy. *Journal of Consulting Psychology, 13*, 82–94.

Rogers, C. R. (1951). *Client-Centred Therapy: Its current practice, implications and theory*. London: Constable.

Rogers, C. R. (1954). Changes in the Maturity of Behaviour Related to Therapy. In C. R. Rogers & R. F. Dymond (Eds.), *Psychotherapy and Personality Change*. Chicago: University of Chicago Press.

Rogers, C. R. (1957). The Necessary and Sufficient Conditions of Therapeutic Personality Change. *Journal of Consulting Psychology, 21*, 95–103.

Rogers, C. R. (1959). A Theory of Therapy, Personality and Interpersonal Relationships as Developed in the Client-Centred Framework. In S. Kich (Ed.), *Psychology: A study of science: Vol. 3. Formulations of the Person and the Social Context*. (pp. 184–256). New York and Boston: McGraw Hill.

Rogers, C. R. (1961). *On Becoming a Person: A therapist's view of psychotherapy*. London: Constable.

Rogers, C. R. (1966). Client-Centred Therapy. In S. Arieti (Ed.), *American Handbook of Psychiatry*. New York: Basic Books.

Rogers, C. R. (1967). Some Learnings from a Study of Psychotherapy with Schizophrenics. In C. R. Rogers & R. Stevens (Eds.), *Person to Person: The problem of being human*. Layfayette: Real People Press.

Rogers, C. R. (1968). Some Thoughts Regarding the Current Presuppositions of the Behavioural Sciences. In B. Coulson & C. R. Rogers (Eds.), *Man and the Science of Man*. Columbus, OH: Charles E Merrill.

Rogers, C. R. (1977). *Carl Rogers on Personal Power*. New York: Delacorte Press.

Rogers, C. R. (1980). *A Way of Being*. Boston: Houghton Mifflin.

Rogers, C. R. (1981). Notes on Rollo May. *Perspectives, 2*(1).

Rogers, C. R. (1982). Reply to Rollo May's Letter. *Journal of Humanistic Psychology, 22*(4), 85–89.

Rogers, C. R. (1986). Rogers, Kohut and Erickson. *Person-Centred Review, 1*(2), 125–140.

Rogers, C. R. (1987). Transference. *Person-Centred Review, 2*(2), 182–188.

Rogers, C. R., & Dymond, R. F. (1954). *Psychotherapy and Personality Change*. Chicago: University of Chicago Press.

Rogers, C. R., Gendlin, E. T., Kiesler, D. J. & Truax, D. J. (1967). *The Therapeutic Relationship and its Impact: A Study of Psychotherapy with Schizophrenics*. Madison, WI: University of Wisconsin Press.

Rogers, C. R., & Sanford, R. (1984). Client-Centred Psychotherapy. In B. J. Kaplan & B. J. Sadock (Eds.), *Comprehensive Textbook of Psychiatry IV*. Baltimore: Williams and Wilkins.

Roth, A., & Fonegy, P. (1996). *What Works for Whom: A critical review of psychotherapy research*. New York: Guilford Press.

Rowan, J. (1998). Depression and the Question of Labelling. *Self and Society, 26*(5), 25–27.

Russell, J. (1999). Counselling and the Social Construction of Self. *British Journal of Guidance and Counselling, 27*(3), 339–443.

Rustin, M. (2001). Research, Evidence and Psychotherapy. In C. Mace, S. Moorey & B. Roberts (Eds.), *Evidence in the Psychological Therapies: A critical guide for practitioners*. Hove: Brunner-Routledge.

Sachse, R. (1998). Treatment of Psychosomatic Problems. In L. S. Greenberg, G. Lietaer & J. C. Watson (Eds.), *Experiential Psychotherapy: Differential intervention*. New York: Guilford Press.

Sachse, R., & Elliott, R. (2001). Process-Outcome Research on Humanistic Therapy Variables. In D. Cain & J. Seeman (Eds.), *Humanistic Psychotherapies*. Washington DC: American Psychological Association.

Sampson, W. E. (1989). The Deconstruction of the Self. In J. Shotter & K. Gergen (Eds.), *Texts of Identity*. London: Sage.

Samuels, A. (1997). Pluralism and Psychotherapy: What is a good training? In R. House & N. Totton (Eds.), *Implausable Professions: Arguments for pluralism and autonomy in counselling/psychotherapy*. Ross-on-Wye: PCCS Books.

Sanders, p. (2000) Mapping Person-Centred Approaches to Counselling and psychotherapy. *Person-Centred Practice, 8(2)*, 62–74.

Sanders, P. (2004). History of CCT and the PCA: Events, dates and ideas. In P. Sanders (Ed.), *The Tribes of the Person-Centred Nation*. Ross-on-Wye: PCCS Books.

Sanders, P. (2005). Principled and Strategic Opposition to the Medicalisation of Distress and all of its Apparatus. In S. Joseph & R. Worsley (Eds.), *Person-Centred Psychopathology: A positive psychology of mental health*. Ross-on-Wye: PCCS Books.

Sanders, P. (2006). Politics and Therapy: Mapping areas for consideration. In G. Proctor, M. Cooper, P. Sanders & B. Malcolm (Eds.), *Politicising the Person-Centred Approach: An agenda for social change*. Ross-on-Wye: PCCS Books.

Sanders, P. & Tudor, K. (2001). This is Therapy: a Person-Centred Critique of the Contemporary Psychiatric System. In C. Newness, G. Holmes & C. Dunn (Eds.), *This is Madness Too: Critical Perspectives on Mental Health Services*. Ross-on-Wye: PCCS Books.

Sanders, P., & Wyatt, G. (2001). The History of Conditions One and Six. In P. Sanders & G. Wyatt (Eds.), *Contact and Perception*. Ross-on-Wye: PCCS Books.

Sartre, J. P. (1956). *Being and Nothingness: An essay on phenomenological ontology*. New York: New York Philsophical Library.

Schlien, J. M. (1984). A Countertheory of Transference. In R. F. Levant & J. M. Schlien (Eds.), *Client-Centred Therapy and the Person-Centred Approach*. New York: Praegar.

Schmid, P. F. (2001). Authenticity: Dialogical and ethical perspectives on therapy as an encounter relationship. And beyond. In G. Wyatt (Ed.), *Rogers' Therapeutic Conditions Volume 1: Congruence*. Ross-on-Wye: PCCS Books.

Schmid, P. F. (2002). The Necessary and Sufficient Conditions of Being Person-Centered: On Identity, Integrity, Integration and Differentiation of the Paradigm. In J. C. Watson, R. Goldman & M.S. Warner (Eds.), *Client-Centred and Experiential Psychotherapies in the 21st Century*. Ross-on-Wye: PCCS Books.

Schmid, P. F. (2003). The Characteristics of a Person-Centred Approach to Therapy and Counselling: Criteria for Coherence and Identity. *Person-Centred and Experiential Psychotherapies, 2(2)*, 104–120.

Schmid, P. F. (2004). Back to the Client: A phenomenological approach to the process of understanding and diagnosis. *Person-Centred and Experiential Psychotherapies, 3*, 36–52.

Scott, M. J., & Dryden, W. (2003). The Cognitive-Behavioural Paradigm. In R. Woolfe, W. Dryden & S. Strawbridge (Eds.), *Handbook of Counselling Psychology*. London: Sage.

Seager, M. (2003). Problems with Client-Centred Therapy, letter in *The Psychologist, 16*(8), 401.

Seeman, J. (2001). Looking Back, Looking Ahead: A synthesis. In D. Cain & J. Seeman (Eds.), *Humanistic Psychotherapies*. Washington, DC: American Psychological Association.

Seligman, M. E. P. (1995). The Effectiveness of Psychotherapy: The Consumer Reports study. *American Psychologist, 50*, 965–974.

Shotter, J. (1993). *Conversational Realities: Constructing life through language*. London: Sage.

Singh, J., & Tudor, K. (1997). Cultural Conditions of Therapy. *The Person-Centred Journal, 4*(2), 32–46.

Skinner, B. F. (1917). *Verbal Learning*. New York: Appleton.

Skinner, B. F. (1953). *Science and Human Behaviour*. New York: Macmillan.

Smail, D. (2001). *The Nature of Unhappiness*. London: Robinson.

Snyder, W. U. (1945). An Investigation into the Nature of Non-Directive Psychotherapy. *Journal of General Psychology, 33*, 193–223.

Snygg, D., & Combs, A., W. (1949). *Individual Behaviour: A new frame of reference for psychology*. New York: Harper and Brothers.

Sommerbeck, L. (2003). *The Client-Centred Therapist in Psychiatric Contexts: A therapists' guide to the psychiatric language and its inhabitants*. Ross-on-Wye: PCCS Books.

Sommerbeck, L. (2005). The Complementarity between Client-Centred Therapy and Psychiatry: The theory and the practice. In S. Joseph & R. Worsley (Eds.), *Person-Centred Psychopathology: A positive psychology of mental health*. Ross-on-Wye: PCCS Books.

Speirer, G. W. (1998). Psychopathology According to the Differential Incongruence Model. In L. S. Greenberg, J. C. Watson & G. Lietaer (Eds.), *Handbook of Experiential Psychotherapy*. New York: Guilford Press.

Sperry, L., Gudeman, J. E. & Blackwell, B. (2000). *Psychiatric Case Formulations*. Washington, DC: American Psychiatric Association.

Spinelli, E. (1989). *The Interpreted World: An introduction to phenomenological psychology*. London: Sage.

Spinelli, E. (1994). *Demystifying Therapy*. London: Constable.

Spinelli, E. (2001). *The Mirror and the Hammer: Challenges to therapeutic orthodoxy*. London: Continuum.

Spinelli, E. (2003). The Existential-Phenomenological Paradigm. In R. Woolfe, W. Dryden & S. Strawbridge (Eds.), *Handbook of Counselling Psychology*. London: Sage.

Standal, S. (1954). *The Need for Positive Regard: A contribution to client-centred theory*. Unpublished PhD, University of Chicago, Chicago.

Stern, D. (1986). *The Interpersonal World of the Infant*. New York: Basic Books.

Stevens, R. (1983). *Freud and Psychoanalysis*. Buckingham: Open University Press.

Stock, D. (1949). An Investigation into the Interrelations Between the Self Concept and Feelings Directed Toward Other Persons and Groups. *Journal of Consulting Psychology, 13*, 176–180.

Strawbridge, S., & Woolfe, R. (2003). Counselling Psychology in Context. In R. Woolfe, W. Dryden & S. Strawbridge (Eds.), *Handbook of Counselling Psychology*. London: Sage.

Stumm, G. (2005). The Person-Centred Approach from an Existential Perspective. *Person-Centred and Experiential Psychotherapies, 4*(2), 77–89.

Swildens, H. (2002). Where Did We Come From and Where Are We Going? The development of person-centred psychotherapy. *Person-Centred and Experiential Psychotherapies, 1*(1 & 2), 118–131.

Taft, J. (1937). *The Dynamics of Therapy in a Controlled Relationship*. New York: Macmillan.

Takens, R. J., & Lietaer, G. (2004). Process Differentiation and Person-Centredness: A contradiction? *Person-Centred and Experiential Psychotherapies, 3*(2), 77–87.

Teasdale, J. (1999). Metacognition, Mindfulness and the Modification of Mood Disorders. *Clinical Psychology and Psychotherapy, 6*(2), 146–155.

Thomas, K. (1996). The Defensive Self: A psychodynamic perspective. In R. Stevens (Ed.), *Understanding the Self*. Milton Keynes: Open University Press.

Thorne, B. (1992). *Carl Rogers*. London: Sage.

Thorne, B. (1994). Brief Companionship. In D. Mearns (Ed.), *Developing Person-Centred Counselling*. London: Sage.

Thorne, B. (1999). The Move Toward Brief Therapy: Its dangers and its challenges. *Counselling, 10*(1), 7–11.

Thorne, B. (2002). *The Mystical Power of Person-Centred Therapy*. London: Whurr.

Timulak, L. (2003). Person-Centred Therapy as a Research Informed Approach: Evidence and possibilities. *Person-Centred and Experiential Psychotherapies, 2*(4), 227–241.

Tolan, J. (2002). 'The Fallacy of the "Real' Self". In J. Watson, R. Goldman & M. S. Warner (Eds.), *Client-Centred and Experiential Psychotherapy in the 21st Century*. Ross-on-Wye: PCCS Books.

Tolan, J. (2003). *Skills in Person-Centred Counselling and Psychotherapy*. London: Sage.

Tudor, K. (1996). *Mental Health Promotion: Paradigms and Practice*. London: Routledge.

Tudor, K. (2000). The Case of the Lost Conditions. *Counselling, 11*(1), 33–37.

Tudor, K., & Merry, T. (2002). *Dictionary of Person-Centred Therapy*. London: Whurr.

Tudor, K., & Worrall, M. (1994). Congruence Reconsidered. *British Journal of Guidance and Counselling, 22*(4), 197–206.

Tudor, K., & Worrall, M. (2004). Person-Centred Philosophy and Theory in the Practice of Supervision. In K. Tudor & M. Worrall (Eds.), *Freedom to Practice: Person-centred approaches to supervision*. Ross-on-Wye: PCCS Books.

Tudor, K., & Worrall, M. (2006). *Person-Centred Therapy: A clinical philosophy*. London: Routledge.

Vahrenkamp, S., & Behr, M. (2004). The Dialog with the Inner Critic: From a pluralistic self to client-centred experiential work with partial egos. *Person-Centred and Experiential Psychotherapies, 3*(4), 228–244.

van Deurzen, E. (2002). *Existential Counselling and Psychotherapy in Practice, (2nd ed)*. London: Sage.

Van Kalmathout, M. (1998). Personality Change and the Concept of Self. In B. Thorne & E. Lambers (Eds.), *Person-Centred Therapy: A European perspective*. Sage: London.

Van Werde, D. (2005). From Psychotic Function: Person-centred contact work in residential psychiatric care. In S. Joseph & R. Worsley (Eds.), *Person-Centred Psychopathology: A positive psychology of mental health*. Ross-on-Wye: PCCS Books.

Vanerschot, G. (1993). Empathy as Releasing Several Microprocesses in the Client. In D. Brazier (Ed.), *Beyond Carl Rogers*. London: Constable.

Wampold, B. (2001). *The Great Psychotherapy Debate: Models, methods and findngs*. Mahwah, NJ: Lawrence Earlbaum Associates.

Warmoth, A. (1998). Humanistic Psychology and Humanistic Social Science. *Humanity and Society, 22*(3). www.sonama.edu/users/w/warmotha/awhumpsy.html

Warner, M. S. (1996). How Does Empathy Cure? A theoretical consideration of empathy processing and personal narrative. In R. Hutterer, G. Pawlowsky, P. F. Schmid & R. Stipsis (Eds.), *Client-Centred and Experiential Psychotherapy: A paradigm in motion*. Frankfurt-am-Main: Peter Lang.

Warner, M. S. (1999). Person-Centred Psychotherapy: One nation, many tribes. In C. Wolter-Gustafson (Ed.), *A Person-Centred Reader: Personal selection by our members*. Boston: Association for the Development of the Person-Centred Approach.

Warner, M. S. (2000). Person-Centred Therapy at the Difficult Edge: A developmentally based model of fragile and dissociated process. In D. Mearns & B. Thorne (Eds.), *Person-Centred Therapy Today: The frontiers in theory and practice*. London: Sage.

Warner, M. S. (2002). Luke's Dilemmas: A Client-centred/Experiential Model of Processing with a Schizophrenic Thought Disorder. In J. Watson, R. Goldman & M. S. Warner (Eds.), *Client-centred and Experiential Psychotherapy in the 21st Century: Advances in Theory, Research and Practice*. Ross-on-Wye: PCCS Books.

Warner, M. S. (2006). Toward an Integrated Person-Centred Theory of Wellness and Psychopathology. *Person-Centred and Experiential Psychotherapies, 5*(1), 4–20.

Waterhouse, R. (1993). Wild Women Don't Have the Blues: A feminist critique of 'person-centred' counselling and therapy. *Feminism and Psychology, 3*, 55–71.

Watkins, C. E. (1993). Person-Centred Theory and the Contemporary Practice of Psychological Testing. *Counselling Psychology Quarterly, 6*(1), 59–67.

Watson, J. B. (1917). Psychology as the Behaviourist Views It. *Psychological Review, 20*, 158–177.

Wessley, S. (2001). Randomised Controlled Trials: The gold standard? In C. Mace, S. Moorey & B. Roberts (Eds.), *Evidence in the Psychological Therapies: A critical guide for practitioners*. Hove: Brunner-Routledge.

Wetherell, M., & Maybin, J. (1996). The Distributed Self: A social constructionist perspective. In R. Stevens (Ed.), *Understanding the Self*. Milton Keynes: Open University Press.

Wetherell, M., & Potter, J. (1992). *Mapping the Language of Racism*. Hemel Hempstead: Harvester Wheatsheaf.

Wexler, D. A. (1974). A Cognitive Theory of Experiencing, Self-Actualisation and Therapeutic Process. In D. A. Wexler & L. N. Rice (Eds.), *Innovations in Client Centred Therapy*. New York: Wiley.

Wexler, D. A., & Rice, L. N. (Eds) (1974). *Innovations in Client-Centred Therapy*. New York: Wiley.

Wheeler, S., & McLeod, J. (1995). Person-Centred and Psychodynamic Counselling: A dialogue. *Counselling, 6*(4), 283–287.

Wilkins, P. (1997). Toward a Person-Centred Understanding of Consciousness and the Unconscious. *Person-Centred Practice, 5*(1), 14–20.

Wilkins, P. (2000). Unconditional Positive Regard Reconsidered. *British Journal of Guidance and Counselling, 28*(1), 23–36.

Wilkins, P. (2003). *Person-Centred Therapy in Question*. London: Sage.

Wilkins, P. (2005a). Assessment and 'Diagnosis' in Person-Centred Therapy. In S. Joseph & R. Worsley (Eds.), *Person-Centred Psychopathology: A postive psychology of mental health*. Ross-on-Wye: PCCS Books.

Wilkins, P., & Gill, M. (2003). Assessment in Person-Centred Therapy. *Person-Centred and Experiential Psychotherapies, 2*(3), 172–187.

Williams, F., Coyle, A., & Lyons, E. (1999). How Counselling Psychologists View their Personal Therapy. *British Journal of Medical Psychology, 72*, 545–555.

Woolfe, R., Dryden, W. & Strawbridge, S. (2003). *Handbook of Counselling Psychology*. London: Sage.

Worsley, R. (2002). *Process Work in Person-Centred Therapy: Phenomenological and existential perspectives*. Basingstoke: Palgrave.

Worsley, R. (2003). Small is Beautiful: Small-Scale Phenomenological Research for Counsellor Self-Development. *Person-Centred and Experiential Psychotherapies, 2*(2), 121–132.

Wyatt, G. (2000). The Multifaceted Nature of Congruence. *The Person-Centred Review, 7*(1), 52–68.

Yalom, I. (1980). *Existential Psychotherapy*. New York: Basic Books.

Yalom, I. (1989). *Loves Executioner and their Tales of Psychotherapy*. Harmondsworth: Penguin.

Yontef, G. (1998). Dialogic Gestalt Therapy. In L. S. Greenberg, J. C. Watson & G. Lietaer (Eds.), *Handbook of Experiential Psychotherapy*. New York: Guilford Press.

Zeigler, D. J. (2002). Freud, Rogers and Ellis: A comparative analysis. *Journal of Rational-Emotive and Cognitive Behaviour Therapy, 20*(2), 75–90.

Zimring, F. (1974). Theory and Practice of Client-Centred Therapy: A cognitive view. In D. A. Wexler & L. N. Rice (Eds.), *Innovations in Client-Centred Therapy*. New York: Wiley.

Zimring, F. (2000). Empathic Understanding Grows the Person. *The Person-Centred Journal, 7*, 101–113.

Zohar, D. (1990). *The Quantum Self*. London: Bloomsbury.

Index